HEBREWS

Verse by Verse

OSBORNE • NEW TESTAMENT • COMMENTARIES •

HEBREWS

Verse by Verse

GRANT R. OSBORNE

WITH

GEORGE H. GUTHRIE

LEXHAM PRESS

Hebrews: Verse by Verse
Osborne New Testament Commentaries

Lexham Press, 1313 Commercial St., Bellingham, WA 98225
LexhamPress.com

Print ISBN 9781683595373
Digital ISBN 9781683595380
Library of Congress Control Number 2021934330

Lexham Editorial Team: Elliot Ritzema, Karen Engle, Mandi Newell, Abigail Stocker
Cover Design: Christine Christophersen
Typesetting: Justin Marr

CONTENTS

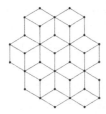

SERIES PREFACE

There are two authors of every biblical book: the human author who penned the words and the divine Author who revealed and inspired every word. While God did not dictate the words to the biblical writers, he did guide their minds so that they wrote their own words under the influence of the Holy Spirit. If Christians really believed what they said when they called the Bible "the word of God," a lot more would be engaged in serious Bible study. As divine revelation, the Bible deserves, indeed demands, to be studied deeply.

This means that when we study the Bible, we should not be satisfied with a cursory reading in which we insert our own meanings into the text. Instead, we must always ask what God intended to say in every passage. But Bible study should not be a tedious duty we have to perform. It is a sacred privilege and a joy. The deep meaning of any text is a buried treasure; all the riches are waiting under the surface. If we learned there was gold deep under our backyard, nothing would stop us from getting the tools we needed to dig it out. Similarly, in serious Bible study, all the treasures and riches of God are waiting to be dug up for our benefit.

This series of commentaries on the New Testament is intended to supply these tools and help the Christian understand more deeply the God-intended meaning of the Bible. Each volume walks the reader verse-by-verse through a book with the goal of opening up for us what God led Matthew or Paul or John to say to their readers. My goal in this series is to make sense of the historical and literary background of these ancient works—to supply the information that will enable the modern reader to understand exactly what the biblical writers were saying to their first-century audience. I want to remove the complexity of most modern commentaries and provide an easy-to-read explanation of the text. I have read nearly all the recent literature and have tried to supply a commentary that sums up the state of knowledge attained to date on the meaning and background for each biblical book.

But it is not enough to know what the books of the New Testament meant back then; we need help in determining how each text applies to our lives today. It is one thing to see what Paul was saying to his readers in Rome or Philippi, and quite another thing to see the significance of his words for us. So at key points in the commentary, I will attempt to help the reader discover areas in our modern lives that the text is addressing.

I envision three main uses for this series:

1. **Devotional Scripture reading.** Many Christians read rapidly through the Bible for devotions in a one-year program. That is extremely helpful to gain a broad overview of the Bible's story. But I strongly encourage another kind of devotional reading—namely, to study deeply a single segment of the biblical text and try to understand it. These commentaries are designed to enable that. The commentary is based on the NIV and explains the meaning of the verses, enabling the modern reader to read a few pages at a time and pray over the message.

2. ***Church Bible studies.*** I have written these commentaries
   also to serve as guides for group Bible studies. Many Bible
   studies today consist of people coming together and sharing what they think the text is saying. There are strengths
   in such an approach, but also weaknesses. The problem
   is that God inspired these scriptural passages so that the
   church would understand and obey *what he intended the text
   to say.* Without some guidance into the meaning of the text,
   we are prone to commit heresy. At the very least, the leaders
   of the Bible study need to have a commentary so they can
   guide the discussion in the direction God intended. In my
   own church Bible studies, I have often had the class read
   a simple exposition of the text so they can all discuss the
   God-given message, and that is what I hope to provide here.

3. ***Sermon aids.*** These commentaries are also intended to help
   pastors faithfully exposit the text in a sermon. Busy pastors
   often have too little time to study complex thousand-page
   commentaries on biblical passages. As a result, it is easy to
   spend little time in Bible study and thereby to have a shallow sermon on Sunday. As I write this series, I am drawing on my own experience as a pastor and interim pastor,
   asking myself what I would want to include in a sermon.

Overall, my goal in these commentaries is simple: I would
like them to be interesting and exciting adventures into New
Testament texts. My hope is that readers will discover the riches
of God that lie behind every passage in his divine word. I hope
every reader will fall in love with God's word as I have and begin
a similar lifelong fascination with these eternal truths!

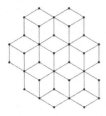

PREFACE TO THIS COMMENTARY

I had the great privilege of knowing Grant Osborne as my professor, my friend, and a longtime colleague on the board of an international ministry to Asian house church pastors. When Grant died in November of 2018, he had made it through almost all of his commentary on Hebrews, lacking only a few summary/application sections in chapters 10–13, commentary on the final verses of chapter 13, and the commentary's introduction. At Grant's request, Lexham Press asked if I would be willing to finish this book, and it has been a great honor to do so.

I first met Grant in the fall of 1985. I had moved to Trinity Evangelical Divinity School in Deerfield, Illinois, to work with Robert Coleman in the area of Christian discipleship, while my academic work centered on a ThM degree in New Testament. Grant, a respected professor at Trinity, served as the supervisor for my thesis and thus became my academic mentor right from the start. I remember a moment early in my first semester when we were both doing research in the library and were sitting side by side using the resources in front of us on the table. With a big smile, Grant turned and said something to the effect of, "I can't think of anything better than this!" I smiled back and responded, "Well, I can think of a few things!" He laughed out loud, and our friendship took off from there. Grant *loved* studying the Bible and had great *joy* in God's word. From the start, I was impressed with Grant's deep devotion to Christ, his integration of Christian faith with scholarship, and his generous posture of encouragement toward students. In fact, for the next three-and-a-half decades, Grant would be a consistent source of encouragement to me personally.

It was in working on my master's thesis that our paths first intersected in the pages of Hebrews. The previous year, while translating an article for a German class, I had become intrigued with the use of the Psalms in Hebrews and decided to write my master's thesis on the use of Psalm 110:1 in the book. Grant was enthusiastic and, once the thesis was finished, encouraged me to consider writing my doctoral dissertation on the structure of Hebrews when I returned to a PhD program in Texas the following year. I took his advice, and, by God's grace, the dissertation was eventually published, and a good bit of my life's work has focused on this fascinating and encouraging book. So helping my dear brother with the completion of this commentary has brought us full circle.

Grant Osborne was an outstanding New Testament scholar, trained at the University of Aberdeen under I. Howard Marshall. He was a leading member of the translation team for the New Living Translation and edited or wrote numerous respected books, including commentaries on the New Testament, as well as a major work on hermeneutics called *The Hermeneutical Spiral.* You can trust his scholarship (so go buy the other volumes in the Osborne New Testament Commentaries series!), but through his reflections on the text, you can follow him into a life of faithful discipleship. For, like the greats of Hebrews 11, Grant is a prime exemplar of the faith—a hero of the faith, in my book. Those of us who knew him knew that he struggled with his health in his final years. Yet he kept teaching and kept traveling to Asia, at times under difficult circumstances, because he believed in the power and importance of the word of God for the church. And Grant kept writing commentaries, like the one you are reading, all the way to the very end. So value this commentary. Use it well in ministry. Allow it to offer you strong encouragement until you, like Grant, step into the presence of Jesus, our great high priest, in the heavenly city.

George H. Guthrie
Regent College
Vancouver, British Columbia

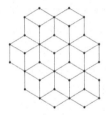

INTRODUCTION TO HEBREWS

Have you ever traveled to a new city and felt disoriented until you started to find your way around, the lines and boxes on your GPS gradually morphing into real, three-dimensional places with which you were familiar? I remember the first time I traveled to San Francisco. The bus ride from the airport was a blur of interstates, passing neighborhoods, glimpses of the ocean, and then the labyrinth of crowded streets laid out in what seemed to be a spaghetti-type pattern! Yet as I attended a professional meeting over the next few days, the area of the city in which the conference was being held gradually took shape. The streets around the hotel and the conference center began to feel familiar. I knew how to get from one place to another without a map. Having traveled to that beautiful city many times through the years, I now have a general idea of how the city "works." The layout makes sense.

As we become familiar with the New Testament book of Hebrews, we may have a similar sense of disorientation until we begin to know our way around. The outline in a commentary or a study Bible will start to fill out with powerful and practical passages, "landmarks" in our understanding of the book. When we travel to a new city, it helps to have a local or even a professional guide show us around. The commentary you have in your hand is meant to be such a guide to this wonderful yet complex book. It has been said that "Hebrews is a delight for the person who enjoys puzzles."[1] But if you are willing to put the time in to walk through the fascinating twists and turns of this ancient Christian text, you will begin to discover its theological riches and relevance for today.

Hebrews is worth the effort for several reasons. First, *Hebrews is unique among the New Testament writings in terms of its message.* For instance, no other book focuses on the high priesthood of Jesus. In fact, the author's interaction with the Old Testament Scriptures shines a light on Christology that offers a unique perspective on both Jesus' identity and his sacrificial work in dealing with our sins. Second, unlike any other book in the New Testament, *many scholars believe that Hebrews originally was a sermon,* which the author crafted for the congregations addressed. The move back and forth between exposition about Jesus and exhortation to the church follows the form of a Jewish synagogue sermon, or homily, of the first century AD. So Hebrews gives us a unique glimpse into one aspect of worship in the early church. Third, *Hebrews was written to address real-life, nitty-gritty challenges that believers faced at a critical time in the church's development.* It is easy to approach Hebrews as a heady, theologically-oriented "lecture," meant to impress with deep theology and high-sounding rhetoric. But Hebrews is both *pastoral* and *relevant* for both the life of the individual believer and the church as a whole. The author uses solid teaching to address crying needs, especially the need to "hang in there" in following Jesus when life becomes difficult. In this book, we find profound help on our journey to the heavenly city (11:10, 16). But if we are to get that help, we need to understand some things about the book.

---

1. William L. Lane, *Hebrews 1–8*, Word Biblical Commentary (Waco, TX: Word Books, 1991), xlvii.

The introduction that follows considers the authorship, date and destination, purpose, structure, and theology of Hebrews.

THE AUTHOR

WRITTEN BY PAUL?

Undoubtedly, the question that I have been asked far more than any other about Hebrews is, "Who do you think wrote it?" It seems that if someone knows little about the book, they at least know that the question of authorship has been controversial. In the first centuries of the church, leaders in the East, centered especially in Alexandria in Egypt, recognized that Hebrews was not written in Paul's style but suspected that Paul had crafted the content of the book. For instance, Clement of Alexandria (AD 150-215) believed Paul wrote this work in Hebrew, and Luke translated for those who spoke Greek. Origen (AD 185-253) thought the book written by a disciple of Paul, but he also gave us the famous quip, "But who wrote the epistle, in truth God knows." Early on, Hebrews started circulating with Paul's letters. For instance, Papyrus 46, crafted in about AD 200, places Hebrews just after Romans. Other manuscripts place Hebrews after Paul's letters to churches and before those to individuals. By the time of Augustine (AD 354-430) and Jerome (AD 347-420), most saw the book as Pauline, and that position dominated in the church for a millennium until the time of the Protestant Reformation. Since the church had long assumed Pauline authorship, this view also made its way into the King James translation of the Bible, which calls the book "The Epistle of Paul the Apostle to the Hebrews."

Yet, in the earliest centuries of the church, not everyone understood Hebrews to have been written by Paul, especially in the West. For example, Tertullian (AD 155-220) believed that the apostle's companion, Barnabas, a Levite who had come to believe in Jesus (Acts 4:36), crafted the book. The church historian Eusebius reports that the presbyter Gaius did not include Hebrews in his list of Paul's writings at the end of the second century or the beginning of the third. He also notes that others among the Romans believed someone other than Paul wrote Hebrews.

There are reasons why this view, regardless of the theological orientation of the scholar, has come to dominate modern scholarship on Hebrews. First, the style of writing in Greek is among the best in the New Testament, very different from Paul's style, and the vocabulary is not characteristic of Paul. About 170 terms in the book are not found anywhere else in the New Testament. Further, the word pictures used are different from those used by the apostle, and Hebrews focuses on key themes that don't show up in Paul's writings. For example, as pointed out above, Hebrews alone focuses on the high priestly ministry of Christ.

Second, Paul and the author of Hebrews have very different ways of introducing Old Testament quotations. Whereas the apostle typically uses the formula "It is written" over and over again, Hebrews presents the Scriptures as falling from the lips of God, introducing quotations with, "He says." Moreover, the Father, Son, and Spirit are presented as speaking Scripture, demonstrating a basic orientation to Trinitarian thought. When a passage of the Old Testament clearly is written from the standpoint of a human being—as is the case with the quotation of Psalm 8:4-6 in Hebrews 2:6-8a—Hebrews uses an ambiguous formula: "But there is a place where someone has testified" (2:6). This is not because the author did not know the location of Psalm 8, for it was an important psalm in Judaism and early Christianity! Rather, the author introduces it ambiguously to focus on the fact that ultimately God is the speaker of Scripture!

Finally, in Hebrews 2:3, the author presents himself as having received the gospel from the original witnesses: "This salvation, which was first announced by the Lord, was confirmed to us by those who heard him." This does not sound like Paul, who insists that he received the gospel directly from the Lord himself (Rom 1:1; 1 Cor 15:8; Gal 1:11-16).

OTHER SUGGESTIONS?

As noted above, the question of authorship began to be reconsidered at the time of the Reformation. Since that time, a number of other possibilities have been suggested in addition to Barnabas or Luke, such as: Apollos, Clement of Rome (who quotes Hebrews extensively in an early letter), Silas, Philip, Stephen, Jude, Timothy, Priscilla, and even Mary, the mother of Jesus. Most of these suggestions are mere speculation with little, if any, evidence to back them up. The other New Testament writings are the only evidence we have in hand that could lead us to real possibilities. Modern scholars suggest there are Pauline elements in the theology of Hebrews, thinking perhaps that an associate in Paul's mission wrote the book. Yet if we consider Luke, Barnabas, or Silas, for instance, one characteristic of Hebrews calls such choices into question, for Hebrews clearly was written by someone with advanced skills in public speaking (rhetoric), the book showing evidence of the highest level of education offered in the ancient world. Yet in the mission endeavors we see in Acts, for example, Luke, Barnabas, and Silas normally are in the background, treating Paul as the main public speaker. By contrast, Hebrews was produced by someone who was a powerful preacher of Scripture.

For this reason, many commentators today name Apollos as one of the most likely candidates in the search for Hebrews' author, a suggestion first made by Martin Luther. We know that Apollos was such an effective leader in Corinth that some in the church preferred his leadership to Paul's (1 Cor 1:12; 3:4-6, 22). Yet, more significantly, the New Testament depicts Apollos as a highly trained and effective public speaker. Acts 18:24-26 describes him as follows:

> Meanwhile a Jew named Apollos, a native of Alexandria, came to Ephesus. He was a learned man, with a thorough knowledge of the Scriptures. He had been instructed in the way of the Lord, and he spoke with great fervor and taught about Jesus accurately, though he

knew only the baptism of John. He began to speak boldly in the synagogue. When Priscilla and Aquila heard
him, they invited him to their home and explained to
him the way of God more adequately.

Notice that Apollos is described as "a learned man," a description
used in the first century of a person with advanced education.
Notice also that he had a "thorough knowledge of the Scriptures"
and "began to speak boldly in the synagogue." A bit later, in
verse 28, Luke tells us that in Achaia the Alexandrian "vigorously
refuted his Jewish opponents in public debate, proving from the
Scriptures that Jesus was the Messiah." All of these descriptions
match what we have in the book of Hebrews. So Apollos is a "good
guess" on the book's authorship.

WHAT CAN WE KNOW FOR SURE?

At the end of the day, we have to agree with Origen that "only God
knows" who wrote this book! Yet there are at least three things we
can know for sure about the person used by God to give us one of
the richest writings of the New Testament. First, as already noted,
the author was very well educated. The style of Greek, the use of
many rhetorical devices, and the overall crafting of the book are
remarkable. Second, the author seems to have had a lot of training in Jewish synagogues of the Mediterranean world. Many of
the arguments in Hebrews are shaped by rabbinic techniques of
argumentation. For instance, we see an "argument from lesser
to greater" in Hebrews 2:1-4, which was a common method used
by rabbis. The author at times pulls two Old Testament passages
together based on a common word (like the word "son" in the two
texts quoted at Heb 1:5), and this too was a technique used by the
rabbis. In fact, the use of Scripture in general, and the "sermon"
form of the book as a whole, suggest that the author had grown up
and been trained in a synagogue setting. Finally, the author was a
concerned Christian minister who cared deeply about the spiritual

condition of the congregation to whom he wrote. He longed for them to endure in following Christ! So we should hear Hebrews as both a highly crafted theological discourse and a warm, relevant sermon on endurance in the Christian life.

DESTINATION, ORIGINAL AUDIENCE, AND DATE

DESTINATION AND ORIGINAL AUDIENCE

Another puzzle surrounding Hebrews concerns the original audience for this book. Most commentators today believe that the writing was sent to the church in Rome, which had been established after Jews and God-fearers, who, having believed in Christ at Pentecost, returned home and founded a Christian community in the empire's capital (Acts 2:10). A Roman destination seems indicated by the greeting in Hebrews 13:24: "Those from Italy send you their greeting." The statement can be understood as referring to those in the presence of the author, from the Italian peninsula, who sent their greetings back to Italy. Also, Clement, a church leader in Rome at the end of the first century, is the first ancient writer to quote Hebrews. He does so extensively in 1 Clement, a letter written to the church in Corinth. Also, Hebrews refers to the overseers of the church as "leaders" (13:7, 17), a designation distinct from the primary labels used in the Pauline literature and other New Testament writings, yet one that Hebrews shares with 1 Clement and the Shepherd of Hermas, another early Christian writing associated with Rome.

Second, Hebrews is profoundly *Jewish*, both in its orientation to the Jewish Scriptures and in its theology. This does not mean that there were not gentiles in the church, for it probably was a mixed congregation (compare Rom 1:13–16). Many gentiles in the early church had a background as "God-fearers," gentiles who worshiped the God of Israel and had belonged to Jewish synagogues of the Mediterranean world. Yet in the mid-first century, there were between 40,000 and 60,000 Jews in Rome, and the church to whom Hebrews was originally sent likely had a strong contingent of Jewish believers in Jesus.

Third, it is clear that those to whom Hebrews was written were struggling with persevering in the Christian faith. In 2:1 the author exhorts them, "We must pay the most careful attention, therefore, to what we have heard, so that we do not drift away." This threat of apostasy, of falling away from the living God, recurs throughout the book, especially in the sections of exhortation (for example, 6:4-8; 10:26-31). The author warns, "It is a dreadful thing to fall into the hands of the living God!" (10:31). Yet he also gives a lot of encouragement, including promises, positive examples, and especially a robust theology of who Jesus is and what he has accomplished on our behalf.

DATE

As for the date that Hebrews was written, we also have several clues in the book. For one thing, it seems that the people being addressed had been believers for a while. In 5:11-6:3 the author chastises them, stating that their spiritual condition did not match the length of time they had been Christians. In essence, he tells them, "You should be teachers by now, but you need someone to teach you the ABCs of the faith!" (5:12). Second, at some time in the past, they had faced persecution and stood boldly with Christ and fellow believers (10:32-35). If we are indeed dealing with the church in Rome, this could be a reference to the expulsion of Jews from Rome in AD 49 (Acts 18:1-2), recounted by the historian Suetonius. In his *Lives of the Caesars*, Suetonius says that the expulsion took place during the reign of the emperor Claudius and was due to riots at the instigation of a person named Chrestus, a common slave name in Rome.[2] Yet it may be that the name was confused with "Christus," and the riots occurred because of conflict within the Jewish community over belief in Jesus. If this lies

---

2. Suetonius, "Life of Emperor Claudius," 25.4.

behind the situation described in 10:32–35, the expulsion would have been a number of years prior to the writing of Hebrews. There is yet another point of reference in Hebrews that may narrow the timeframe further. In 12:4 the author says that the readers are being persecuted but had not yet faced martyrdom: "In your struggle against sin, you have not yet resisted to the point of shedding your blood." Again, if the writer addresses the church in Rome, this would place the composition of Hebrews prior to the onslaught of violent persecution of believers at the hand of the emperor Nero, in which many Christians were killed. The martyrdoms began in AD 64 in conjunction with a fire in Rome that burned a large section of the city. Given the historical reference points of the Claudian expulsion and the Neronian persecution, several commentators have suggested a date for Hebrews in the early-to-mid 60s, just prior to the escalating persecution of the church in Rome under Nero.

PURPOSE

Hebrews is one of the most beautifully crafted books in all of Scripture. Yet we need to understand that the theological depth, the exegetical brilliance in dealing with the old covenant Scriptures, the powerful examples, and stern warnings all work together for a single purpose—to encourage those who were struggling spiritually to endure in following Jesus. As with virtually every church, the community of faith to whom Hebrews was written evinced a spectrum of spiritual conditions, including those who had "one foot out the door" and were considering abandoning the faith altogether (3:6, 14; 4:1–2; 6:4–12; 10:26–27). It is instructive to see how Hebrews addresses the problem. As the sermon develops, the detailed expositions on Christ and his superior work (1:5–14; 2:5–18; 5:1–10; 7:1–10:18) *lay the foundation* for the author's exhortations (2:1–4; 3:1–4:16; 5:11–6:20; 10:19–13:24). In other words, the author uses *Scripture* and *theology* to lay down a firm basis for the *exhortation* to endure in faithfulness to Christ. At the heart of Hebrews' message stand two key themes:

- God has spoken through his superior Son!
- Listen and respond to his word of salvation!

Further, Hebrews unpacks the implications of how people respond differently to the message of Christ. For those who respond positively, enduring in the faith and standing with Jesus and his church, there will be a wonderful, eternal inheritance, a place in the heavenly city (Heb 9:15; 12:22). For those who reject the message, there will be judgment and devastation away from the presence of the Lord (2:1-4; 6:7-8; 10:26-31; 12:25-29).

Today we can draw this key teaching from Hebrews, a teaching that has inestimable relevance for our spiritual lives: *Your perseverance in the Christian faith will be in direct proportion to the clarity with which you see **who** Jesus is and **what** he has accomplished on our behalf.* If you and I really grasp (1) **Christ's identity**, that he is the eternal Son of God, Creator of the world, Lord of all that is (1:1-14), who became incarnate (2:10-18), and who (2) **lived and died for us as our high priest and great sacrifice for sins** (2:17-18; 5:1-10; 7:1-28; 9:1-10:18), it will help us greatly in enduring in the Christian life. This was the purpose for which Hebrews was written.

STRUCTURE AND OUTLINE

The commentary that follows divides Hebrews into two great movements, 1:1-10:18 and 10:19-13:25.[3] The first of these movements runs back and forth between exposition about Christ and exhortations

---

3. Since Grant had already written the commentary in accordance with the outline of the book presented here, I felt that the simplest approach would be to offer a brief description of his outline. For those interested in my take, I have written about the structure of Hebrews in a major academic book entitled *The Structure of Hebrews: A Text-Linguistic Analysis* (Leiden: Brill, 1994), as well as my own commentary on Hebrews in the NIV Application Commentary Series (Grand Rapids: Zondervan, 1998), 27-31. I actually owe Grant a great debt in my work in this regard. As pointed out in the preface to this commentary, he was my supervisor for a master's thesis in which I grappled for the first time with the structure of Hebrews.

to endure in the faith. Yet a key theme of the whole concerns Christ's superiority to various Jewish conventions found in the Old Testament. Christ has brought a superior revelation (1:1-3), is superior to the angels (1:5-14), is superior to Moses and brings a superior rest (chapters 3-4), and is a superior high priest (5:1-10; 7:1-28) who made a superior offering (8:1-10:18). The second great movement of the book constitutes a call to proper Christian living, including the danger of falling away (10:19-39), the wonderful example of heroes of the faith (chapter 11), endurance in kingdom living (chapter 12), and sacrificial living (chapter 13).

I. Christianity superior to Judaism (1:1-10:18)
   a. The superiority of the Son (1:1-14)
      i. Introduction: revealed in the Son (1:1-4)
      ii. Old Testament proof for the superiority of the Son (1:5-14)
         1. His status (1:5-6)
         2. His glory (1:7-9)
         3. His majesty (1:10-12)
         4. The exalted and victorious Lord (1:13)
         5. The task assigned to the angels (1:14)
   b. Focusing on the suffering Messiah (2:1-18)
      i. Warning to pay attention (2:1-4)
         1. Principle: focus rather than drift (2:1)
         2. The danger of ignoring God's salvation (2:2-3a)
         3. The twofold confirmation of this salvation (2:3b-4)
      ii. Superiority via incarnation (2:5-18)
         1. Humiliation by means of incarnation (2:5-9)
         2. Solidarity with humanity as Savior and high priest (2:10-18)
   c. The danger of losing God's rest (3:1-19)
      i. Moses and Jesus: faithful to their calling (3:1-6)
         1. The comparison made (3:1-2)

2. Faith and Abel and Enoch (11:4–5)
3. Thesis: Faith and pleasing God (11:6)
4. Faith and Noah (11:7)

iii. Faith among the patriarchs (11:8–22)
   1. Abraham and Sarah (11:8–19)
      a. Call to a promised land (11:8–10)
      b. Sarah and the Abrahamic progeny (11:11–12)
      c. Wanderers in search of a home (11:13–16)
      d. Faith and the sacrifice of Isaac (11:17–19)
   2. Faith and Isaac (11:20)
   3. Faith and Jacob (11:21)
   4. Faith and Joseph (11:22)

iv. Faith and Moses (11:23–28)
   1. Faith and Moses' birth (11:23)
   2. Faith and refusing the world's riches (11:24–26)
   3. Faith and leaving Egypt (11:27)
   4. Faith and the Passover (11:28)

v. Faith and the exodus events (11:29–31)

vi. Further examples of faith (11:32–38)
   1. The wondrous deeds they performed (11:32–34)
   2. The wondrous deeds of the person of faith (11:32–35a)
   3. The terrible suffering of the people of faith (11:35b–38)

vii. The promised culmination (11:39–40)

c. A call to disciplined action (12:1–29)
  i. Persevering in the race (12:1–3)
  ii. Discipline and sonship (12:4–13)
    1. Their limited experience (12:4)
    2. Challenge: reflect on your sonship (12:5–6)
    3. The universal need for discipline (12:7–8)
    4. Human fathers and the heavenly Father (12:9–11)
    5. The corporate dimension in the race (12:12–13)

KEY THEOLOGICAL THEMES

GOD THE FATHER

For Hebrews the living God is the ground of all reality (1:1; 3:4; 11:3; 12:22), and references to God permeate the book, the author using the Greek word *theos* sixty-eight times.[4] This general designation for God refers to God the Father, who is both the Father of the divine Son (1:5) and of believers (12:7, 9). God puts things

---

4. For example, Heb 1:1, 6, 8-9; 2:4, 9, 13, 17; 3:4, 12; 4:4, 9-10, 12, 14; 5:1, 4, 10, 12; 6:1, 3.

in motion in the world and reveals truth by his powerful, spoken word (1:1-2; 4:11-12). He has "testified" about the truth of the word of salvation given through the Son, by signs, wonders, miracles, and by gifts of the Holy Spirit. God the Father has the authority to exalt the Son to the highest place in the universe (1:6-13), and he brings sons and daughters to himself through the work of the Son (2:10-13). In fact, God is drawing people to himself through his covenants into his presence (4:15-16; 7:19; 8:10; 10:21-24) and does not want them to fall away from him (4:1-2; 6:4-8; 10:26-31). God is just, remembering the good works people do (6:10) and commending those of faith (11:4-5, 39). God is a God of grace and peace (Heb 2:9; 4:16; 10:29; 12:15, 28; 13:9, 20, 25) and judgment (9:27; 10:27), and he has a kingdom that cannot be shaken (12:28).

Hebrews demonstrates a Trinitarian theology by presenting the Son as identified with the Father (1:2b-3), as being addressed as God (1:8), as the Creator of the world (1:2, 10-12), and as the one who shares the Father's throne (1:3, 13). The Spirit distributes gifts to the church (2:4), speaks Scripture (3:7; 10:15), reveals truth through the Scriptures (9:14), and offers grace to people (10:29).

The Son's Nature, Exaltation, and Incarnation

Both the introduction and the great expositional movements of Hebrews are focused on the Son of God. In the introduction, the Son is the dividing point of history (1:1-2), sustains the world through history (1:3), and is both the Creator of the world (1:2, 10) and the heir who will wrap up the world at its end (1:11-12). The Son is identified with the Father and has been seated at the Father's right hand (1:3, 13; 8:2; 10:12; 12:2). The first main movement of the sermon concerns the Son's exaltation above and superiority to the angelic beings, as revealed in the Old Testament Scriptures (1:5-14). The Son is superior because of his unique relationship with God the Father (1:5), the fact that the angels themselves are servants who worship him (1:6-7), and his status as ruler and Creator of the universe (1:8–12). Finally, quoting Psalm 110:1, the author focuses on the Son's sitting at the right hand of God (Heb 1:13).

The second movement of Christology in the book has a transition (2:5–9) and then a section focused on the incarnation (2:10–18). The Son has become fully human in order to die for the "sons and daughters," who he brings into relationship with the Father (2:10–14). He accomplishes this through solidarity with them, taking on the role of high priest (2:17–18).

THE SON AS HIGH PRIEST AND HIS SUPERIOR OFFERING

The high priesthood of Jesus is another key theme of Hebrews, the focus of the great center section of the book (4:14–10:25), and, as noted above, it is a theme unique to this book in the New Testament. After discussing general principles concerning high priests under the old covenant (5:1–3), the author introduces another part of Psalm 110, specifically verse 4, a part of which reads, "You are a priest forever, in the order of Melchizedek" (5:6). The author uses Psalm 110:4 to focus attention on the qualifications of the Son for high priesthood and especially on his appointment as the high priest (5:7–10). Having introduced the topic, the author breaks off to focus on the problem with the hearers (5:11–6:20), but then returns to the appointment of the Son in 7:1–28. Using Psalm 110:4, he demonstrates that Jesus is a superior high priest because he is a priest in Melchizedek's order (Heb 7:1–15) and is a "priest forever" since he has an indestructible life (7:16–25).

Moreover, as a superior priest, Jesus had to have a superior offering (8:3–6). Now the author, using Jeremiah 31:31–34, turns to the topic of the new covenant (8:7–13). The priests of the old covenant had offerings made in their worship system and a place to offer them (9:1–10), yet Christ's offering was superior in three ways. (a) It was made with his own blood, not the blood of animals (9:12, 25); (b) it was made in the heavenly tabernacle rather than the earthly (9:11–12, 23–24; 10:12); and (c) unlike the offerings of the older covenant, which had to be made year after year, Jesus' new covenant

sacrifice only had to be made once for all time (9:12, 25-28; 10:11-12).
One of the most encouraging things about the sacrifice of Christ is
how decisive it is in cleansing new covenant people from their sin,
for when Jeremiah says, "Their sins and lawless acts I will remember no more" (Jer 31:34; Heb 10:17), this means that God's people
have absolute forgiveness; sacrifices for sins are "no longer necessary" (10:18). Although the author draws on a variety of sacrificial
images from the Old Testament, one of the most important is the
Day of Atonement, during which the high priest entered the holiest place of the tabernacle and offered a sacrifice for sins. Rather
than being offered year after year, Christ's Day of Atonement sacrifice only had to be offered once, the Son entering into the heavenly
holy of holies with his own blood and then sitting at the Father's
right hand, demonstrating that the work was finished (10:11-12).

THE WORD OF GOD

Hebrews' treatment of the word of God shows that communication
transcends the created order, being used by God in the creation of
the world (11:3). God speaks Scripture throughout Old Testament
history (1:1-2), as the quotations of the Old Testament throughout
the book demonstrate, and God preeminently reveals his word in
his Son (1:2-4). The Son and the Spirit also speak Scripture (2:12-13;
3:7; 10:5, 16). The word of salvation was originally delivered through
Jesus, but then testified to by the first witnesses and finally by God
himself (2:3-4). The word, therefore, is to be taken seriously and
obeyed (2:2-3), for it is "alive and active," a word of judgment as
well as promise that can penetrate the depths of a person's spiritual
life (4:11-12). God's word, therefore, is to be learned by God's people
(5:11-6:3) and is foundational for a healthy life in the church (13:7).

FAITHFULNESS/ENDURANCE AND FALLING AWAY

The need for faithful endurance in following Christ stands at the
heart of the exhortation material in Hebrews, and the author uses a
rich mix of warnings and promises, negative and positive examples,

and various forms of instruction. The warnings in Hebrews are both striking and sobering, calling for obedience to God's word of salvation and reverence and awe for God himself (2:2-4; 12:28-29). Those who reject God's word are under judgment. They drift away from the word of salvation (2:1), falling away from God (3:12-14; 6:4-8) and falling short of God's rest (4:1-2), because their hearts are hardened by the deceitfulness of sin (3:13), causing them to rebel and disobey God's word (2:3; 3:15-19). In effect, such people reject the word of salvation (2:3), stand with those who crucified Jesus, holding him in contempt (6:6), and trample him with their feet, treating his blood as if unfit for sacrifice (10:29). All must give an account before the penetrating gaze of God (4:13), and those who have rejected the word of salvation will face the word of judgment "and the raging fire that will consume the enemies of God" (10:27), for "our God is a consuming fire" (12:29).

On the other hand, there are encouraging words of hope and promise for those who endure in faithfulness to Jesus and in standing with the people of God (Heb 10:32; 12:2-3, 7). They heed such encouragement by paying careful attention to the word of salvation (2:1-3; 13:7), indeed by growing in the word of truth (5:11-6:3), looking to Jesus (3:1; 12:1-3) and other appropriate examples (6:12-14; 10:32-39; 11:1-40), by encouraging one another in the community of faith (3:13; 10:24-25), by holding onto the confession (3:6, 14; 4:14; 10:23) and drawing near to God (4:16; 10:22), and by striving to enter his rest (4:1-10). Christ-followers can keep perspective on the persecution they face by remembering that God redeems suffering, using it to discipline his true children (12:3-11). They also can live out their faith practically by loving one another, showing hospitality, caring for those who are persecuted for the faith and in prison, honoring marriage and sexuality, and thinking correctly about money and possessions (13:1-6). Believers honor God by continually offering up sacrifices of praise, by doing good and sharing with one another, and by following faithful leaders well (13:15-17). God rewards such faithfulness with his Sabbath rest, by which the people of faith cease from their own works (4:1-11); they receive an inheritance from God (9:15)—an eternal kingdom (12:28-29)—and, because of their forgiveness in the new covenant, they know God face to face, having the ability to enter right into God's presence (4:14-16; 10:19-25). Thus they know the joys of the new covenant, the dwelling place of God, and the celebration of the angels. They have their names written in heaven, have been vindicated by God, having been made perfect by Christ—knowing him in his mediatorial role over the new covenant. Whereas Abel's blood says, "The price must be paid," the blood of Jesus speaks a better word, saying over those of the new covenant, "The price has been paid!" (12:22-24).

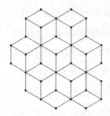

THE SUPERIORITY OF THE SON
(1:1–14)

The danger of these Christians giving up on their walk with Christ is incomprehensible to the author, and he has to remind them forcefully of what they have in Christ and what they will lose if they "drift away" (2:1). So the first ten chapters are devoted to proving Jesus the Son of God superior in every way over the Judaism they would return to if they deserted the Christian faith. The key term is introduced in 1:4, "superior" (*kreittōn*), appearing twelve more times throughout the letter at critical junctures (6:9; 7:7, 19, 22; 8:6; 9:23; 10:34; 11:16, 35, 40; 12:24) and establishing the major point: the incomparable greatness of the Son of God over everything this world or Judaism has to offer. They do not want to join the wilderness generation in disobedience and rebellion (3:1–4:13) and have to face an angry God, suffering the consequences.

INTRODUCTION: REVEALED IN THE SON (1:1–4)

Most New Testament letters follow the precedent of both Jewish and **Hellenistic** first-century letter-writing practice and begin with the author, the recipient, the greeting, a thanksgiving, and an opening prayer. When that is omitted, as here and in 1 John, it is evidence that the situation is so dire that the author must dispense with the normal courtesies and get right to addressing the serious problem. Here it is so serious that the author doesn't even name himself. Nothing matters except "rescuing the perishing" while he still can. This carefully constructed passage functions as both the introduction to the entire treatise and as the first section detailing the superior nature of the Son—superior to the old covenant revelation (1:1-4), to the angels (1:5-2:18), to the promise of rest in the wilderness (3:1-4:13), to the high priesthood (chs. 5-7), and to the sanctuary and the sacrifices (chs. 8-10).

These opening verses are some of the most beautifully written in all of Scripture. God himself has mounted the rescue operation and has done so by revealing the greatest eternal reality this world will ever know. In fact, he has revealed these wondrous truths not only "through the prophets" but even more wondrously "by his Son." There are three parts to this opening material:

1. The revelation through the Son fulfilling the old covenant revelation through the prophets (1:1-2a)

2. The incredible "hymn" to the ministry of the Son in the world (1:2b-3)

3. The superior results of the coming of the Son (1:4)

Within this, I agree with those who find a **chiastic**[1] arrangement in this marvelously constructed paragraph:

> A Revelation via the Son in continuity with the prophets (1:1-2a)
> > B Heir of all things (1:2b)
> > > C Creator of the physical world (1:2c)
> > > > D The threefold work of the Son (1:3a-b)
> > > C' Savior of the spiritual world (1:3c)
> > B' Exalted Ruler over all (1:3d)
> A' His person and name superior to the angels (1:4)

---

1. Terms in bold type are discussed in the Glossary (pages 321-23).

Some have called this an early Christian **christological** hymn similar to Colossians 1:15–20, Philippians 2:6–11, or 1 Timothy 3:16 because of its poetic air, its high christological language, and its parallelism of thought. While it certainly has the air of a hymn about it, it is probably better to see this as the author following the creedal traditions of the early church in creating a theological masterpiece.

Many have called 1:1–2a a threefold contrast in methods (many revelations versus one), times (old at various occasions in the past versus new "in these last days"), and agents (the prophets versus the Son). However, it is doubtful that there is any idea of inferiority here, and it is better to see this as a point of continuity and fulfillment. The incredible process of revelation by which God spoke to his people continues and is finalized in that which has now come through the Son of God. The emphasis at the outset is on the multiple occasions and multiple forms by which God has revealed his divine truths. Over a period of centuries and via a wondrous and complex variety of ways (law, poetry, wisdom, prophecy), God has personally drawn his people to him and told them how they could remain close to him. There is no attempt to denigrate the old covenant revelation in any sense, but rather to rejoice and glory in all God has done throughout the history of his people. Still, it was not complete until the coming of the Son.

All the authors of the Old Testament writings are placed under the category of "prophets," not because they were all prophets but because of the prophetic revelation that took place through their writings. Still, throughout these chapters the citations of prophets continually reverberate, and so the divine revelations through both the prophets and the Son dominate the whole work. Some see significance in the preposition *en*, as if the revelation inhered "in" the arrival of the prophets. However, it often has an instrumental force, "by," indicating emphasis on both the prophets and their writings. God chose the people who would bear the messages as well as the messages themselves.

There is a great deal of emphasis on "these last days" (*toutōn eschatou tōn hēmerōn*), stressing Christ's arrival at the end of time when all will be fulfilled. These are the climax of the ages and the finalization of God's salvation. In ancient times, God's revelation came one piece at a time and was not drawn into a whole and final truth until the arrival of his Son in the "last days" to bring final fulfillment to God's purposes. The prophets were the channel of revelation, but the Son was, along with his Father, the source of revelation. There had to be many prophets, but there was need of only one Son, and he completed the age of the prophets—though he didn't end prophecy altogether, for it continued in Agabus and others (Acts 11:28; 21:10).

The stress is on the fact that we are now living in the last days, the time when God's redemptive purposes and revelatory work have been fulfilled in Christ. The end time has entered the here and now, and the final period of history has been inaugurated. It has been initiated by the One who has been awaited from the dawn of time, and the rest of this incredible passage (vv. 2b–3) will explain his significance for all of us.

Christ as "heir of all things" (1:2b) will become a major thrust in this letter (1:14; 6:17; 9:15; 11:7–9), and this parallels Colossians 1:15–20, Philippians 2:6–11, and 1 Timothy 3:16 with its emphasis on the exaltation of the Son. Normally, this was used of the Caesar dynasty and imperial succession. However, it also had been used of the inheritance of the promised land by Israel as the children of God (Lev 20:24; Deut 1:38; 3:28) and is now seen in its fullness of expression as a statement of the exaltation of the Son by the Father, who "appointed" or "anointed" him heir. Sonship involves by its very nature being an heir (Gal 4:7; Rom 8:17), but this reverses the process, for the inheritance now occurs not when the Father dies but when the Son dies.

The Son partakes of his royal inheritance at his death. His is a heavenly reign, as is made evident in its parallel in the chiasm, "sat down at the right hand of the Majesty in heaven." The "all things" looks to him as David's heir who will inherit the nations (Ps 2:8). In Romans 4:13 (see Gen 17:5), Christ also is "heir of the world" as Abraham's offspring. In Hebrews 2:5 and 8, this will be finalized at the **eschaton** (the end of all things) when he will have "everything under his feet"—in other words, when he will inherit all of God's creation.

The author ends verse 2 with "through whom also he made the universe." Christ as the divine instrument of creation is seen elsewhere in the New Testament (John 1:3; 1 Cor 8:6; Col 1:15–16) and demonstrates the splendor and glory of his preincarnate state. His divinity is eternal and an integral part of Trinitarian theology. The following formula for the interrelationship within the Trinity is apropos—the Father proclaims, the Son performs, the Spirit perfects. The term here for "the universe" is *tous aiōnas*, literally, "the ages" (used later in 6:5; 9:26). It combines the temporal with the spatial sphere; that is, it refers not just to the physical world but to the epochs of time that together constitute history. Still, it is a euphemism for the entire universe and everything in it down throughout the ages. Jesus will, in reality, inherit that which he originally made. At both the beginning and the end of all that is, the Son of God as Alpha and Omega ("the beginning and the end," Rev 1:8; 22:13) has been completely sovereign.

At the center of the chiasm and providing the core of the person and work of Christ in these verses is what could be called "the threefold work" of the Son in verse 3, the essence of who he is and what he does in his incarnate state:

1. He is "the radiance of God's glory." There is some question whether the stress in *apaugasma* ("radiance") here is on the passive side of "reflecting" the glory of God (stressing subordination) or on the active "radiating" his glory (stressing the glory of the Son as coequal with the Father). In the context, the active side is more likely, and the emphasis is on the deity of Christ. He is the

living presence of the **Shekinah** glory, stemming from the glory of God dwelling on earth among his people (from the Hebrew *shakan*; to "dwell"), as in the pillar of fire by night and the cloud by day in the exodus (Exod 13:21) and the idea of the cloud filling the temple in Exodus 25:8–9 and Ezekiel 43:7 (also John 1:14).

2. He is "the exact representation of his being," meaning Christ embodies in himself all that God is. The Greek term *charaktēr* ("representation" or "image") was used of coins or seals in the first century that bore images or impressions meant to represent the emperor exactly. This is often stressed in the New Testament (John 1:1–4; Phil 2:6–7; 2 Cor 4:4; Col 1:15) and looks to the Son as the perfect imprint of God in this world. "Of his being" is *tēs hypostaseōs autou*, literally, "of his substance." It connotes not only that the Son shares the very "being" of God but that everything that makes God to be God (his true essence) is inherent in the Son as well. These two descriptions (radiance of glory, imprint of essence) are ontological (who he is) but, at the same time, functional (what he does), for the Son is portrayed as acting as God's regent on earth, his very presence in this world.

3. He "sustains all things by his powerful word." The one who created the world and was heir to everything in it (the beginning and end; see above) is at the same time the power that binds together every single part of his created world. The emphasis throughout this incredible paean to Christ is on "all things," the universal effects of his presence and power in this world. He created everything in this world, it ultimately belongs to him, and he sustains or upholds it

as the life-force that holds it together. Once more the
thrust is active rather than passive and stresses his
work, as seen in the verb chosen, *pherōn*, to "bear" or
"carry" ("sustains, upholds" in most translations) the
world on his shoulders, so to speak. The preexistent
Son in all his glory is presently at work both as the
presence of God making him known in this present
world and the one "bearing" it to completion and its
intended end in eternity. So his past, his present, and
his future are intimately connected to the past creation and future destiny of this world as we know it.

Parallel to Christ as Creator of the physical world (C and C' in the
chiasm), he is also Savior of the spiritual world, accomplished by
the fact that he "provided purification for sins"—namely, his salvific work on the cross. This will be perhaps the most discussed
part of the list and will dominate Hebrews. Christ's death on the
cross as the atoning sacrifice that enables forgiveness of sin, and
the gift of salvation is the most important event in the history
of this world. Some have mistakenly interpreted the aorist tense
"provided" or "made" as a once-for-all event, but the actual stress
is on the event as a completed whole, stressing the eternal effects
of Christ's sacrifice. By focusing on Jesus' act as "purification"
(*katharismos*), the author brings in the Old Testament imagery of
sin as defilement and Christ's death on the cross as atoning or
making pure the forgiven sinner who has repented and believed.

When he "sat down at the right hand of the Majesty in heaven,"
he fulfilled Psalm 110:1, as his death is followed by his glorious exaltation and seat to the right hand of God and his throne. The humiliation followed by the exaltation of Jesus comes full circle here, and
the victory and glory of Christ ensue. The rest of Hebrews could
be called a **midrashic** expansion of the themes introduced here,
namely that Jesus died for our sins and then entered his exaltation and reign of power at the right hand of God.

Several have recognized that Psalm 110:1 is at the heart of the organizational framework of this letter. It also occurs at Hebrews 1:13; 8:1; 10:12; 12:2, mainly because this is the primary prophetic text in Scripture that predicted the future exaltation of God's Messiah and set the stage for the twofold victory at the cross and then at the **parousia** (coming) of Christ. The "right hand of the Majesty in heaven" is the place of power and pictures Jesus as the conquering King, head of heaven's armies. When he "sat down," his work was finished, and he assumed his eternal place on the Bema or royal throne with his Father as the "Majesty in heaven." When he returns, he will move from his heavenly throne to sit atop his white horse (Rev 19:11) as the conquering King. At that time, Psalm 110:1 tells us, God will make his enemies the footstool of his feet.

In the first element of the chiasm, Christ was seen in continuity with and at the same time above the prophets, for he culminated the revelation of God in this world. Parallel to that here is the final element in verse 4, that he is superior to the angels.[2] The "superiority," as I said there, is *kreittōn* and becomes the key term in the book for remaining true and faithful to him. In his glory and exaltation he has been lifted far above everything Judaism could offer, and there is no reason ever to abandon Christ and embrace any other notion for salvation and meaning in life.

When Christ ascended to heaven and entered his exaltation by sitting at God's right hand, that meant he rose to a position "as much superior to the angels as the name he has inherited is superior to theirs." This is a reference to his Sonship,[3] vastly superior to the "messenger" title the angels have (the meaning of their name, "angel"). Since his Father has exalted him to heaven and sat him

---

2. For many years, I have believed that verse 4 begins the next section (1:4–14), but it seems clear to me that this is not true, for grammatically verses 3 and 4 form a single sentence, and all the clauses of verse 3 modify this verse. So it culminates the chiasm of verses 3–4 as a whole unit.

3. The superior name could be "Yahweh," stressing him as Lord of the universe—but in the context, Christ is presented as the royal Son, and that is more likely here.

at his right hand on the throne, he has reentered his preexistent glory as Sovereign over heaven, thus as "superior to the angels." Some think this emphasis stems from the occasional Jewish worship of angels.

There is an interesting development between these first two chapters regarding the Son's relationship with angels. In 1:4-14, the stress is on his exaltation, and he is seen as vastly superior to angels (highlighting his deity), with seven citations supporting this contrast. However, in 2:5-18, he is seen as "lower than the angels" (Ps 8:5, highlighting his humanity) in his priestly work of bringing fallen humanity back to God. Truly in 1:2-4, Jesus is presented as prophet (receiving revelation), priest (mediating God's salvation), and king (receiving honor and glory).

OLD TESTAMENT PROOF FOR THE SUPERIORITY OF THE SON (1:5-14)

It is often thought that this section is responding to a "worship of angels" cult (see Col 2:18), but there is little evidence for such a cult within Judaism in the first century. More likely, this reflects angels' elevated role in Judaism as the messengers of heaven, mediating the law at Sinai (Jubilees 1:27, 29; Deut 33:2; Acts 7:38, 53) and taking on mediatorial roles in making God known to humankind. The seven citations form a three-part message regarding the Son's status (vv. 5-6), his glory (vv. 7-9), and his majesty (vv. 10-13). The author may be following a Jewish messianic "testimonia" collection—that is, an accumulation of prooftexts attesting to a common theme. The **Qumran** document 4Q Florilegium has the order 2 Samuel 7:10-14 followed by Psalm 1:1 and Psalm 2:1-2, and then it is broken off. The author here may be using this tradition.

His Status (1:5-6)

The first two Old Testament quotations are introduced with a rhetorical question that emphasizes the disparity between the Son and the angels: "to which of the angels did God ever say ... ?" The father/son relationship belonged only with Jesus, and no angels could ever achieve that status. The quotes from Psalm 2:7 and 2 Samuel 7:14 form another brief chiasm: Son to Father and then Father to Son, stressing the oneness between the two. On the other hand, angels are called "sons of God" (Gen 6:2, 4; Job 1:6; 2:1; Ps 29:2), but never is one labeled a "son of God." Jesus' special filial relation to his Father made him unique in God's creation.

The second part of the sentence, "today I have become your father," stems from Psalm 2:7, a coronation psalm fulfilled especially in Jesus as Davidic Messiah. The cited portion here needs explanation and has been variously interpreted, especially in light of the "today." Augustine understood this as a reference to the eternal generation of the Son, the church fathers saw it as linking Jesus' baptism with his coronation, and others have taken it as a reference to Jesus' incarnation, resurrection, exaltation to the right hand of God, or second coming. Clearly it is meant to designate when Christ was presented as "Son of God." He was Son in his preexistence (1:2), his earthly work (1:3a), and his future glory (1:3b–4), but this designates when God presents him to this world as such. However, the author is most likely highlighting his exaltation in heaven as the "today" moment when all the facets of his Sonship came together in the final fulfillment of his filial role.

Parallel to Psalm 2:7, 2 Samuel 7:14 stresses Jesus' unique Sonship anew. This was used originally of Nathan's prophetic promise to David that his house would reign forever (see also Jer 33:17), and his son would build a house for God, the temple. Solomon built the temple, but this promise was never fulfilled in David's seed, and it disappeared when his line ended with the last of the kings of Judah (Jehoiachin and Zedekiah in 2 Kings 24–25) with the exile. The prophets looked for a greater son of David, the Messiah, who would return that promise to God's people (Jer 23:5–6). So it was fulfilled in Jesus Messiah (Rom 1:3; 1 Tim 3:16). In Jesus, as Son of

God, the promise rings true: "I will be his Father; and he will be my Son." The angels have no such relationship and can make no such claim. Jesus reigns supreme over this world.

The third passage (1:6) brings in the other side of the contrast, the relationship of the angels to the Son. It is similar to Psalm 97:7 ("worship him, all you gods!") but even closer to the **Septuagint** (Greek Old Testament) and Qumran (4QDeut32) versions of Deuteronomy 32:43, which has "Rejoice, O heavens, along with him, and let the sons of God [= the angels] worship him."[4] I agree with those who surmise that this was the reading in the author's Greek Bible, and that Qumran had the correct reading rather than the Masoretic tradition that is behind most English versions. In the Song of Moses here, the call to "worship him" is directed toward the worship of Yahweh, but the author applies it to the Son with the opening declaration that this worship is to take place "when God brings his firstborn into the world."

"World" is *oikoumenē*, referring to the world inhabited by men and women. So this could refer to the incarnation and the angelic worship of Luke 2:13–14, but it could also refer to the revelation of Jesus' true significance at either his exaltation or second coming. "Firstborn" seems to indicate that this worship takes place at his exaltation, which is likely in this context where Jesus' ascension to glory is featured.

Most see Psalm 89:27 echoed here as well: "I will appoint him to be my firstborn, the most exalted of the kings of the earth." As firstborn, he is both eternal Son and incarnate Redeemer, with dominion over the nations as well as heavenly authority. So the angels not only carry messages from Father and Son but also worship the Son and the Father. His superiority could not be presented more forcefully.

---

4. Many scholars believe this may well represent the original text written by Moses rather than the Masoretic translation found in most English Bibles.

HIS GLORY (1:7-9)

This is another place where the author is using his Greek Old Testament, for the Hebrew Bible for Psalm 104:4 has, "He makes winds his messengers, flames of fire his servants," while the Septuagint is the same as here, "He makes his angels spirits, and his servants flames of fire." This contrasts with verses 8-9 and stresses the temporary, changing character of angels. Fire and wind were symbols of ever-shifting forces in rabbinic literature. While angels were extremely important beings, they were "made" what they are by God, and everything they became was at his bidding. The Son is the opposite. He partakes of the deity of his Father and has his role intrinsically as a member of the Trinity. Angels are part of God's created order, while the Son stands with the Father above the created order and is sovereign over it. The servant-Son contrast is at the core of this.

The Son, on the other hand, is not just exalted as the Sovereign in heaven or God's viceroy ruling over this world. He is God himself, inhabiting his very throne. The citation (the fifth one) is taken from Psalm 45:6-7, a hymn to celebrate the royal wedding of the Davidic king. The wording here, "Your throne, O God," was a problem for several ancient scribes, who changed the wording to "Your throne is God" to avoid labeling the king God. However, while unusual, it was not unheard of; it simply viewed the king as God's regent and representative on earth, an extension of God himself. In fact, in John 10:34, Jesus cites Psalm 82:6 in terms of calling all true Israelites "gods" because they constituted the children of God, part of his family.

In this context, however, it is a clear ascription of deity to Jesus as the royal Messiah on the divine throne. At the Father's right hand, he partakes of the Father's essence and authority, and his is an eternal throne. The rest of this (vv. 8b-9) is a near word-for-word citation of the Septuagint of Psalm 45:6-7 and establishes the tone of the reign of God-Messiah over this world.

In verses 8b–9a there are two ascriptions. First, the royal scepter defining the kingdom he has established on earth—that is, his sphere of rule—is to be a "scepter of justice" or "uprightness," with *euthytētos* emphatic and denoting perfect moral rectitude and upright behavior. This directly contrasts the immorality and depravity of nearly all the kings of the divided monarchy and describes the messianic age when all God's promises would be fulfilled.

Second, within this high moral atmosphere, the royal Messiah-God would "love righteousness and hate wickedness." This must define his rule, and it is the opposite of how nations have acted throughout history. Here *dikaiosynē* intends both aspects of its meaning: spiritual righteousness and social justice. The second flows out of the first, and you cannot have the one without the other. Obviously, this will only predominate when the Messiah establishes his kingdom, but it is the goal of God's people at all times.

Because his messianic reign was characterized by righteousness and justice, God has "set you above your companions by anointing you with the oil of joy" (v. 9). The king's companions here are probably not the angels but the "sons and daughters" who are members of his family (2:10–11) and "share in the heavenly calling" (3:1). In the wedding setting of the psalm, this means the bridegroom is elevated above the others who participate in the wedding. "Messiah" means "anointed one," and it is significant that his sovereign rule is to be characterized primarily with "gladness" or the joy of heaven. His will be a reign of joy and peace unlike any other this world has ever known. To be a part of God's family and enjoy the reign of his Son will truly be a foretaste of heaven. This should be a goal of both worship and fellowship in the church as the body of Christ. We strive to allow his "joy" to govern our time together as a church family.

HIS MAJESTY (1:10–12)

After establishing Jesus' status above the angels as the object of angelic worship in 1:6–7 and his glory as not only God's anointed but as God himself in 1:7–9, here the author turns to proclaiming his majesty as creator and destroyer of worlds as in Psalm 102:25–27. This fits like a glove with Psalm 45:6–7, as it, too, centers on the divine sovereignty he enjoys and the eternal nature of his work. The fact that the two are connected with "and" demonstrates that they serve the same powerful message: the divine majesty of the Son. The two together reaffirm and deepen the picture of the Son as Creator and Sustainer of the universe. The changeable nature of creation echoes that of the angels and sets in antithetical contrast to the immutable nature of the Son.

Psalm 102 is a lament psalm and calls itself a "prayer of the afflicted." The psalmist personifies Jerusalem and the nation, with national sin bringing about divine wrath and judgment, leading to the people calling themselves "the destitute" (v. 17). The psalmist contrasts his frail, finite body with the eternal throne of God (compare Heb 1:8 above), prays for restoration, and praises God for creating both earth and the heavens and ending this finite world in his own time. Once more, what Psalm 102 ascribes to Yahweh is applied to the Son as coequals in the divine reality. Hebrews 1:10 centers on the Son's work at the beginning of creation, and verses 11–12 on his work at the end of creation. In both parts the Son is timeless and eternal, without beginning or end, in contrast with the impermanence of creation.

In John 1:3–4, Jesus is the twofold Creator, bringing life and light into this physical world at creation and bringing spiritual life and light into this world at his incarnation (the new creation). Here in Hebrews 1:10, the author repeats what he said in 1:2–3, that all the universe, both the earth and the heavens, was the product of his hands. He laid the foundation and created the vast reaches of the heavens. Christ is addressed as "Lord"—Yahweh, Lord of heaven and earth. Yahweh as Father and Son has created both the heavens and the earth, and the Triune Godhead will bring them to an end at the proper time.

This latter point is the subject of the second half of the quote (1:11–12). The eternal nature of the Son and his office is in polar contrast with the temporality and changeable nature of his creation. Due to sin, this world is finite. It will "perish" and "wear out like a garment." The basic thesis is stated ("they will perish"), and then three successive images of worn-out garments flesh out the premise. The verb is "growing old" (*palaioō*) like a garment does, and it is a common metaphor, picturing both life itself (Isa 50:9) and this world as a whole (Isa 51:6) as a gradually decaying old threadbare garment that has become moth-eaten and worth only throwing away.

Three successive pictures show this: this world is in the process of growing old and wearing out; it is ready to be "rolled out like a robe," that is, removed from the clothing hook, rolled up, and thrown away (compare Rev 6:14, the "heavens receded like a scroll being rolled up"), then finally "changed." In this third image (the changed garment), the picture switches from negative to positive, for in Isaiah and here this depicts the renewal of God's creation and people. This is the day of the Lord, when the present earth and heaven will perish and pass away (2 Pet 3:7, 10) and the "new heavens and new earth" will come (Rev 21:1). The emphasis here, though, is on the changeable nature of finite creation. Only the eternal, sovereign Son could accomplish this and bring life out of death. No angel could do so, for angels, though not temporary, are still created beings and limited in their power and authority.

In contrast, the Son "remains the same" (Heb 1:11a, 12b), permanent rather than gradually deteriorating like creation. Further, he is not only never-changing but eternal, and his "years will never end." Angels do not participate in the world's sin and so do not partake of its impermanence and doomed nature; though they are part of God's creation, they lack the power to bring about the eschaton (or end). Nevertheless, they will be the servants of God and Christ and will accompany Christ at his return as part of heaven's army (Matt 13:41, 49; 24:31; Rev 19:14). Still, they are servants and not equals with Christ.

THE EXALTED AND VICTORIOUS LORD (1:13)

The seventh and final citation provides the proper conclusion and echoes the citation of Psalm 110:1 in Hebrews 1:3c above. As the primary prooftext for the doctrine of the exaltation of Christ by the early church, it is the most oft-quoted Old Testament text in the New (over twenty times). An **inclusio** is formed between verses 5–6 and verses 13–14. Verses 5 and 13 both begin with "to which of the angels did God ever say" and then describe the exalted nature of the Son. Verses 6 and 14 center on the angels as the Son's servants (v. 6) and followers (v. 14).

Psalm 110 shows par excellence why the Son is superior to the angels. They can never attain his glory and splendor. The psalm is perhaps the greatest example of a royal psalm, with the introductory "The LORD said to my lord" going beyond the Davidic king to the Davidic Messiah and looking to the fulfillment of the Davidic promises in the Christ. In Hebrews 1:3c the first half of Psalm 110:1 is the focus (exaltation to the right hand of God), and in Hebrews 1:13 the second half comes to the fore in the final victory of King Messiah: "Sit at my right hand until I make your enemies a footstool for your feet." Presently the Son is the enthroned Lord of all, and at the end of history at his return he will become victor over Satan and all the forces of evil.

As many have pointed out, Psalm 110 presents the Davidic Messiah as prophet, priest, and king, and this is a central point in Hebrews. His royal work is seen in the citations of Psalm 110:1 in Hebrews 1:3, 13; 8:1; 10:12; 12:2; and he is priest-king in the Melchizedekian quotes of Psalm 110:4 in Hebrews 5:6, 10; 6:20;

7:11, 17, 21. Here the emphasis is on the fact that he alone has the sovereign power to defeat the evil that currently has a strange hold on this world and is causing so much pain for God's people.

THE TASK ASSIGNED TO THE ANGELS (1:14)

As so often in the letters, the end of a section is designated by a rhetorical question, which focuses the reader on the central thesis—in this case, the place of angels in God's plan as servants of both his Son and his Son's followers. They are, at heart, "ministering spirits sent to serve those who will inherit salvation." The Son is sovereign over the nations, while angels are servants of the Son's followers among the nations. The Son as Creator and Sustainer is in absolute control of the present and future of God's creation, and the angels minister within his creation.

This is a significant passage on the question of "guardian angels," the fact that God created his angels to watch over or guard as well as serve and minister to his people (see Ps 91:11; Dan 3:28; Matt 18:10; Acts 12:15). It is debated whether angels are greater than humans in God's created order. They were created, are heavenly rather than earthly beings, and appear to have a higher function. As we will see in 2:7, Psalm 8:5 states we were created "a little lower than the angels." However, here and elsewhere they serve God's people. In the Old Testament and here, they are "sent to serve," which in the Greek is *eis diakonian apostellomena dia*, "sent for the sake of" or "to help" the saints. My view is that angels and humans are coequal beings and will live together in eternity. Here the emphasis is on their God-chosen purpose as "ministering spirits," *leitourgika pneumata*, a phrase that connotes priestly service. In the book of Revelation, angels are the priests of heaven (Rev 5:8; 8:3-4), and this "ministry" is continued in their work on earth.

The believers to whom they minister are described as those who "will inherit" (actually "about to inherit," *mellontas klēronomein*) salvation, combining imminence and the certainty of their future salvation. The angels help them spiritually and physically in their struggle against the powers of evil in the world. This is the second time the inheritance motif has been stressed (Christ as "heir" in 1:2). Christ has become "heir" of his creation at his own exaltation to God's right hand, and when he returns his followers will accompany him to glory. Our "salvation" has already been inaugurated—for we experience it spiritually now, and in the future, when he initiates his eternal reign, we will enjoy it with finality. This is labeled "so great a salvation" in 2:3. All the magnificent truths of Hebrews 1 flesh it out and fill it with meaning and power.

The author of Hebrews has made his point and prepared his readers with his wondrous tribute to the superiority of Christ and the magnificence of the salvation he has made available to us. It is now time to underscore the danger of a shallow reception of these truths that might jettison all that Christ has done for us. The author will do that in two stages in Hebrews 2, first with the initial warning (2:1-4) against wandering away and failing to persevere and second with a lengthy description (2:5-18) of the salvation Christ has provided for his followers. So let us move on to the next incredible section of this exciting exhortation.

In Hebrews, we have a somber letter to a weak congregation in serious danger of losing it all. At the same time, we have a literary masterpiece, both in the quality of its writing and the depth of its theology. To wake up these dullards and get them growing in Christ, the author has woven together a magnum opus, especially in its christological and **soteriological** meditations. The first section (1:1-4) replaces the standard letter opening (author, recipient, and all) to remind the readers what they have in the new covenant age—namely, a new revelation that fulfills and completes the old in nearly every facet.

The first two titles (heir and creator) trace the glory of God's Son both in his post-incarnate state (at his exaltation to glory he will be "heir of all" that he has just saved) and in his preincarnate state (he created the very world he will later inherit). These are incredible truths in chiastic form, telling all readers the true significance and splendor of the One who entered this world to save us. Then at the center of the chiasm and the heart of the description of the Christ is his threefold work that depicts his incarnate state: he perfectly radiates the glory of God, completely represents God in this world, and sustains this world by his strength. He is the perfect embodiment of God in this world.

The final elements of this hymn-like chiasm constitute the bottom half of the chiasm, paralleling the top half in reverse order (see above, intro to the section). The first pair (C, C') depicts the Son as sovereign over all of creation, both creating the physical world (v. 2c) and providing forgiveness as Savior of the spiritual side of creation (v. 3c). He is the source of life and salvation. The second pair (B, B') centers on his exaltation to glory following his death on the cross. At that time, he inherits (v. 2b) all that he had created (showing him as Lord of all, both before and after his incarnation) and sits "at the right hand of the Father" as exalted Ruler (v. 3d). The final pair (A, A') provide the titles for the first two sections of this letter, declaring him the source of the new revelation of the new covenant age (vv. 1–2a) and superior to the angels (v. 4). This section provides a magnificent panorama of virtually all facets of the person and work of the Son of God and demands extensive meditation of its depths on our part.

The second part of this opening chapter expands on Jesus' superiority to the angels from 1:4, providing seven Old Testament citations that prove that this was an established theme from the old covenant revelation. The first two (v. 5) show that Jesus as royal Messiah was indeed God's Son, finalized in his exaltation when he was formally presented as "my Son" (Ps 2:7); and this was anchored in the Davidic covenant of 2 Samuel 7:14, promising that the Christ would return the Davidic dynasty to the throne.

In Deuteronomy 32:43 (and Ps 97:7) in Hebrews 1:6, it is clear that angels worship him, not the other way around. As the object of worship, even by the heavenly beings, he is truly exalted. He has dominion over earth and heaven and alone is worthy of worship. The question to us is: How can we revere anyone other than him?

From his status as Son of God, we now turn to his glory as the Exalted One in verses 7–9. Two citations dominate this section. First, in Psalm 104:4, he has greater glory than the angels because they are created beings, "made" to be spirits and servants of both God and his people. Second, Psalm 45:6–7 shows that he is deity on an eternal throne and establishing righteousness and justice over God's kingdom. Through him, wickedness will be removed and joy will reign. Our task then is to allow this scenario to play itself out as we accept our place in God's kingdom and allow Christ to reign over us.

The next section (Heb 1:10–12) builds on this theme of glory and reveals the majesty of the Son, centering upon Psalm 102:25–27, which traces the beginning and end of this creation, from its foundations at the hand of God to its close as a worn-out garment. Creation ever changes, but the Godhead does not and remains the same for eternity. The only power we can truly rely upon is that of the immutable God, not the ever-changing face of life on this earth. We must depend entirely on him.

The final citation (Heb 1:13) is the key passage for the message of this letter, Psalm 110:1, establishing the Son as the Exalted One at the right hand of God. This quote frames the arguments thus far, beginning in Hebrews 1:3 and concluding in 1:13: Jesus is King Messiah, in the place of glory and power at the right hand of his Father on high, and thus vastly superior to the angels. Why would any weak Christian return to their Jewish roots and desert Christ? He is God-Messiah, the only One who has the strength to bring us victory in the war against evil.

The concluding point (v. 14) is that angels are sent into this world to "minister to" God's people. Christ controls them and gives them their marching orders as to their work in this world. They are messengers and servants. So once again, why would anyone allow themselves to drift away and turn their backs on the One who alone is sovereign and who is totally focused on providing salvation and giving help to all who follow him?

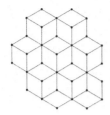

FOCUSING ON THE
SUFFERING MESSIAH
(2:1–18)

The introduction to Hebrews consists of 1:1–2:18, yet at the same time, it is the first part of the central section of the book (1:1–10:18) and will be listed that way in the outline of this letter in the introductory chapter. There is a kind of A-B-A-B pattern, with a shorter section fleshed out in a lengthy one: A (1:1–4), B (1:5–14), A (2:1–4), B (2:5–18). The two lengthier parts center on the superior work of Christ in contrast to the angels, with an incredible irony here in 2:5–18. In 1:4–14, the stress was on the superiority of Christ over the angels, and that continues here, but it comes by way of the teaching that in his incarnate state, he was rendered "a little lower than the angels" (v. 7, from Ps 8:5). In his humility he accomplished his great work of bringing God's salvation to sinful humanity.

WARNING TO PAY ATTENTION (2:1–4)

This is the first of five major warning passages, which could be seen more broadly as macro-units (2:1–4; 3:7–4:13; 5:11–6:12; 10:19–39; 12:14–29) or more intensely as micro-units (2:1–4; 4:12–13; 6:4–8; 10:26–31; 12:25–29). However we perceive it, at critical junctures throughout the letter, the author pauses and applies the material to the great danger that lies behind the letter: falling away from salvation. He sees in these shallow, lazy Christians a new wilderness generation like the one following the exodus that failed to enter the promised land (see especially 3:1–4:13). In the same way, these dullards could fail to enter their heavenly destiny.

Principle: Focus Rather Than Drift (2:1)

In 1:1–14 we see the superior work of Jesus the Son of God both in providing a new revelation for God's people and in ascending to the right hand of God as the one exalted above the angels. In light of both important truths, Jesus' followers must "pay the most careful attention to what we have heard" in that revelation. Both the Son and the salvation he has wrought make it necessary to focus as never before on this revelation of God in him. The "therefore" is *dia touto* and is first for emphasis. Let me paraphrase: "Because Christ is completely superior to the angels, it is absolutely necessary (*dei*, "must") that we concentrate closely on his revealed truths regarding himself and salvation." Careful attention is not a mere option but a serious requirement for every believer. The readers have grown lax in their spiritual concerns and focus on the things of the world rather than the things of God.

So, as a result, they have fallen into danger—namely, that of "drifting away" from the faith. Literally, the construction commands the people to "continue to hold fast (present-tense *prosechein*) lest we drift away," a strong nautical image of a ship slipping away from its moorings and drifting away to sink on the rocks. Some also take this picture as a ring slipping off the finger to be lost in the grass. After I suddenly lost weight due to illness, I lost my wedding ring in exactly this way.

The Danger of Ignoring God's Salvation (2:2–3a)

This is a single conditional sentence, with *ei* ("if"), a condition of fact translated by the NIV as "since." The "message spoken through angels" stems from the Jewish tradition that when God gave the torah, it was mediated through angels. This is based on the **Septuagint** of Deuteronomy 33:2, "The LORD came from Sinai ... myriads of holy ones with him," with the Septuagint adding that "angels were with him at his right hand." In Acts 7:38, Stephen spoke of Moses as the one to whom the angel spoke on Mount Sinai, and in Acts 7:53, of the law as "given through angels" (also Gal 3:19). So while not explicitly mentioned at Sinai, tradition firmly places the angels implicitly at Sinai.

The point highlighted here is that the message was given at Sinai through God's angels, and therefore, "was binding," holy, and completely valid legally. As a result, "every violation and disobedience received its just punishment" (Heb 2:2). Technically, this was more than just a refusal to obey a precept of torah; it constituted an act of rebellion against God. Thus divine justice demanded that a proper "punishment" (*misthapodosia*, often used positively for rewarding good deeds, as in 10:35) be given for such deliberate transgressions.

If this firm and just penalty came through the law, how much more is it certain to come when Christ's great salvation is ignored (2:3a). The lazy, unresponsive people in the church had better worry, for there is "no escape" for that kind of person. Since their salvation is incomparably greater, and the penalty for jettisoning it correspondingly greater as well, they should not think there is any way out. Their punishment is doubly certain. In fact, this idea of certain punishment becomes a mega-theme that will be repeated in 4:11; 6:6; 10:28–29, 31; 12:25.

THE TWOFOLD CONFIRMATION OF THIS SALVATION (2:3B–4)

The penalty for disregarding this great salvation was certain because this salvation itself was certain. It was both "announced by the Lord" and doubly confirmed, first by "those who heard" and then by the Godhead themselves. The first "salvation" or "deliverance" had come through Moses at the exodus and Sinai, the second and final proclamation through the Son via his incarnation and the cross. These two "revelations" were the subject in 1:1-3. As several have pointed out, the time and content through which the proclamation of the Son took place do not constitute a single announcement but the incarnation, life, death, and ascension to glory of his earthly work. The Son is revealed as "the Lord," the same Sovereign who "laid the foundations of the earth" in 1:10.

The first confirmation by "those who heard" likely refers to the apostles and others whom Christ taught in his earthly ministry. So the truth of Jesus is affirmed not only by apostolic witness but by all those privileged to sit at his feet and observe his wondrous deeds. While his earthly ministry consisted of words and deeds, the message itself is highlighted here because it constituted the revelation of the gospel truths by the Son himself. The fact that it is "confirmed" (bebaioō) means that its truthfulness and accuracy has been guaranteed by a countless number, many of them followers and even apostles.

Second, God himself provides testimony as to the validity of the new revelation, witnessing to its reality via "signs, wonders and various miracles," echoing the "signs and wonders" of the exodus from Egypt (Exod 7:3; Deut 4:34; 7:19; Ps 135:9; Jer 32:20-21). These were miracles that packed a message and signified God's presence and power behind his people. Here in Hebrews, they indicate that the divine revelation through Jesus continued through the ongoing miraculous ministries of the apostles.

Then the work of the Holy Spirit completed the Trinitarian involvement of the Godhead in the church's witness. The "gifts of the Holy Spirit distributed according to his will" echoes Paul in 1 Corinthians 12:11-30. Christ provided the revelation, God confirmed it by pouring out signs and wonders, and the Spirit continued its effects via spiritual gifts distributed among the people of God. What greater confirmation could there be than this? No rational person could doubt the reality and power of the Christian life after this. "Distributed according to his will" here, echoed in 1 Corinthians 12:11, brings out the sovereign control of all spiritual gifts by the divine will as conveyed by the Spirit. Each of us receives exactly those gifts the Spirit determines we should have. All the gifts are available to us, but all are not meant for us. More importantly, by receiving these wondrous gifts, we *all* have a role in the proof and confirmation of the work of the Son in us.

At the same time, this means that each of us, building on the original recipients of this letter, is responsible for living up to the privileges Christ has given us. We, too, are "hearers," since we have received this letter and studied it. "How shall we escape" is meant for us as well. There is no excuse for shallow, unresponsive hearers who live for the world rather than the Lord. This is a sober warning intended to wake up those who are pretending they can't hear the message. Their danger could not be greater.

SUPERIORITY VIA INCARNATION (2:5-18)

HUMILIATION BY MEANS OF INCARNATION (2:5-9)

Christ's greatness and exalted glory came through humiliation and suffering. The author continues his emphasis on the superiority of the Son over the angels by showing how he has deliberately lowered himself by undergoing incarnation into a human body that is "lower than the angels" (vv. 7, 9). After an excursus to warn the readers of the dangers of ignoring the new revelation via God's Son, the author now returns to the subject of the superiority of the Son and his revelation over the angels from 1:5-14. There the emphasis was on his exaltation to the right hand of God, and here we are told the process by which he arrived at that point—namely, his incarnation and the fact that he joined humanity as "lower than the angels."

Quote from Psalm 8:4-6 (2:6-8a)

The author does not comment about authorship but instead calls it simply "a place where someone has testified" (Heb 2:6). Throughout Hebrews, he cares little about authorship issues but believes the authority lies in the message more than the person who wrote it. Its power stems from its nature as the word of God—and God, rather than the human author, is the one who matters. Psalm 8 is a creation hymn praising God in amazement that humans, made lower than the angels, should have dominion over God's creation.

In looking at human beings both as a corporate body ("mankind") and as individuals ("a son of man"), the psalmist is filled with wonder at God's concern and care for them. He doesn't understand why humans should have such worth. In the creation account of Genesis 1:26–28, humans had been created in God's image and given authority and responsibility to care for his creation. Yet because of sin, they had failed to meet the divine expectations and were made to reside in finite bodies "lower than the angels" (Heb 2:7). Still, they were remembered, loved, and cared for deeply by God even though they deserved none of that. In fact, God "crowned them with glory and honor." The psalmist marvels at that. There is little hope or future for humanity as observed in action. Yet the ideal human being as portrayed here is the object of divine care and glory. They deserve nothing but have been given everything. The Creator has invested in them and raised them up, giving them "glory and honor," which but for God's compassion would never be theirs. They have been given dominion, God has "put everything under their feet" (v. 8), yet it has been marred by sin. They are existing in the frustration of sin at the present time.

There is considerable debate regarding the significance of "son of man" in verse 6. In Psalm 8:4, it is a euphemism for the individual human being, but for the early church, it was a major title of Christ. So several scholars believe it should be capitalized in Hebrews 2:6 and refers to Christ: "What is mankind that you are mindful of them, or the Son of Man that you care for him?" However, that reads too much into the psalm. In the Gospels, the title always has the definite article ("*the* Son of Man"), while here it does not ("*a* son of man")— and it is better to leave it as originally intended in the psalm. Christ is not introduced until verse 9, and the message is that only in him is humanity's dominion returned.

Explanation of the quote (2:8b–9)

The fact is that, because of their depravity, human beings have diminished the dominion God had given them over his creation. That tension is made clear in 2:8b. On the one hand, from the ideal perspective, "God left nothing that is not subject to them." This is stated emphatically with a double negative—there is "nothing that is not under his control." Yet at the "present," due to sin, "we do not see everything subject to them." The image of God in humans has been marred, and they do not have dominion. This seems an oxymoron. Humanity has universal dominion and yet doesn't.

The dilemma is clear. The solution is even more clear (v. 9), for Jesus now enters the equation. In the humiliation he received from his incarnation, life of opposition, and death on the cross, he, too, endures a life "lower than the angels"—yet in the results of his sacrificial death and exaltation to his session at the right hand of God, he experiences the "glory of honor" that is his. Here we see the reality of the already and the not yet. "At present we do not see everything subject to them" (v. 8c) but we *already* see Jesus, and through him the process of recovery has been inaugurated and is soon to be realized.

There is a further question as to how to interpret "a little" (*brachy ti*) in the psalm's citation of verse 7 and the application of it to Jesus in verse 9. It can be understood as time ("lower for a little while") or degree ("a little lower"), and scholars have taken it both ways, usually with both verses translated the same. If time, the emphasis is on the temporal nature of the dilemma; if degree, it is on the limits of his subjection. My developing understanding is to see the description of humanity as stressing the limits (humanity made just "a little lower" than the angelic realm) but the application to Jesus stressing the temporal nature of the incarnation ("just a short while")—namely, until his sacrificial death brought about his exaltation to heavenly glory. That makes slightly better sense to me.

The result is twofold, and this is what the author wants us to "see." Jesus' incarnate ministry to humanity ended when he "suffered death," which led to him being "crowned with glory and honor" by his Father. His humiliation produced his exaltation. We are at the true heart of the message of Hebrews; it is the core of everything. All that has been said prepares for this. His incarnation and life on earth were vehicles for his greatness, and his exaltation and **parousia** (second coming) flow out of it. He died as the suffering servant of Isaiah 52–53 for our sake.

The purpose is then given, "so that by the grace of God he might taste death for everyone." At first glance this seems confusing, for this seems to be saying that he "received his crown for dying in order that he could die." He hardly was to die twice. The key is that the purpose statement covers all that has been said thus far about the Son. He became a lowly human and identified with us, came to earth, performed his messianic work, and lived a life of suffering, all so that he could die not just a humiliating death but a vicarious death "for everyone" (*hyper pantos*)—meaning, dying in our place.

This says that he "tasted death," a strong ancient idiom stressing that he experienced the full enormity of the cross in all its ignominy and pain on our behalf. To "taste" is to experience fully. Moreover, all this came "by the grace of God,"[1] a frequent New Testament emphasis pointing to the divine mercy and love of the Godhead that led the Father to send his Son to die so that we sinners could find salvation.[2]

SOLIDARITY WITH HUMANITY AS SAVIOR AND HIGH PRIEST (2:10–18)

Perfected through sufferings (2:10–13)

God's choice of suffering as the vocation of his Son for his incarnate work on earth was perfect and "perfected" or "completed" the work

---

1. A few older manuscripts omit this phrase, but by far the best manuscripts include it.
2. See Rom 3:24; 1 Cor 1:4; 3:10; Gal 2:21; Eph 1:6, 7; 2:7; 2 Thess 1:12; 1 Tim 1:14; Heb 12:15.

of salvation set for him to accomplish. The goal is established at the beginning—namely, "bringing many sons and daughters to glory." The point of verses 6–8a was that sin has marred the image of God in humankind and brought these sinners low, removing the glorious state they would have enjoyed. There was no hope for humankind, and that is why the grace and compassion of God led him to send his Son to pay the price for them and thereby restore them to the "glory" God intended for his people.

The message of verses 7 and 9 was that Jesus, the Son of God, came and suffered death so he could return the "glory" to created humanity that they had lost due to sin. He did this by "tasting death" as a vicarious sacrifice for them. The results of that act are now explored further, and again the purpose is to "bring them to the glory" they had lost. Moreover, they are now "sons and daughters" because they have also been brought back into the family of God, the subject of the next verse (11).

All this, the author insists, shows how "fitting" or "appropriate" it was for God to do all that he chose to do in 2:5–9—namely, to have his Son suffer so that his work could come to completion (be perfected) through it. The focus is not on his person or character but on his messianic office. Christ was born into this world to die for this world. Without his suffering and death, there could be no salvation, and heaven would have been depopulated of all human life. In fact, the Greek *eprepen* shades over into *dei*—that is, divine necessity. It was both completely "proper" and necessary to God's purposes that Christ suffer and die for the salvation of fallen humanity.

The very character and purpose of God in this world was at stake. We are told he is the One "for whom and through whom everything exists" (v. 10). In 1:2b–3, 10, the emphasis was on the Son as the instrument of creation, and now here it is the Father who is the cause (*di hon*) and the instrument (*di hou*) by which creation took place. This doxology praises God for placing the suffering of his Son into his creative purposes, for it ensured that humanity could now have a part in the final eternal creation when evil has finally been removed from this world. What could possibly be more "appropriate" for God's redemptive purposes in creation?

As such, Christ is now labeled "the pioneer of their salvation," with "pioneer" (*archēgon*) connoting a leader or champion, often a major figure like Hercules who accomplishes great feats. In the New Testament, it always refers to Jesus in terms of his death, resurrection, and glory (Acts 3:15; 5:31; Heb 2:10; 12:2). It fits well here because it depicts Jesus as the One who leads or pioneers God's people in a new exodus, delivering or saving them for God. "Champion" also works well, as it pictures him as the Victor who triumphs through suffering and death. He is the New Moses (3:1–6) who is guiding God's family to their final redemption.

God achieves this by "perfecting" this pioneer "through sufferings" (*dia pathēmatōn*; niv, "what he suffered"). The plural "sufferings" encompasses Jesus' whole life of suffering as a fulfillment of the Isaianic Suffering Servant (Isa 52–53). As stated above, it is not that Jesus was a finite, fallen creature but that his messianic office needed to be completely finalized, as when a priest was commissioned (Exod 29:9, 33; Lev 8:33; 21:10; Num 3:3). His personhood is not brought to perfection, but he is equipped and consecrated for office through it.

In verse 11 the author turns to language of sanctification and consecration for his next point. There is some question whether *hagiazōn* here connotes "making holy/sanctification" or "consecration." Nothing in the context suggests Christian growth, and a great deal favors consecration, as the author uses the imagery of consecrating a priest into his office in verse 10. So it is probably better to translate, "Both the one who consecrates and those who are consecrated." The One consecrated to his priestly work in verse 10 is now consecrating his followers into the sacred family of God. The emphasis is on their unity and oneness. In the Old Testament, it is God who consecrates his people to himself (Exod 31:13; Lev 20:8), while here it is Jesus. His followers are clearly the ones who are consecrated. The point here is that they are "of the same family" or "of one origin" (*ex henos pantes*).

The question is the origin and basis of this solidarity. Some take "of one" as a neuter and believe the message is that they share a common humanity. Others take it as masculine and see it as Adam (one race) or Abraham (one people), but that is unlikely here. Most take this rightly as masculine and a reference to God, specifically to their union with him as "sons and daughters" (v. 10) of his family. We have been redeemed by the blood of Christ and made a part of his sacred family.

The result is that "Jesus is not ashamed to call them brothers and sisters" (v. 11; see its parallel with God in 11:16). Honor and shame provided the backbone of the social fabric of the ancient world. For Jesus not to be ashamed of his followers conferred both honor and status on them. This is especially true of those of low social status, especially slaves. All relationships relied on such social distinctions, and Christ has just removed them entirely, rendering every one of his followers his brother or sister and part of his family. This was unheard of in the ancient world (for the reciprocal nature of this, see Mark 8:38; Luke 9:26). Jesus has not only accepted them but raised them to an incredible level, as the King of the universe has just included them in his family. This is covenant theology at its best.

The three citations in verses 12–13 develop the three primary themes and provide messianic prooftexts to support them, and a good part of the meaning stems from the context of each psalm. At the same time, they demonstrate the solidarity between Christ and his followers.

1. In Psalm 22:22, the Messiah praises God in the midst of suffering. This is the psalm of Christ's cry of agony on the cross, "My God, my God, why have you forsaken me?" (Mark 15:34 and parallels). This citation begins the second half of Psalm 22 when the

psalmist's lament transforms into a cry of thanksgiving, for God has been faithful and delivered him
from his enemies. The first half of the psalm was seen
by the early church as a foretaste of Jesus' suffering
on the cross, and here it provides parallels between
Christ and the suffering of his messianic community.

God has responded to the cries of his Suffering
Servant, and the pioneer who has been exalted is
responding with a twofold act of "proclaiming" and
"praising" the name of Yahweh to his "brothers and
sisters"—namely, the new people of God established
under the new covenant. The "assembly" would
include both the messianic community on earth
and the angelic worshipers in heaven, the "thousands upon thousands of angels in joyful assembly,"
as well as "the church of the firstborn, whose names
are written in heaven" (Heb 12:22–23). It is these who
are being warned of the danger of drifting away (2:1),
and they need to be made aware of the God who is
faithful and can bring them through the hard times.

2. Isaiah 8:17b ("I will put my trust in him") seems out
    of place but, when seen in the light of its context,
    makes a lot of sense. Often the New Testament pas-
    sages from the Old are used in light of the whole con-
    text of which they are a part. In this passage, Isaiah
    is sealing up his prophecies (8:16) so they may indict
    the stiff-necked generation when they are fulfilled.
    His fellow Israelites, including the king, may disre-
    gard and mock his prophetic warnings from God, but
    Isaiah will "put [his] trust" in God and his oracles (see
    also 2 Sam 22:3; Ps 18:3). Jesus did exactly as Isaiah,
    and in all his sacrifice and suffering, trusted implic-
    itly in God. So likewise must his followers in the midst
    of the opposition they face.

3. Isaiah 8:18a ("Here am I, and the children the LORD
   has given me") is the following clause in Isaiah 8 but
   is intended to be a separate citation here. It is making
   a different point, moving from trust to celebrating the
   promises of God. Isaiah had two children: one meaning "the spoil speeds, the prey hastens" (8:3, my translation) and the other "a remnant shall return" (7:3,
   my translation). The thrust is that while God's judgment on the nation will speedily fall, he has promised
   mercy for his faithful remnant. Isaiah was the greatest exponent of the righteous remnant concept. There
   were a faithful few in the midst of the rebellious and
   apostate people. Those who maintained their trust
   (v. 17b) have been given by God to his Messiah (v. 18a)
   and will be redeemed. The community of the saints
   has been formed not by their worthiness but by the
   salvific actions of God and Christ. A new community
   has been formed and guaranteed by their redeeming
   work, and they are watching over it and pouring out
   their promised mercy upon it.

Solidarity in his high priestly work (2:14-18)

Jesus had to become incarnate and take on "flesh and blood" so he
could share in the humanity of sinners and liberate them from sin
and death. The reasoning behind this lies at the heart of the whole
biblical portrait. Humankind is totally under the power of sin and
cannot find forgiveness because the only possible payment for sin
is eternal damnation. God had to assume the guilt and pay the penalty himself and so sent his Son into this world to pay the price
for sinful humanity. As 9:22 states, "without the shedding of blood
there is no forgiveness." In order to pay the penalty, Jesus "shared
in their humanity" and become the blood sacrifice for sin. So this
mandated his incarnation, which would enable him to die in our
place and liberate us from the power of sin and Satan.

The purpose (Greek: *hina*, "so that") is that his sacrificial death might not only atone for sin but also "break the power of him who holds the power of death—that is, the devil" (2:14). "Break the power" is *katargeō*, "destroy, nullify." In Romans 6, sin is pictured as an invading army, part of the forces of darkness, that has taken human beings captive and enslaved them in sin. Christ has defeated this evil war machine and removed its power over those who come to him in faith, liberating them as a result. This spiritual war against the satanic powers was a common depiction in both Jewish and Christian writings (1 Enoch 10:13; 4 Ezra 13:1; Matt 12:25–30; Eph 6:10–17; Rev 12:7–12). There is a twofold victory: breaking Satan's power and freeing enslaved humanity to live for God. For the believer, death is nothing to fear, for it means resurrection to life eternal and the final victory over this evil world.

The human dilemma is clear—sin has "enslaved" every human being "all their lives" to "the fear of death" (2:15). They are bound with the chains of sin and hounded with fear every conscious moment without surcease, and there is no hope—apart from Christ. For the unsaved, death is a fear-ridden concept from start to finish, for it is completely uncertain, the end of everything held dear in life and with absolutely no guarantees (or much hope) for what lies ahead. Only with Christ does hope enter the picture, and with his death on our behalf, hope becomes certitude. Our future is filled with promise and wonderful beyond belief. Anticipation replaces fear for the believer.

In verse 16 the author reminds his readers of the general topic for this section: Christ's superiority over the angels. He wants them to be aware that Christ's primary purpose was not ministry to angels but to sinful humanity. As the "pioneer of their salvation" (2:10), Christ is depicted as "taking hold of" (*epilambanetai*) them or grasping them by hand to "help" them over obstacles (see Jer 38:32). The present tense emphasizes the ongoing nature of this help. Angels are already eternal beings dwelling in heaven, so they do not need this help. It is human beings mired in sin who desperately need their champion (2:10) to grab them by the hand and lead them to the eternal "promised land" of heaven. Calling them "Abraham's descendants" stresses the Abrahamic covenant made to Israel as Abraham's seed, promising God's help in their struggles (Gen 12:3; 22:18; 26:4; 28:14), and may well point to Isaiah 41:8–10.

To help them, he had to be "made like them" (Heb 2:17). He had to die in their place as their atoning sacrifice, and to die he had to be "fully human in every way." He could not remain a heavenly being, for they are eternal beings and will never know death (that includes fallen angels like Satan, for they, too, will not cease to exist but spend eternity in the lake of fire [Rev 19:20; 20:10]). At his incarnation, the God-man Jesus became completely human in every way, including finite physical characteristics like illness and hunger. We will see in the next verse, Hebrews 2:18, and in 4:15, that this included temptation to sin with one proviso—he never gave in to it and was without sin.

Two primary purposes of his earthly ministry, stated in 2:17, demanded the incarnation:

1. The first is "that he might become a merciful and faithful high priest." Only a human being and an Israelite could be the high priest, whose work is presented in 9:7, with Jesus fulfilling it (especially the Day of Atonement ritual) in 9:11–14. This is another of the major emphases in this letter, for as high priest, he brought salvation to a fallen humanity. As a "merciful" (*eleēmōn*) high priest, he mediated God's mercy to an undeserving people. In the Old Testament it reflects *chesed*, a covenant concept in which God accepts his people as covenant partners and graciously helps them in their time of need. God's compassion flows out and embraces his people, bringing

them redemption.[3] Here divine mercy is mediated
through the high priestly work of Christ in bringing
atonement and forgiveness to sinners. As a "faithful"
(*pistos*) high priest, he fulfills 1 Samuel 2:35, where,
after Eli's evil sons failed, Yahweh promised to "raise
up for myself a faithful priest" who turned about to
be Zadok (1 Kgs 22:26–27) and reestablished the true
line of the priesthood. Jesus will be the eternal high
priest, the One who faithfully brings salvation into
this world, as emphasized in Hebrews 3:1–6, where he
is faithful to God's appointment (v. 2) and over God's
house (v. 6). He is faithful to his Father in discharg-
ing his office and trustworthy to his people in meeting all their spiritual needs.

2. The second purpose is to "make atonement (*hilask-
    esthai*) for the sins of the people." It is quite debated
    whether atonement language means expiation
    (removing sin) or propitiation (satisfying God's
    demands for sin by a sacrificial act). Most agree that
    both are part of the meaning here. In Romans 3:25
    we are told God "presented Christ as a sacrifice of
    atonement," meaning that he is the counterpart of
    the mercy seat on the ark where the blood of the sac-
    rifice was poured on the Day of Atonement (Lev 16:14)
    and sins were covered by Yahweh. Christ, by his sac-
    rifice on the cross, became the means of atonement
    or forgiveness for those who turn to him by faith for
    forgiveness of sins. Because of his blood sacrifice, sin-
    ners can find forgiveness and attain salvation.

Christ does not only help when people seek forgiveness over sins,
he also helps before sins are committed when the temptation

---

3. Exod 34:6; Ps 25:6; 40:11; 103:8; 116:5; Isa 14:1; 54:8; Jer 3:12.

comes (2:18). Amid constant temptation from self, Satan, and the world, Jesus is there to provide the strength to overcome. As in the Lord's Prayer (Matt 6:13), "lead us not into temptation" actually means, "Give us strength to triumph when we are tempted." Jesus, because he endured every temptation we face and overcome them all, is "able to help those who are being tempted." He has defeated sin on our behalf, and that gives us the strength to defeat sin in our lives.

"Suffered when he was tempted" (Heb 2:18) centers upon the end of his life and all he went through in his mission with the disciples and especially in the passion events. His rejection by his own countrymen and his death on the cross meant a climax of temptation reflected at Gethsemane when his "sweat was like drops of blood" and he prayed, "Father if you are willing, take this cup from me" (Luke 22:42, 44). This intense suffering was a powerful source of temptation, more than we will ever have to endure. So he understands what we are going through and is thereby able to help us through it. "Able" in verse 18 is *dynatai* and emphasizes his powerful strength available to empower us as we resist temptation. In 4:15 he is able to "empathize with our weakness," and in 7:25, he "is able to save completely" when we come to him.

———

In 2:1–18 we are presented with the heart of the letter to the Hebrews—namely, the danger of these weak Christians succumbing to the pressures they are facing and giving up on their Christian faith (2:1–4)—followed by the response exposing the foolishness of any such thing because of Jesus' transcendent supremacy, as the author begins a series on the greatness of Christ by extolling his deity and superiority over the angels of heaven (vv. 5–14).

In light of Jesus as the source of new covenant revelation and as the One elevated to the right hand of God after dying and rising again, the readers are challenged to pay close attention and make certain they do not drift away from the faith, for the superior greatness of the salvation that has come through him mandates an even more certain punishment for vacating it (vv. 1-3a). There is no escape for those who refuse this great salvation, for its glory was announced by God from heaven and confirmed on earth by the miraculous Spirit-given gifts (vv. 3b-4). For us in the twenty-first century as well, it is essential to direct our lives based on the Spirit's work within us.

For the rest of the chapter, the author returns to the subject of Christ's superiority to the angels, but now, in ironic fashion, as he explores the theme of glorification through humiliation, as also seen in the hymn of Philippians 2:8, "being found in appearance as a man, he humbled himself." Jesus entered this world via incarnation and was made like all humanity, "a little lower than the angels," by assuming a finite body (Heb 2:5-9). This is explored via a quote from Psalm 8:4-6 in which we see humanity, although being given dominion over creation, losing it due to sin (Heb 2:6-8a). Yet Christ, in assuming human flesh, has returned that dominion to God's people (vv. 8b-9). His humiliation and sacrificial death have produced his exaltation to and glorification at the right hand of God, and this has led to humanity's lost dominion being returned. This means we live in eternal victory rather than defeat entirely as a result of what he has done for us.

The results come in the second half of the chapter (vv. 10-18), as his incarnation meant solidarity with humanity and became the vehicle for his work of Savior and high priest. First, his office or work in this world is brought to completion or "perfected" in all he has accomplished in his suffering and sacrificial death. It is not his person but his work that is perfected, for he is perfect throughout his incarnate life on earth. He is consecrated as high priest and consecrates his followers in turn as united with him in solidarity as the family of God (vv. 10-11). The author then anchors this in Old Testament prophecy (vv. 12-13). From Psalm 22:22, he praises God that his messianic community has faithfully joined him in suffering. From Isaiah 8:17b, he joins his people in placing his trust wholly in God, and in Isaiah 8:18a, he pours out his promised mercy upon his righteous remnant in the midst of their suffering.

The final section (2:14–18) establishes the results of this solidarity with Christ. First, we are redeemed by his sacrificial death on our behalf and liberated from the power of sin, for Satan's stranglehold over us has been broken and we have been freed (vv. 14–15). Next, his incarnation meant he had to be "made like them" in order to die on their behalf (vv. 16–18) to become a "merciful and faithful high priest" and provide salvation for faithless sinful humanity. In his high priestly work he "made atonement" for our sins and placed these sins under God's mercy seat, making forgiveness possible. He has gone through every temptation we face and done so victoriously, and he has the strength to empower us so we, too, can triumph over our temptations.

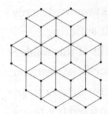

THE DANGER OF LOSING
GOD'S REST
(3:1–19)

T he opening chapters of Hebrews achieve a virtual historical
tracing of the story of God's creation and, in particular, of his
people, beginning with creation (1:3-4) and the place of the angelic
realm as sent to minister to his chosen people (1:14). The turning
point in the history of the human race is God's Son made like them
in his incarnation in order to bring them to God (2:14-18). So it is
a natural segue to center now on the reason why Christ had to
become incarnate, namely the systemic failure of God's people in
the wilderness wanderings as proving the terrible effects of sin
in this world and setting the pattern for the generations to come
(3:1-4:13). As the New Moses, he fulfilled Moses' ministry at Sinai
(3:1-6) and in the wilderness, leading God's people to overcome
their failures (3:7-4:13). In this letter, the shallow Christians being
addressed are a new wilderness generation in great danger of succumbing to their temptations (see 2:18) and joining ancient Israel
by perishing in their own wilderness.

This section also provides a twofold contrast, first between
faithful Moses and unfaithful Israel, disobedient in the wilderness,
and second, between faithful Jesus and the unfaithful, disobedient

Christians in the churches of the author's acquaintance. These contrasts control the organization of the material, with the first part presenting the faithful service of Moses and Jesus (3:1-6), the second part citing Psalm 95:7-11 and tracing the terrible results of the wilderness generation's unfaithful disobedience (3:7-19), and the third part promising a Sabbath rest for those who turn to God in this time (4:1-13).

MOSES AND JESUS: FAITHFUL TO THEIR CALLING (3:1-6)

THE COMPARISON MADE (3:1-2)

This section begins with a solemn address to challenge the readers concerning the serious nature of their status as Christians. They are "holy brothers and sisters who share in the heavenly calling." There are three truths here: (1) They belong to God as members of his family and, as such, are spiritual siblings to one another. (2) They have been "set apart" (the meaning of *hagios*) from this world, "made holy" by the sanctifying work of Christ (2:11) and set aside for God's use. (3) With their conversion, they have become "sharers" (*metachoi*), removed from their former earthly allegiance and set aside for a "heavenly calling." It is Christ who has made this possible for the rest of God's people with whom they share it. In reality, this defines what it means to be a part of Christ's body, the church. We no longer belong to this world and its twisted values, for our new home and calling is "heavenly," and that is our true home *now*, not just in the distant future. This is where the strength to be victorious over the pressures of this world originates, but it is a calling, a demand from God that must guide our choices and preferences. The emphasis here is on the positive side, stressing our privileges in Christ. It is both an invitation and an election (the predestinarian air will come to the fore in 9:15). God is calling us to himself.

In light of this, we must "fix our thoughts" or "consider carefully" (*katanoēsate*) who it is we follow. This asks for careful reflection on the spiritual realities behind our Christian faith. In particular, we meditate on Jesus "whom we acknowledge as our apostle and high priest." "Acknowledge" (or better, "confess") is not just a description of what we do but means Jesus is the subject and heart of all formal Christian confession or belief systems. There is a liturgical air to this confession, with the vertical dimension of a solemn pledge made in the presence of God and a horizontal dimension of a corporate promise made as God's united people.

The two titles are unusual. This is the only place in the New Testament where Jesus is called "apostle," although he is described as God's "sent one" (John 3:17, 34; 6:29; 8:42; 10:36)—that is, the verbal form (*apostellō*) of "apostle." Some think this image arose due to reflection on Exodus 23:20, where Israel was promised, "See, I am sending an angel ahead of you to guard you" as they traveled to the promised land. Jesus goes before his people to guide them on the new exodus. As the source of divine revelation in the new covenant age (1:1-2), he is designated as God's "apostle" here, as the Father sends the Son to bring salvation to the world. He is God's representative—in fact, "the exact representation of his being" (1:3) and has been "sent" into the world as the presence of the Godhead in it, the pioneer/champion (2:10) and apostle (3:1) of God.

Jesus as "high priest" is also a title unique to Hebrews. The two titles could almost be put together—"sent as the divine agent to be high priest." The high priestly office in Hebrews especially centers on the Day of Atonement ceremony when the high priest placed the sins of the nation on the scapegoat and cast it into the wilderness to atone for God's people and bring them forgiveness. Hebrews 5-7 will be devoted to this emphasis. Jesus as high priest enables us to achieve our "heavenly calling," and as apostle and pioneer, he is sent by the Father to bring us there. In short, he is depicted here as a twofold representative—as apostle representing God to people and high priest representing people before God.

In verse 2 he is seen as faithful to both offices, as already stated in 2:17. The author doesn't explain this further, but we would assume that both offices are in mind, and the focus is on his Father's "appointment" or calling of his Son to fulfill these duties. As such, he fulfills the calling of Moses, who also was sent by God to Pharaoh (Exod 3:10) and was promised God's presence with him in carrying out this appointment. Then, in Numbers 12:7, God told Miriam and Aaron that Moses was greater than a prophet. Since Moses was "faithful in all my house," God spoke with him not through visions but face-to-face. So Jesus is seen as the New Moses, faithful to his calling as God's apostle or agent. The readers are being challenged to carefully study the models that both Moses and Jesus provided of those who are faithful to God's call on their lives. The lesson should not be lost on them, for at the moment, they resemble not faithful Moses but the faithless wilderness generation. Things had better change, or they are in serious trouble.

THE CONTRASTS DEVELOPED (3:3-6)

Servant to builder (3:3-4)

In the first two verses, the readers are asked to follow the example of Moses in his faithful discharge of his duties. Now he turns to his overall theme of the superiority of Christ, developing two contrasts between himself and Moses, both in antithesis to Moses' ministry as a "servant in God's house," while Christ was first the builder of the house (v. 3) and second the Son over that house (v. 6). Moses was entirely faithful and deserving of honor, but he served rather than led God's house. Jesus therefore was worthy of the greater glory. While Moses was identified with the house, Jesus was "the builder of the house" and therefore "has greater honor" (doxa, "glory"). Moreover, as we have already been told, this glory was recognized in a heavenly ceremony when he sat down at the right hand of God (1:3, 13).

In the first antithesis, the builder of a house has greater honor than the house itself, a point that can be proven simply by a name— Frank Lloyd Wright. I live on the outskirts of Chicago, where he established a large part of his reputation. You can drive by several homes in the area simply known as a "Frank Lloyd Wright home" and worth a lot more money as a result, even designated as historical landmarks. That is the message here; the builder who created a house has greater glory than the house itself. Once more, they are warned not to turn back to Moses from their allegiance to Jesus, for he is incomparably greater and alone is worthy of worship. Moses ministered in God's house and was identified with that house—namely, with Israel as the house of God. Jesus, however, built that house with his high priestly work and is the only one worth following.

It is somewhat difficult to ascertain the meaning of verse 4 in this. The first statement, "every house is built by someone," is not just a throwaway statement but an essential point. God's house, like any house, had to have a builder, but Israel was not just any "house," and did not have just any builder. The One who constructed this edifice was God in the flesh—Jesus, Son of God and God of very God—for "God is the builder of everything," meaning Jesus is the divine builder. As Jesus was creator of the universe (1:2, 10), so he as the Son is the builder of God's house. This verse implicitly affirms Jesus' deity as the instrument of his Father who constructs the house of Israel.

Servant to Son (3:5–6a)

The next part of this section (3:5–6a) develops the second antithesis, Moses as servant to Jesus as Son over God's house. Moses ministered as steward while Jesus reigned as Son. It is important to realize that Moses is in no way denigrated, for this builds entirely on Numbers 12:1–16, where Moses' greatness is affirmed in no uncertain terms after Miriam and Aaron turned against him and were soundly castigated by God for doing so. The incredible status of Moses is used here to establish the even greater glory of Jesus the Son of God.

Moses as "faithful" (*pistos*) sums up what has been said above, that he was appointed by God as steward and was faithful to his calling. The term for "servant" is only here in the New Testament, picked up from the **Septuagint** of Numbers 12:7 (also Exod 4:10; Deut 3:24; Josh 1:2), stressing the honor his office held and the trust God placed in him.

Thus far, the author has been speaking of Moses' historical ministry as leading Israel to the promised land and being a servant of God in so doing. Now, in the latter part of this verse, he turns to his prophetic function and centers on his official "witness" (*martyrion*) to God's future (to him) revelations, that is, prophetic witness to the coming Messiah (the prophet like Moses of Deut 18:15; see Mark 9:7; John 6:14; 7:20; Acts 3:22; 7:37). First Peter 1:11 speaks of the "Spirit of Christ," predicting in such prophetic witness "the sufferings of the Messiah and the glories that would follow," and this makes that very point about Moses.

Christ's superior position is seen in the fact that his faithfulness was as "Son over God's house" (Heb 3:6a). Christ not only fulfilled the ministry of Moses (the early church believed Christ fulfilled the whole history of Israel) but went beyond it because his calling was to be the Son who reigned over God's house. For the first time in the letter, the author switches from "Jesus" to "Christ" to center on his office as Messiah. Moses is the essential steward who administers God's house, but Jesus is both Son and Messiah who is sovereign over every facet of that house.

Exhortation to persevere (3:6b)

Israel was the house of God in the old covenant era, and the church is in complete continuity as the New Israel under the new covenant. The readers are now warned anew that they can only count themselves as being part of the house of God if they persevere in faithfulness to the divine mandate or "appointment" (v. 2) they have received as Christians. The "if indeed" (*eanper*) shows that their current status as believers depends on their continuing in their faithful adherence to Christ. It is one of many conditional statements regarding salvation (Rom 8:9, 17; 2 Cor 13:5; Col 1:23; Heb 3:14; and others), a key warning passage in this letter. Of the metaphors used to define the church (assembly, community, family, body of Christ, temple), the picture of the church as the house of God provides one of the deepest portraits, connected to the idea of the church as God's family and also with the temple in the Old Testament as the house of God (and the sacrifices as sharing meals with God). So those who fail to persevere are warned that they are on the verge of being kicked out of their home.

The only possible solution to this danger is to "hold firmly" or "steadfastly" (*kataschōmen*) to the truths of the gospel. The thrust is to hold fast and retain tightly the body of truth the readers have received. Here this is presented in terms of the results of these truths, namely the "confidence and hope" they instill in a person. There is a double meaning in the first term, with *parrēsia* connoting both "confidence" in God and the "boldness" that results. The image is of a person facing troubles after a lifetime of experiencing God's faithfulness and so assured that he will never leave nor forsake them (Deut 31:6, 8; Josh 1:5), leading them to boldly "cast all [their] anxiety on him because he cares for" them (1 Pet 5:7).

The final result of this process of persevering in confidence is to attain "the hope in which we glory" (Heb 3:6). The literal Greek of the clause translates, "hold fast to confidence and to boasting in hope" (*to kauchēma tēs elpida*). God's faithfulness so anchors our confidence in him that our hope turns into an absolute certainty that the future lies entirely in his hands (see 6:11, 18; 7:19; 10:23). No matter how dark the "valley of the shadow of death" (Ps 23:4, KJV, ESV) appears to be, our trust in God does not waver, and we boast of (or "glory in") his guiding presence through it all. This is the theme that will predominate in the "roll call of heroes" in chapter 11, and it virtually becomes the theme of the entire letter. The negative side of this theme, failure to persevere, will now be explored in the next section (3:7–19) as we consider Psalm 95:7–11.

THE GENERATION THAT REJECTED MOSES AND GOD (3:7–19)

Israel's sordid history of committing apostasy again and again was encapsulated in the rebellion at Kadesh-Barnea in Numbers 14. The author uses extensive coverage of this incident in three parts, due to how well-known this incident was to the Israelites (see also Ps 106:24–26; Neh 9:15–17; 1 Cor 10:5): (1) the citation of Ps 95:7–11 (Heb 3:7–11); (2) a **midrashic** commentary on the psalm, centering on the negative results of their past unbelief (3:12–19); and (3) further commentary, centering on the positive future promise of a Sabbath rest (4:1–13). As a result, this is by far the lengthiest exposition of an Old Testament text in the entire letter and one of the longest in the New Testament.

THE TEXT OF PSALM 95:7-11 (3:7-11)

Testing God in the wilderness (3:7–10a)

Psalm 95 was likely written as the Israelites were preparing to return from the Babylonian exile and challenges the people to remember past failures to triumph in the present as they returned to their homeland. The new generation addressed in the psalm and the even newer generation addressed in Hebrews needed to learn from the failures of the past. Thus the author reminds his readers that this is not just an Old Testament psalm but was actually penned by the Holy Spirit, addressing us in the present as directly as it did Israel in the past.

Moreover, the opening address in Psalm 95:7, "Today, if you hear his voice," was perfect for these dull Jewish Christians. "Today" is often used in this section (Heb 3:13, 15; 4:7) for the "now"-ness of decision, stressing the urgency of getting right with God. They dare not emulate the failed wilderness people and must "hear [God's] voice" anew. The past Israelites refused to hear or obey the voice of God (Num 14:22) and suffered terrible consequences. These followers in the author's generation dare not make the same sad mistake. "Today" is the time of present exhortation and calls for spiritual renewal. "If [ean] you hear" is the second conditional clause, and as in Hebrews 3:6b, it constitutes a critical warning to become spiritually alert while there is still time.

The present danger (for the psalmist as well as for the author of Hebrews) is found in the terrible failure of the wilderness generation who hardened their hearts in the rebellion, further defined as "the time of testing in the wilderness" (Heb 3:8). Three separate terms are used to depict the massive failure—hardened, rebellion, and testing. The "hardened" heart (sklērynēte) refers to a person who is "stubborn and unyielding," refusing to give way to God's truth. It described Pharaoh (Exod 7:22 and eleven more), Israel in the wilderness (Deut 10:16), and those who put themselves above God in their priorities. It could also describe the Jewish leaders (Mark 3:5) and the disciples (Mark 6:52; 8:17). It is synonymous with the unbelief that frames the exposition in verses 12 and 19. Both in Moses' day and the time when this letter is being penned, it describes apostates.

The Kadesh-Barnea incident of Exodus 17:7 is labeled "the rebellion" and "the testing" here, when the Israelites complained of thirst and Moses struck the rock, assuaged their thirst, and named the place Meribah ("contention," or "rebellion") and Massah ("testing") to depict the people's sin. This became almost the title for the entire wilderness period (as seen in verse 8b, "in the rebellion, during the time of testing"), and as a result, virtually no Israelite was allowed to enter the promised land. They all died and were buried in the wilderness, except the two spies, Caleb and Joshua.

The people's guilt is depicted in verses 9–10a in three statements. First, the people of Israel who engaged in the exodus "tested and tried me," which echoes the message of Psalm 78:17–18. In Numbers 14:22 we are told Israel tested God ten times, and each was linked to a demand for God to provide what Israel wanted and an unwillingness to obey his dictates. Second, they did so despite the fact that "for forty years they saw what I did." The forty years was the period of the exodus, and for that entire time, they had watched God's miraculous provision for his people, sending plagues to force the Egyptians and Pharaoh to let them go, providing food and water to nourish the beleaguered people, and performing miracle after miracle to lift them out of troublesome situations. So third, God was "angry with that generation" for ignoring all he did and complaining when they failed to receive their selfish demands.

God's wrath and solemn oath (3:10b–11)

The rest of 3:10b–11 describes God's wrath as it descended on the rebellious nation. It tells first why they faced his wrath and then what constituted that judgment. His anger was kindled because "their hearts are always going astray." The "always" isn't really hyperbole, for every time the people of Israel turned around, they were rebelling and complaining and "going astray" from the Lord. Interestingly, the period between the return from exile and the coming of Jesus was the only extended period in the history of the Jewish people when they failed to have generations that fell into apostasy. They only had two faithful kings in the entire history of the divided monarchy—Josiah and Hezekiah. Then when Jesus arrived, the nation fell into apostasy again and rejected their Messiah.

The judgment is the result (*hōs*, "so"), as God declares "on oath in my anger." Normally ancient oaths were taken in the name of God, but the Lord himself would often take one on his own authority when he wished a particularly solemn declaration. The Greek follows the Hebrew idiom, "If [*ei*] they will enter," which actually means, "They shall *never* enter my rest." By "rest" the author meant life in their promised homeland when they would find rest from their wandering and difficult life (Deut 25:19). This will be explored further in 4:1. It was not a single sin that produced so extreme a judgment but an accumulation of incidents where the wilderness people consistently refused to obey and kept on grumbling about every little hardship. They never followed his directions, so they would never enter the land.

THE RESULTS OF UNBELIEF (3:12-19)

The paragraph here (vv. 12-19) forms a rabbinic-style commentary on the Psalm 95 passage called a "midrash." The author chooses a few key ideas and phrases from the psalm and draws implications from it for his readers.

The warning and solution (3:12-13)

From the example of the wilderness wandering, he draws the application of verses 12-13, beginning with the warning that encapsulates the whole, the supreme danger that will lead to spiritual disaster. The opening "See to it" (*blepete*) is the regular particle for admonition and means, "beware lest" or "be careful to." It calls for spiritual vigilance and frames this section (vv. 12, 19), along with the term that defines the danger itself, *apistia* ("unbelief"). The "hardened heart" by definition will be characterized by unbelief and will result in the wrath of God bringing eternal judgment down upon their heads.

The "sinful, unbelieving heart" will always turn "away from the living God," with the infinitive *apostēnai* meaning to "fall away" or "apostatize" from their faith in God. These weak Christians are committing the same sins that destroyed the Israelites in the wilderness, so the warning is desperately needed. At present they are still believers and part of God's family and thus can be addressed as "brothers and sisters." He hints that in the same way that the hardened hearts of all the spies except Caleb and Joshua turned the nation from God at Kadesh-Barnea (Num 14:36-38), the unbelief of a few in the church can turn many "away from the living God" at the present time. Unbelief was at the heart of the problem in the wilderness generation (Num 14:11), and it led to disobedience and to their perishing in the wilderness (Num 14:22-23).

It is critical to realize that unbelief is not simply a passive failure to understand or trust God's promises but an active, willful rebellion and refusal to allow God into one's life. Israel did not simply live in discouragement but wanted nothing to do with God and the life he had chosen for them. As we will see in Hebrews 6:4-6, this is active apostasy rather than passively being overwhelmed by sin as in James 5:19-20. The lazy, weak Christians here, as at Kadesh in Numbers 14, are turning "away from the living God," rejecting God's dynamic presence among them. He is the "living God" because he is at work on behalf of his people, unlike the pagan gods who don't care. So they were engaging in a new kind of idolatry, worshiping themselves and their earthly desires rather than the God of heaven. They would be no better off than the pagans around them.

After spelling out the danger, the author turns to the solution (3:13), the way they can avoid the crevasse into which they were about to plunge. The answer is found in the corporate side of the Christian life, that is, our life as part of the church. There are two dimensions to spiritual growth: the vertical or individual aspect—namely, our personal commitment and confession of our faith in God and Christ—and the horizontal or corporate aspect—the involvement of the community in the life of the believer. This is a critical passage for the church today, as all too often we fail in this very area of admonishing each other in love.

This is the horizontal side, as the community "exhorts one another" (ESV, KJV, NKJV). The NIV translates "encourage," but that only fits in a positive context. This has a more negative connotation

and is better "exhort" or "admonish, warn" (the term is used positively in 10:25). The danger of being "hardened by sin's deceitfulness"
persists and calls for strong warning (see Gal 6:1). Moreover, these
weak readers are characterized by spiritual lethargy (Heb 5:11; 6:12)
and in great danger of allowing sin to deceive them and cause them
to "fall away" into "unbelief" (3:12, 19). All God's people need, from
time to time, to be challenged by their brothers and sisters as they
inadvertently succumb to the blandishments of sin. It is a constant
battle, and we cannot fight it alone.

In 13:22 the author calls this letter a "word of exhortation," which
is the language he uses here as well. He wants all the believers in
his churches to "exhort one another" on a "daily" basis, meaning
regularly, and following the meaning of *parakaleō*, that means positive encouragement when it is needed and negative admonition
when circumstances call for it. Ancient Israel failed to do so, and the
nation fell in the wilderness as a result. The author does not want
that sad history to repeat itself in his churches and is admonishing
them to react very differently in the present situation. They must
do so "as long as it is called 'Today,'" meaning, as in 3:7, the present
opportunity to get right with God. This hints that there may not be
another such opportunity, so they had better make sure they make
the most of today's chance.

Sin never rests from the pressure of suborning the believer with
repeated temptations and "deceives" step by step, gradually harden-
ing the weak by continuous exposure to self and to life's pleasures
until God no longer has a place in their lives. The present is not just
the time of decision; it is the time of deception by sin. God is at work,
but so is self and Satan, and it is up to the believer and the community as a whole to make this time count by the spiritual admonition
that leads to revival and the rejection of sin's deceptive strategies.

The need for perseverance (3:14)

Still centering on the corporate side of the Christian life, we start
with the basic premise that "we have come to share in Christ," with
the perfect tense *gegonamen* stressing the state of things, that we

who are followers of Christ can be described as *metachoi tou Christou*, "sharers/partners in Christ." It is two-dimensional—we share the life of Christ and share Christ with one another. It is often used in business relationships with those who are partners in a business and share the profits. Christ is our senior partner and has brought us onto the team, sharing the benefits with us. There may also be an **eschatological** dimension, with the idea that we have joined "the church of the firstborn" in heaven (12:22-23) and have become part of the heavenly hosts, indeed the meaning of sharing in the heavenly calling of 3:1.

However, this is only the case if we persevere in the faith, and this repeats 3:6b by tying the promise that we are his people to our responsibility to persevere, here "if indeed we hold our original conviction firmly to the end." Like verse 6b, *eanper* demonstrates a strong conditional sense. To be true companions of Christ and one another, we must remain faithful to our Christian convictions. The language of this conditional clause is very interesting, as it speaks of holding "*the beginning* [*tēn archēn*]" of our conviction firm to "*the end* [*mechri telous*]" (my translation). From start to finish, we must dedicate our lives to maintaining our convictions in Christ.

It is somewhat debated as to whether we should read "conviction" (*hypostasis*) as subjective ("confidence, assurance") or objective ("conviction"), but it is likely a blend of the two sides. Our assurance of the reality of the Christian faith leads to a settled confidence in God and our walk in him. It is our steadfast confidence that produces the kind of convictions that carry us through difficult times. We are called to persevere in this day by day and grow in the certainty of our convictions so that we may do so. No one ever said the Christian life should be easy, and we need all our determination to remain faithful at all times.

Repeating the warning (3:15)

This is a critical time to remind everyone of the central issue, so he repeats Psalm 95:7 for effect, beginning, "As has just been said," to make more emphatic the citation already found in Hebrews 3:7b-8

above. He especially wants them to take note of the danger, as
"in the rebellion," for they were on the verge of joining together
in a new rebellion against the will of God. This will be the point
of the rest of this chapter and the three rhetorical questions and
answers in verses 16–19 below. So this verse both sums up what
precedes and leads into the longer summary that follows. The
whole (vv. 15–19) provides a transition into chapter four and the
conclusion of the "rest" theme.

The three questions (3:16–19)

The key terms in these verses all relate to the danger these churches
are facing, reflecting both the sinful actions (rebelled, sinned, disobeyed, unbelief) and the judgment that resulted (angry, perished,
never enter his rest, never able to enter). The author brilliantly
pens a series of questions and a final statement that concludes it
all, with an A-B-A-B-A organization. The first two sets (A-B [v. 16],
A-B [v. 17]) are in a question-answer format, and then a final question (v. 18) has an obvious answer that is part of the question.

The first set of questions (3:16) refers to the "rebellion" of
Kadesh in verse 8 ("Meribah" in Ps 95:8) portrayed in Numbers 14,
itself the result of a series of grumblings during the wilderness
wanderings. These ancient Israelites had heard his promises and
were the recipients of divine revelation regarding all he was about
to do for them, but they still rebelled against those very things. God
had rescued and redeemed them from slavery under the Egyptians;
yet, at every stage, they complained about their hardships and
refused to believe his promises that he would bring them safely
through the wilderness and into the promised land. They even set
up a golden calf and tried to return to Egyptian idolatry, thinking
that would be easier than learning the lessons the Lord had for
them via the exodus travels.

The author answers his own question with another: "Were
they not all those Moses led out of Egypt?" Note the emphatic "all
those," meaning, every single Israelite set free from Egypt and

experiencing miracle after miracle in the process. They are labeled "all the members of the community" and "all the Israelites" in Numbers 14:1-2. Moreover, they all had heard Joshua and Caleb's report that the land was very fruitful and that God would indeed lead them into it (Num 14:7-8), as well as the warning not to rebel (14:9), but they ignored that and rebelled anyway.

The second set of questions (3:17) centers on God's response, namely his anger that lasted for forty years, the entire time of the wilderness wanderings. The Kadesh incident occurred close to the beginning of their sojourn and initiated the wilderness wanderings as judgment against the rebellious nation. The answer then speaks further of their sad fate—because of their sin, their "bodies perished in the wilderness," and they never entered Canaan. Both the question and the answer reflect Numbers 14:26-35, where God skewers the nation for its wickedness and tells them none of them would enter the land except Caleb and Joshua, but their children under twenty years of age would enjoy the plenty that could have been theirs. They would wander for forty years and die there. The Greek behind "bodies perished" is *ta kola epesen*, *"fallen corpses,"* the punishment for apostasy in Isaiah 66:24, often with the bodies left unburied for the wild dogs and birds to eat (Gen 40:19; Deut 28:26; Jer 7:32-33; Ezek 29:5).

The final question (3:18) combines the question and the answer, focusing on the disobedient who would "never enter his rest," quoted from Psalm 95:11 and reflecting Numbers 14:41-43, where God tells the people that their disobedience meant that they would all "fall by the sword" against the Amalekites and Canaanites. Clearly disobedience is considered a type of rebellion and has the same serious consequences. Together they constitute apostasy, and the wilderness generation has become enemies of God, no longer deserving to live.

The final verse (Heb 3:19) draws verses 15-18 together and provides the main conclusion: "they were not able to enter, because of their unbelief." Let us note the four terms that sum up what has taken place: the very people who had been redeemed by God from Egypt *refused to believe* God's promises and, as a result, *disobeyed* his demands, *rebelling* against him and thereby *apostatizing*—or falling away from—their faith. Looked at as cold hard facts, their hubris is absolutely shocking. How could anyone receive so much and not just ignore all that God had done but act as if he had mistreated them and turn against their divine benefactor? They didn't just fail to understand out of ignorance but deliberately refused to believe what was obvious—that God had rescued them from the Egyptians—because of a few temporary hardships that any rationally thinking person would know was soon to pass.

The warning to the Jewish Christians of these churches is also perfectly clear. If they continue to react to their own hardships with the same unbelief and rebellion as the wilderness people, they will suffer the same penalty. This will come up several more times in this letter (chapters 6, 10, 12), and they had better heed the admonition while there is still time. The ancient Israelites could not enter their rest—namely, the promised land—and the current generation would also fail to enter their rest—namely, eternal heaven. It is up to us to apply this to ourselves and realize we are under the same pressures. Our responsibility is spiritual vigilance, to watch out for each other spiritually and make certain these tragedies do not take place in our lives and churches.

————

In 3:1–4:13 we come to another of the major themes in this letter—namely, the tendency of God's people to fall into failure as a result of disobedience and unbelief. The paradigm for failure is the wilderness generation at the time of the exodus, who, due to sin and the national narcissism it produced, fell into unbelief and were denied entrance into God's rest in Canaan, perishing in the sands of the wilderness floor.

The opening verses (3:1-2) remind us of both who we are and who Jesus is and thereby prepare for the study of the danger of spiritual failure in this chapter. Along with previous generations of Christians, we are partners with Jesus, no longer mere earthlings but called to be citizens of heaven and serve our heavenly Father. We follow the Jesus who reveals his Father and takes his place as Son of God in chapter 1 and was sent to earth as God's divine agent and high priest to enable us to experience God's salvation.

Turning to the model of Moses and the Israelites, the author develops two contrasts between Moses and Jesus (vv. 3–6a) to tell the readers why they should cling to Jesus and not give up and return to their former Judaism. Israel here is pictured as God's house, built and placed in this world to glorify him. As great as he was, Moses was merely the faithful servant of that house, while Christ, in twofold contrast, was both builder and Son who reigned over that house. Our call is to be faithful in our own calling and serve God's new house, the church. We are to model ourselves after Moses and not Israel, as will be developed in the rest of this chapter. Our mandate is to persevere (v. 6b) in boldness and hope to God in us, maintain our walk with him, and serve both him and his house faithfully.

The rest of the chapter (vv. 7–19) develops the negative paradigm of Israel's apostasy and failure, showing the readers what they must avoid at all cost and providing the major warning of the letter. The author begins by citing Psalm 95:7–11, where the psalmist used Numbers 14 and Israel's apostasy in the wilderness to challenge the people returning from exile to avoid Israel's rebellion and testing of God in their lives (Heb 3:7–11). The author of this letter applies it to his readers as well, and we must apply it to ourselves, lest we, too, bring God's wrath down upon ourselves and perish as outsiders to the kingdom. Theirs was an ongoing rebellion in which they repeatedly grumbled against God and disobeyed his commands. As a result, he refused them entry into the promised land, and their bodies lay in the wilderness.

Sermonic application follows as the writer draws out the meaning of the psalm passage (vv. 12–19), beginning with the serious danger of allowing an "unbelieving heart" to dominate and turn them into apostates (v. 12). The solution is true Christian fellowship which loves our brothers and sisters enough to admonish them when they are succumbing to sin (v. 13). We need each other in this endeavor, for we too easily ignore unbelief in our lives. As in verse 6b, we all must persevere and "hold firmly" to our Christian convictions in the midst of pressure from self and the world to abandon Christ.

The rest of the chapter (vv. 15-19) consists of a series of questions designed to draw the conclusion for the readers. They must be fully aware of the tragic story of these wilderness people who failed to enter Canaan due to disobedience and rebellion and died in the wilderness as God's enemies, apostate to the very end. As a result, God refused to allow them to enter his rest, pointing to the message of the next chapter. These first-century Hebrew Christians must not allow themselves to fall into the same unbelief, lest they, too, experience God's wrath and rejection.

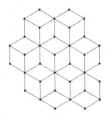

THE PROMISE OF A SABBATH REST
(4:1–13)

Hebrews 3:12–19 developed the end of Psalm 95:7–11, "They shall never enter my rest," while Hebrews 4:1–13 develops the beginning, "Today, if only you would hear his voice," along with Genesis 2:2, "on the seventh day he rested from all his work." The warning of judgment is transformed into a promise of rest. For both the psalmist in Psalm 95:7 and the author of this letter, "Today" refers to the current generation being offered the promise anew that was rejected by the wilderness people. It is also a greater promise, for it now becomes the Sabbath rest of God, as he invites his people anew to join him in not just inheriting a temporary, earthly land but an eternal land as his people rest in him and with him.

There are three parts to this section (vv. 1–5, 6–11, 12–13), as the positive promise is added to the negative warning in verses 1–5 and then is expanded in 6–11 where the significance of "Today" is explored in light of the Sabbath rest in Genesis 2:2. "Today" stresses the now-ness of decision as the people rededicate themselves to God. Finally, in 12–13 the power of the word of God to effect change and anchor the promise is stated unequivocally.

THE PROMISE OF REST WITH GOD (4:1-5)

THE CALL TO BE CAREFUL (4:1)

The caution expressed repeats that in 2:1, and the contents intensify the similar warning in 3:12, which begins *blepete*, "see to it," while 4:1 contains *phobēthōmen*, "let us fear" (ESV, NKJV; the NIV's "be careful" is too weak in my opinion). The verb often connotes reverence, but here the context strongly favors awesome fear in the light of the terrible consequences they face. What they have "seen" in the picture from 3:1-4:13 is as frightening as it gets, with the bodies of an entire generation lying on the desert floor and the warning that this could well depict their future as well. These people inherit the promise of rest from Genesis 2:2, but first, they must wrestle with the danger of Psalm 95. The idea of a healthy fear (see also 10:27, 31; 12:21) is not popular in our postmodern society but is very important biblically, as it relates to the doctrine of judgment and the wrath of God.

This section looks at the positive side. If the readers respond properly to the *fear*some picture, God's promise outweighs the warning and will give them hope. The key idea is that in the midst of the frightening possibility of total destruction, the "promise ... still stands." God has not taken away the hope for those who are willing to respond, but the time is short, and the "Today" demands urgent and immediate repentance. God is offering them not only a chance to discover that rest but to "enter his rest," and it is even stronger than it was in Moses' day, for it is anchored in Christ. The possibility of forfeiting this promise is too terrible to contemplate and demands an immediate response.

We must consider the evolution of the concept of "entering his rest" in Scripture. At the outset it was the land, in particular the land of Canaan. In Deuteronomy 12:9-11 four aspects are highlighted: the promised land, called "the resting place and inheritance"; security—namely, "rest from all your enemies"; safety, or rest from fighting; and God's presence, experienced in religious worship. Then there is the development of this theme through Scripture, and I see four stages here:

1. Again, entering the land and being watched over by Yahweh

2. The Sabbath rest of Genesis 2, related to the present kingdom blessings as well as the promise of the world to come

3. The covenant blessings of being the people of God, developed especially in the prophetic period and following

4. The ultimate blessing of eternal life, developed especially in the intertestamental period and the New Testament

All of these are in the author's mind here.

The fear is made all the greater when we realize what was at stake—namely, that after receiving all of these wondrous blessings, they are "found to have fallen short of it." The passive voice "be found" is a divine passive,[1] referring to the day of judgment when God's people "give account" (13:17; there the leaders are in view but here it is all Christians) of their lives to God. The language reflects the wilderness people who wandered for forty years and then fell just short of their goal, the promised land. Here it is far worse, for they will fall short of eternal life in heaven.

Reasons for Fear (4:2–5)

Three consecutive "for" (*gar*) clauses (vv. 2, 3a, 3b–5) probe more deeply into the serious situation as the people in the "Today"

---

1. Some have instead seen this as the actions of the church that is spiritually vigilant and "finds" these problems. That is an interesting possibility but not as likely as God being the subject, which is better in this context.

reprise the ancients in a new exodus. First, like ancient Israel, the current generation also had "the good news proclaimed to us" (v. 2), literally, "we too were evangelized" (with the perfect periphrastic *semen euēngelismenoi* emphasizing the dynamic proclamation in all its completeness). This gospel message was the promise of entering God's rest as well as their deliverance or salvation from Egyptian bondage (Exod 3:16–17; 4:27–31) and the positive report from Caleb and Joshua that God would lead them successfully into Canaan (Num 14:7–9). The same dual message—salvation and entering God's rest—was given to the Hebrew Christians in the present. The question was not in the proclaiming but the receiving. Would they listen and obey, unlike the Israelites?

Due to unbelief, the promises "were of no value to them, because they did not share the faith of those who obeyed." "Share the faith" is literally "united in faith with those who heard." Two steps are indicated here—hearing and accepting by faith. The ancients heard but failed to have faith and so were guilty of unbelief. As we saw in 3:19, one has not truly heard until they have believed and obeyed. "Those who heard" were Caleb and Joshua, the two faithful spies in Numbers 14, and in this letter they would include the "heroes of the faith" in chapter 11. He wants these weak Christians to find strength by consciously identifying with the faith heroes of the past, thereby defeating the forces that would defeat and destroy them spiritually.

The second *gar* ("for") clause (4:3a) seeks to encourage the readers by declaring that they are not like the failed exodus people, since they "have believed" and thus are in the process of "entering that rest." The author perceives the entrance as a lifelong process rather than a one-time event at conversion. It is a life of ongoing faith and obedience that constitutes experiencing God's rest. The key ingredient indeed is an ongoing faith that puts into practice the initial belief.

The formula here must be understood through what is called "inaugurated **eschatology**," the tension we all experience between the "already" and the "not yet" in our Christian walk. We have believed and so have began the process of entering his rest, but we have not yet finished our walk and look forward to our final victory when Christ returns. In this we are the polar opposite of the wilderness people and will never hear God's dreaded oath from Psalm 95:11, "They shall never enter my rest." In fact, we have already begun to do just that—that is, we have entered Christ's new kingdom by faith. So our future is full of promise rather than terror. God's rest is not purely **apocalyptic**, to be experienced by us only when our eternity in heaven has arrived. It is a present possession, part of the Christian life as a pilgrimage (a major thrust in this letter), with every moment a "Today" experience demanding faithful Christian living.

We should note the shift to positive encouragement. While the danger of 2:7-19 is very real, the message now is that this doesn't at present characterize the readers. They are a new generation, one of promise and hope, and for them the process of experiencing God's rest has indeed been initiated.

So in 4:3b-5 the writer introduces Genesis 2:2. While the ancient Israelites were excluded from enjoying that rest, it had been a reality from the start, since "his works have been finished since the creation of the world" (Heb 4:3). This, of course, refers to the six days of creation followed by God resting "from all his works" in Genesis 2:2 as cited in Hebrews 4:4. God's rest is not a future reality that his people can only wait for but a present reality that has belonged to his faithful followers from the very beginning. God is currently resting from his labors and invites his chosen people to join him in that rest and experience his vigilance over them.

In 3:4-5 the two sides are once more set in antithesis against each other, and the readers are asked to choose which side they wish to follow. The positive side is presented first, and the "somewhere" that introduces the quote from Genesis 2:2 points to a well-known text. God entered his rest "on the seventh day" at the finish of his works of creation and currently exists there with his faithful.

So the fact that the wilderness people never entered his rest (Heb 4:5 from Ps 95:11) does not end the issue. Their failure does not have to be replicated in the current generation (even though it was repeated in generation after generation in the history of the Israelites), for God's rest is still available to the faithful. The seventh day is still open-ended, and the writer is convinced his readers are in the process of enjoying that reality (see also Heb 6:9-12).

THE SIGNIFICANCE OF THE SABBATH REST (4:6-11)

THE NECESSITY OF A FUTURE REST (4:6-8)

Two facts have been established from the first section (vv. 1-5): God has made a promise that his people would enjoy his rest at the "seventh day" of creation. It is open to the faithful, and he has excluded the wilderness people from entering it. In this section, the author asks what implications this reality has for the current generation and argues that a future rest remains. In verse 3 he claimed that they have indeed begun to enter it, and here he will explore the future and final entry available to those who believe.

The *epei* (4:6: "since, because") governs two reasons why the "Today" still points to the offer of God's rest for the current generation. First, the "Sabbath rest" of verses 3b-4 "still remains"; it is open-ended. God's promise is ongoing even if the exodus people failed to receive it. Every generation was offered the opportunity, and it would not be taken away except by unbelief. Second, the fact that one generation who "formerly had the good news proclaimed to them" failed to enter due to their disobedience did not deter the promise. Instead, it reverted to another generation, the current one, and the promise remains. The Sabbath rest, a reality since the days of creation, is offered anew to each generation.

So for rhetorical effect the writer shifts from Psalm 95:11 in Hebrews 4:3a to Psalm 95:7b-8 in Hebrews 4:7 in order to center on the "Today" of the new offer and promise. He treats human history as organized around four "days" in which God's redeeming activity is paramount. The first day ended in failure, as the wilderness people greeted his offer of redemption with unbelief and disobedience and failed to enter his rest in Canaan. The final "day" will mean unparalleled victory as Christ returns and those who have greeted his offer with faith enter eternal rest.

The central focus of this passage is the middle two days: that of David and that of the present time. When David addressed the Jewish people of his time, another "day" calling for repentance and revival was proclaimed, as seen in his reintroducing the quote from Psalm 95:7b–8 here, demanding two things: to "hear" on this "Today" of decision, and to open up to God, as was discussed in Hebrews 3:7–8. The response of the people that David addressed becomes a model for the recipients of this letter in the first century (and for us in our day) for overturning the tragic results in the time of Moses. We do not know for certain the results of David's challenge. It had to have been short-lived, for with Solomon and especially his children, a new level of apostasy came to dominate the divided kingdom.

The fourth "day" is announced here. "Today," when the divine offer is made anew, is the day of decision and opportunity for the readers. Like the people of David's day, they must stop their downward spiral and turn themselves around for God. They have been warned from Psalm 95:11 and given a new chance for redemption with the challenge from Psalm 95:7b–8. It is now up to them to respond with faith and obedience.

To make certain the message is clear, the writer now addresses in Hebrews 4:8 a possible misunderstanding on their part—namely, that God did, in fact, relent when he allowed Joshua to lead the Israelites into the "rest" of the promised land. Deuteronomy speaks of Israel in Canaan as enjoying God's rest (3:20; 12:9–10; 25:19). However, the author sees the answer in the "Today" of Psalm 95, responding, "if Joshua[2] had given them rest, God would not have

---

2. Some see in the introduction of Joshua a new typology, since "Joshua" is the name of Jesus in Hebrew. However, there is no hint that the writer is developing that here. The attention is entirely on the historical event of Israel entering Canaan.

spoken about another day." He develops a two-stage **midrashic** argument based on this. First, if anyone could say anyone had entered the rest, and if the land could constitute that rest, God (the true author of the psalm) would not have spoken of "another day" but instead would have spoken of the day of Joshua. Second, the rest is not the land, for that was merely an earthly sojourn. The rest in Psalm 95 and here in Hebrews 4:8 is the final rest, the spiritual reality, God's eternal kingdom. This reflects a **typology** moving from the earthly rest of Deuteronomy to the heavenly rest of Psalm 95 and here.

GOD'S SABBATH REST (4:9–10)

The answer is found in Genesis 2:2, the open-ended "Sabbath rest" (*sabbatismos*) that God gives to the faithful. The ancient Israelites failed to find their rest, but the New Israel is offered a far greater privilege, to enter the Sabbath-rest of the seventh day of creation. This rest "remains" and is the key offer of this letter, echoing verse 6: "it still remains for some to enter that rest." The term *sabbatismos* was used to connote the Sabbath activity of praise and celebration and here combines Genesis 2:2 with the Sabbath imagery in the Day of Atonement (Lev 23:26–32) in terms of its fulfillment in Jesus. As we will see in Hebrews 12:22–24, this new rest entails us entering in the present as well as the future into the "joyful assembly" of the heavenly Jerusalem, a new life of worship and rejoicing, in Christ. This entails a true rest from sin and the experience of God's peace.

Many recent commentators link this rest entirely with a final eschatology centering on the "new heavens and new earth" of the eternal age and thus a wholly future perspective. I strongly prefer an inaugurated thrust in which these future promises have already "begun" in Christ, and Christ-followers are already experiencing this time of rest and joy. It certainly will not be consummated until Christ returns, but it has been initiated in the new salvation that has come with Christ and is ours from the start to enjoy.

Verse 10 tells how and why the Sabbath-rest is being enjoyed, returning to Genesis 2:2 (Heb 4:4 above). Since on the seventh day of creation God rested from his works, and since that is made available to God's true people, all who enter God's rest in Christ rest from their works. One could argue that "Today" is the time of laboring for Christ, when we turn ourselves over to the Lord and work at our Christian walk. The saints "make every effort" or "work hard" (v. 11) as they live out the process of entering God's rest, but in the end (the eternal kingdom), they will "rest from their work" and receive their reward.

Verses 9–10 speak primarily of the final eschatological rest in eternity, called "a kingdom that cannot be shaken" in 12:28, but they also apply to the believer currently in our "Today" as we rest in God and bask in his empowering presence in our lives (1 Pet 1:5). Do we enter that final rest at death or at our resurrection when Christ returns? The author doesn't say. He may have thought of it in stages—at our conversion, we begin to experience the joy and worship of his Sabbath-rest, but we will experience it fully at death when we enter Christ's presence (2 Cor 5:8; Phil 1:23) and then even more fully when we receive our new bodies and eternity begins (1 Cor 15; 1 Thess 4).

Conclusion: Persevering in His Rest (4:11)

As the author draws this portion of his argument to a close, he once again urges us to take the danger seriously and embrace the promises fiercely and "make every effort to enter that rest" (2:1; 3:1; 4:1). The verb *spoudasōmen* calls for hard work and diligence. This section is framed by two "let us" commands (called "hortatory subjunctives") demanding zealous effort in persevering in the faith. This is the opposite of the shallow laziness that has plagued these Christians heretofore (5:11; 6:12) and is greatly needed lest they fall into the same bad behavior as the wilderness generation.

The terrible example of the failed people of the wilderness journey is motivation enough, for as a result of their "disobedience," the entire generation perished in the wilderness (3:17). Yet as horrendous as that was, it was nothing compared to the danger now, for theirs was an earthly death while eternal punishment awaits this generation. The rest is much greater, involving heaven rather than just Canaan, but the penalty is also that much worse. The Christian life, as a result, demands extremely hard work, but it has correspondingly great rewards.

Note that the goal is that "no one" perish, which matches the same emphasis in verse 1. We are urged to be vigilant over every single member of the congregation. We must not allow a single person to "fall" ("perish"; translated from *piptō*, "fall") like Israel did in the desert. This letter has a great deal to say about the relationship of the individual to the group. The church is responsible for every member, and each of us are part of God's family and siblings of one another. Not one should ever be neglected. This is why admonition is so critical (3:13). Since all people will rationalize away failures, believers should not merely encourage other believers to turn away from sin but instead make each other face failures honestly.

THE STANDARD-BEARER:
THE WORD OF GOD (4:12–13)

These verses provide proper closure to this first major section of the letter, for throughout the letter thus far, the author's narration has centered on Old Testament citations that provide the background for his argumentation. He wants the readers to realize what this signifies, for it is the word of God, and not just human thoughts, that have been quoted. It has been revealed by God's divine Son (1:1–2) and contains God's very mind and thoughts in what it says. Thus it dare not be ignored (2:1–4) nor its commands be neglected. Through it, God's great salvation can be understood and accepted. No one can escape God's great salvation (2:3), and at the same time, no one will be able to escape the judgment that comes through his word. The central citations of Psalm 95:7–11 and Genesis 2:2 are

especially in his mind, which do not merely convey information
but perform a divine action as they convict and challenge us to
consider more carefully our walk with God. While many consider
Hebrews 4:12–13 an early Christian hymn due to its careful construction and parallel clauses, it is more likely a well-crafted piece
of prose the author created to motivate readers to listen carefully
as God speaks to them through it.

There are five steps in the dynamic work of the word in our
lives, moving from general characteristics to personal results—
living, active, sharper than any sword, dividing us asunder (conviction), and discerning our innermost thoughts. As such, it begins
with the character of the word of God as "alive and active," for it
stems from the "living God" (3:12) and is a dynamic, life-changing
force in our lives. Some see in this the *logos* of John 1 and Jesus as
the "word of God" there, but that hardly fits this context. Instead, it
refers to God's revealed truths in Scripture seen in all their magnificent power and force as it speaks to us and changes us. In a sense
this draws out the "Today" theme of Psalm 95—the present time
of decision—and this is the basis of salvation as "now," including
all the covenant promises and responsibility. As an active entity
working in us, it has a moral and intellectual force, including volition and knowledge (see Isa 55:11; Jer 23:29, Wis 18:15–16).

The description of the word as "sharper than any double-
edged sword" (see also Eph 6:17) is a natural metaphor in this
instance, for the punishment of the wilderness people was gen-
erated by the swords of the Canaanites (Num 14:43–45), and the
double-edged swords of the Romans provided the basis of their
invincibility in battle. Yet God's word is "sharper" because it does
far more than any mere human sword and penetrates far more
deeply, effecting eternal realities and not just human flesh. The
"double-edged" element should not be allegorized to mean the
two testaments or any such thing, as many have done; it simply
refers to the razor-sharp Roman sword and its power to "pierce
or penetrate" the heart.

The three areas that are penetrated (soul/spirit, joints/marrow, thoughts/attitudes) are not separate categories. The first two are physical examples of the swords capabilities, and the third defines the metaphor behind the first two. All work together to communicate that the word penetrates and discerns the innermost thoughts so that everything is exposed to the light of God. The two groups correspond to the material and immaterial aspects, meaning the word cuts into every area of our existence and penetrates every area of our being. Nothing is hidden from God's word.

It judges between, or discerns, our thoughts and attitudes—in a sense the third area of our being, the volition and mindset that guides our actions. In other words, the word sifts the wheat from the chaff in our wills (feelings or affections) and reasoning (our thoughts).

Every aspect of our lives, indeed everything "in all creation," is "laid bare" before God. To use a modern equivalent, we might call the word the "ninja sword" of God that can cut through everything and dare not be ignored. We cannot escape God's scrutiny, and his word leaves us powerless and exposed to his truth and the realities we so often try to ignore. This image is taken from wrestling when the opponent is pinned to the ground, helpless and completely exposed. We work very hard to rationalize away our petty sins, but that fails to work with God's convicting presence via the Spirit and the word. We "must give account" to him, a thought that will appear again in 13:17 and is a business metaphor for paying a charge in an account. In a sense, this, too, is inaugurated eschatology, for the reckoning begins now with this convicting presence in our lives but points especially to that final "accounting" at the last judgment when we answer to him for the way we have lived our lives.

Yet just as God's scalpel is cutting through our lives, we—like these Hebrew Christians described in this letter—can be pretending nothing is happening and try to ignore the word's convicting power. Let me apply this to another problem in our day: shallow preaching that bypasses the depths of the word of God and centers on cute little entertaining stories. Little eternal good is produced by pastors who become entertainers. It is the word of God that leads to true conviction, not hollow little anecdotes. This doesn't mean we should stop seeking good illustrations but rather that they should drive home God's truths and develop their meaning rather than become ends in themselves.

———

After the ominous warning of chapter 3, this chapter adds a note of positive promise to those who will heed the warning. It actually begins, "let us fear," which is natural after the lengthy discussion of Psalm 95. All believers need a healthy fear established by their responsibility to be faithful to God. This will make them serious about their walk with Christ. The promise is the incredible blessings to be realized when we "enter his rest," building on Israel's second generation entering Canaan after the wilderness wandering. The basis for that fear is the danger of "falling short," like the first generation who, after forty years, had arrived just at the border of the promised land and yet fell short, perishing in the wilderness. For us it is far worse, for our rest is eternity to heaven. To forfeit that is an eternal nightmare.

In 4:2–5, three reasons (*gar* clauses) are presented for this positive development.

1. We have had the good news proclaimed and have greeted it with faith and obedience (v. 2).

2. We have entered the promised rest and reversed the punishment the wilderness people experienced (v. 3a).

3. The Sabbath rest from God from Genesis 2:2 is now being enjoyed by those among his people who have responded with belief. This Sabbath day rest is ours even now (Heb 4:3b–5).

Then in 7:6-11 the implications of this Sabbath rest are explored as they apply to current believers then and now. First, the promise itself is offered anew to each generation. While the people of the exodus failed to receive it, those of the author's churches (and ours today) can discover those joyous benefits for themselves (vv. 6-8). We are living in a new "Today" with the opportunity of turning it around and entering God's rest, and it is our task to hear, obey, and greet the promise with faith. When that happens, a new day is announced, the "Today" when God's people respond to the offer and enter his rest. In verse 8 the author makes it clear that Joshua did not turn things around. It was the second generation that entered under Joshua, and Psalm 95 still spoke of "another day." The offer still stands.

In verses 9-10 the eschatological nuances of the promise are presented. When we turn our lives over to Christ and greet the promises with true faith and obedience, we enter into an eternal covenant reality that sees us enjoying the benefits of the Sabbath promises in the present with the promise of a final day of glory when they will be completely ours. The implications (v. 11) of these incredibly great promises demand arduous work on our part in living up to his expectations. The danger of failing to enter God's rest is eternal damnation. The demands are greater than they ever were, for the promise is incredibly greater as well.

Finally, in verses 12-13 we are introduced to the dynamic, powerful word of God that has informed and driven every point the author has made in this letter. He wants us to realize that what he has said is not a merely subjective set of ideas he has put onto paper off the top of his head but a message from God that stems from the mind of God. The purpose of God's word is not merely to inform our knowledge but to drive deeply into our hearts and to change our lives. We must respond by acting on what he has said and allowing it to transform the way we think and live our lives.

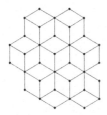

THE SUPERIOR PRIESTHOOD
OF CHRIST
(4:14–5:10)

The author passes from admonition to encouragement, from warning to comfort, by centering on our incredible privileges in Christ. He begins by developing further from 2:17-18 the character of the high priest and our confidence in Jesus fulfilling this office (4:14-16) and in this light showing how Jesus perfectly fits the qualifications (5:1-10). By contrasting the Aaronic with Christ's greater qualifications, he introduces another central text complementing Psalm 110:1 on the exaltation of Christ with the companion Psalm 110:4 on the eternal Melchizedekian priesthood of Christ. All of this prepares for the next warning passage (5:11-6:20) on the foolishness of ignoring the only sufficient salvation in Christ.

JESUS THE GREAT HIGH PRIEST (4:14-16)

THE HEAVENLY DIMENSION (4:14)

This first part is a transition, concluding the section on the new rest Christ has provided as high priest (3:1-4:13), especially this provision as part of Jesus' priestly work (2:17; 3:1). At the same time, it introduces the section on his superior high priestly work

(4:14–7:28), so much greater than the Aaronic priesthood and eternal rather than temporary and passing away. There are two reasons provided why we can place our confidence entirely in his priestly work, for he has ascended into heaven (v. 14) and then has been completely victorious over every temptation we face (vv. 15–16). So we can boldly approach the throne knowing we will receive mercy and grace and the strength we need to face our difficulties. Several scholars have noted the connection between 4:14–16 and 10:19–25, which frame the two-part central section of the letter (4:14–7:28; 8:1–10:18) on Christ's earthly and heavenly priestly ministries.

The "therefore" (*oun*) points back to the earlier discussion of Jesus' priestly work (2:17–3:1) and to the power of the word of God to effect change in God's people (4:12–13). The emphasis is on his "greatness" (*megas*) as high priest, with language of majesty and transcendence throughout. This would be a powerful statement in the first century, when high priests were political appointees given their office by the Romans, and rarely pious. In fact, the high priestly families were among the wealthiest in Jewish society and had their riches at the expense of the other priests who often were virtually penniless and starving.

Jesus, on the other hand, was given his office by his heavenly Father and "ascended into heaven,"[1] pointing back to Psalm 110:1 (Heb 1:3, 13: "sit at my right hand") and his exaltation to heaven. He is "a merciful and faithful high priest" (2:17) as well as "apostle and high priest" (3:1) and now the exalted high priest who reigns in heaven as well as earth. The Aaronic priesthood served in the temple, but Jesus, an entirely unique and divine high priest,

---

1. The Greek is "passed through the heavens," but the plural "heavens" is probably not a reference to multiple heavens (like the "third heaven" of 2 Cor 12:2). In Hebrews, singular *ouranos* occurs in 9:24 and 11:12 and plural *ouranoi* in the others (1:10; 4:14; 7:26; 8:1; 9:23; 12:23, 25–26), and the two forms are likely synonymous. So the NIV "heaven" catches the intended meaning here.

resides in the heavenly sanctuary (6:19–20; 9:12, 24; 10:20). Christ is now in God's temple in heaven where he intercedes for us (8:1–2; 9:1–5, 24–28). Moreover, he is not merely a religious figure but is "Jesus the Son of God" (4:14), the major emphasis earlier (1:2, 5, 8; 3:6), stressing the fact that he is not a mere human being but the God-man whose rightful place is at the side of his Father. Such a claim could be made of no other in the history of this world.

On this basis it is endemic that every reader "hold firmly to the faith we profess." Literally this reads, "hold fast to the confession (*homologia*)," a reference to the creedal confessions of the early church that defined true doctrine. They corporately witnessed to this confession before God and in the presence of both believers and unbelievers (see also 3:1; 10:23; 11:13; 13:15). The emphasis is on divine truth as expounded in God's word (4:12, 13). In their spiritual laziness, many of the readers had fallen back into merely human practices and were in danger of returning to the very Judaism that had shown itself apostate by denying Jesus the Son of God. This dare not go any further, for their very eternity is at stake.

His Earthly Help (4:15–16)

In heaven, he intercedes for us (7:25) and is able to "empathize with our weaknesses"—that is, he identifies with our struggles to defeat sin and triumph over temptation, for he "has been tempted in every way" that we have. The message centers once more on his solidarity with humanity as a result off his incarnation: he has endured every kind of temptation and so can help us in our own weaknesses. Thus we can have complete confidence in his enabling presence. Because he is in heaven at the right hand of God, he has the power to help us triumph, and because he became incarnate on earth, he knows everything we're going through.

He is no outsider to our difficulties but comes to us having suffered in every way we do and far beyond anything we will ever have to endure. The perfect tense "has been tempted" looks at Jesus' life as a whole and stresses that every moment of his earthly existence saw the same battle against temptation that we, too, face. "Just as we are" is *kath homoiotēta*, "according to our likeness," and means that as incarnate, he was as human as we are and was tempted accordingly. In fact, as several point out, he was tempted in ways we will never be, like throwing himself off the pinnacle of the temple or calling for the angels of heaven to come down and defend him.

The great difference with us is that when he experienced these temptations, he never succumbed to them—he was truly tempted but "did not sin," or as often translated, "yet without sin" (see also John 8:46; 2 Cor 5:21; 1 Pet 1:19; 2:22; 1 John 3:5). He never had to offer a sacrifice for his own sins, only for our sins (7:27; 9:14). He was uniquely faithful and obedient to his Father, and in this way, he comes to us as one who was absolutely triumphant and able to give us the help we need.

There has been a major debate regarding Jesus' sinlessness. Theologians have long differed in their answer to the question of whether Jesus was "able not to sin" (he could have sinned but didn't) or "not able to sin" (he could not have sinned). The first is asserted because of his incarnate nature as a human being (stress on his humanity), the second because of his divine nature (stress on his divinity). In the second instance, it is said his human nature was always in union with his divinity, so he would never have been able to yield. Yet Gethsemane shows not only an open choice (as does also the wilderness temptation) but also a human shrinking from the task and prayer for divine help to triumph over the temptation. I agree with those who say that Jesus must have faced a true possibility of yielding if he was to know temptation (the author says, "in every way just as we are"). However, Scripture never truly addresses this issue, so anything we say is somewhat speculative.

The conclusion (*oun*) is drawn in verse 16. Since Jesus has gone through everything, we must endure, and because he both understands our struggles and helps us overcome them, we can "approach God's throne of grace with confidence." "Approach" or "draw near" is a key term in Hebrews for worship and prayer (7:19, 25; 10:22, 25; 11:6; 12:22, 23). This means we can boldly approach God in prayer and expect the empowering presence we need. We are completely confident that he will hear and respond with the strength we lack. This was never possible in the old covenant era. The people were allowed to approach the temple, the priesthood the altar, and the high priest the ark in the holy of holies once a year. However, none came directly to God's throne. Because Jesus has entered through the veil and taken us with him (6:19; 10:20), we come directly before the throne and receive divine grace. Moreover, that grace comes to us at the perfect "time" when our needs are greatest. The Triune Godhead—Father, Son, and Holy Spirit—are always available and there for us.

The throne is also the "mercy seat" and is now open and ready for his faithful people. We now "receive mercy and find grace to help us in our time of need." This takes place because our "merciful and faithful high priest" (2:17) intercedes on our behalf and opens up God's throne for us. "Grace" refers to God's unmerited favor and yet more, for it results in his active work in our lives to lift us above these earthly trials and temptations.

THE QUALIFICATIONS FOR PRIESTHOOD (5:1-10)

The contrast between the Aaronic priesthood and Christ continues, as we see the extent to which the Lord has fulfilled the original qualifications (5:1-4) and gone beyond them (vv. 5-10). The author wants his readers to realize Jesus' faithfulness to his priestly calling and his vast superiority to the Aaronic priests. We are now in the central section of the book, and Christ's high priestly office is at the core of the argument (4:14-10:25), for it encompasses both the christological and **soteriological** dimensions: as high priest, Christ offered himself as the atoning sacrifice and provided salvation for sinful humanity.

So verses 1-4 describe the general qualifications for the Aaronic office of high priest, and verses 5-10 presents the way Christ fulfills those qualities. He goes beyond because he is "a priest forever, in the order of Melchizedek" (vv. 6, 10), from Psalm 110:4. There is a **typological** relationship between Jesus and the office of high priest, and he fulfills that for all eternity. There is no longer a need for an earthly high priest.

QUALIFICATIONS FOR THE HIGH PRIEST (5:1–4)

There are four qualifications that "every high priest" must satisfy to receive his office. He must be: human and Jewish (5:1a); able to fulfill the task of offering sacrifices and atone for sins (v. 1b); sympathetic to the spiritual needs of the people (vv. 2–3); and called by God to the office (v. 4). First, he will be "selected from among the people" (ex anthrōpōn; literally, "taken from mankind"), with the stress pointing to the necessity of Christ's incarnation—an essential part of the comparison. Only a human high priest could represent his fellow human beings (v. 1b) and be truly sympathetic (v. 2), even to the extent of presenting sacrifices for himself (v. 3).

Second, he is divinely appointed for two tasks—"to represent the people in matters related to God [and] to offer gifts and sacrifices for sins." This prepares for verse 4 and stresses God as the true force behind the office. He selects those who will have the spiritual strength to complete the important function of the office. The specific tasks are chosen because they are apropos to the work of Christ as high priest. These tasks allow the priesthood to stand as mediators between God and the people and both represent the people before God and do God's work among them—namely, presenting "gifts and sacrifices" on their behalf. The two categories are not separate items (for example, gifts as cereal offerings and sacrifices as sin offerings) but are synonymous as connoting the entire sacrificial system. The emphasis is on the "for sins," preparing for the atonement and particularly the work of Christ in atoning for sins (see 7:27; 8:3; 9:7; 10:4, 11–12).

Third, as further development of the high priest's "sympathy" for the people (4:15), he must be able to "deal gently with those who are ignorant and are going astray" (5:2). This is a necessary ingredient in both Testaments, for all who minister to people must be understanding and empathetic. "Deal gently" (*metriopathein*) connotes not just gentle actions but moderate attitudes. It means to control emotions, especially anger, in the way we treat those under our care.

Two reasons for such gentle forbearance are provided: First, because the people themselves are often "ignorant and are going astray"—that is, they need understanding and guidance to overcome their human weaknesses and failures. They often inadvertently fall into serious error and must be helped with patience and gentle care. Second, gentleness is mandated because the priest "himself is subject to weakness" (literally, "clothed with human limitations"). High priests wore beautiful robes of office but, in reality, were clothed in sin and needed to maintain their walk with God. Those ministering to others need only look to themselves to realize how deeply every human being needs tender loving care and help.

This is explained further in verse 3: "This is why he has to offer sacrifices for his own sins, as well as for the sins of the people." The high priest himself is at heart a sinner in need of grace and so cannot make sacrifices for others until he has done so for himself (7:27; 9:7) and cleansed himself of sin and guilt (Lev 4:3–23;9:7–14; 16:6, 11; 17:24). This is especially evident in the festival of the Day of Atonement, when the high priest would take a week to purify himself, and before he presented the two goats for the atonement ritual, he had to sacrifice a bull for his own sin offering (Lev 16:6, 11, 15–17). This is a major contrast with Christ who was without sin (Heb 4:15).

The fourth and final qualification for the high priesthood repeats verse 1b. He does not take office on his own initiative or authority but "receives it when called by God, just as Aaron was" (v. 4). The Aaronic priesthood existed only because God had willed it so (Exod 28:1; 29:7–9; Lev 8:1–36; Num 3:10; 16:5; 17:5). In the first century, the high priestly families dominated the office, and they were appointed by the Romans, but this was absolutely counter to the biblical mandate, and everyone realized the corruption of the office. In God's eyes, these were not high priests but charlatans. The principle is important for our day as well. Especially in many mega churches, politics and power control the leadership, and this is just as wrong as it was in the first century. There is no room for dictators in ministry. We all serve God and his people, not ourselves or any power structure in the church.

Christ Fulfilling and Superseding These Qualifications (5:5–10)

There are three emphases with an A-B-A pattern (A = called by God, B = submission to God) in this paragraph: Jesus' calling and exaltation by God (vv. 5–6), his submission to his Father (vv. 7–8), and his appointment by the Father (vv. 9–10). The first aspect centers on two scriptural citations that anchor his God-centeredness and show he "did not take on himself the glory of becoming a high priest" (v. 5), completely unlike the first-century high priests like Annas or Caiaphas. The introductory "God said to him" is significant. His Sonship is directly proclaimed as the spoken word, and as several have noted, it centers not so much on parentage as on Jesus' appointment and exaltation to Sonship. It is the enthroned Son of God who is made the eternal high priest.

The author begins by quoting Psalm 2:7 once more (see Heb 1:5), where God acclaimed him Son. As in 1:5, the "Today" refers not so much to his incarnation (though it is likely included) as to his exaltation to heaven when his glory was demonstrated to all. He was enthroned in heaven and took his place at the right hand of God not only as Lord of all but as the eternal high priest. There is continuity with Aaron in the sense that God appointed Christ to his office and discontinuity with the exaltation and eternal nature of that office. Christ unites the high priesthood with his eternal Sonship (4:14), and the two citations here anchor that, with

Psalm 2:7 in Hebrews 5:5 proclaiming his Sonship and Psalm 110:4 in Hebrews 5:6 proclaiming his high priesthood, both established by the call of God. The basis of Christ's perpetual high priesthood is his eternal Sonship.

As Psalm 110:1 dominated the first chapters and centered upon Jesus' eternal lordship and glory, so Psalm 110:4 will dominate Hebrews 5–7 and center upon his eternal high priesthood (5:6). This text is the core of the argument and will be alluded to numerous times in subsequent chapters. The purpose of Psalm 110, a royal psalm, is to show that the Davidic Messiah has been appointed by God as both exalted king (110:1) and high priest (110:4). The choice of Melchizedek had a twofold purpose: (1) he was the priest-king of Genesis 14 (not a christophany but a historical figure, both king of Salem and priest of God Most High, Gen 14:22) to whom Abraham gave a tithe and so combined the imagery of this psalm; (2) he had no beginning or end in the story (that is, his genealogy is never developed) and so became the "high priest forever," the perfect figure for the Messiah as an eternal high priest.

Hebrews is the only New Testament book to develop this theme, and it is essential for its presentation of the lasting effects of Jesus' atoning work on the cross and in heaven. Many see in this the Jewish development, especially in **Qumran**, of a lay Messiah (the Davidic line) and a priestly Messiah (the Aaronic line). That is difficult to prove but possible. Certainly, the Davidic and the Aaronic are part of the imagery, but here they are part of one figure, not two, as in Qumran. At any rate, this becomes the foundation for Jesus' high priestly office and will be developed in detail in chapter 7. The thrust here is that this was entirely the work of God who made his Son also to be the "high priest forever in the order of Melchizedek."

Second, the author describes Jesus' submission to his Father as the appointed high priest (Heb 5:7–8) and his empathetic union with sinful humanity that resulted. It has often been surmised that the introductory *hos* ("who") at the start of verse 7 plus the parallel participles point to an early Christian hymn behind verses 7–10, but it is more likely that this is high prose penned by the writer. It is rather a beautifully constructed meditation on Jesus' submission to his Father. The Aaronic line was fallible and often unfaithful, giving way to human weakness (5:2b–3), while he, as Son of God, is completely faithful and obedient to his calling. "The days of Jesus' life on earth" (v. 7), of course, refers to his incarnate existence and his solidarity with the human dilemma (see 2:14–18; 4:15). He is the archetype of one submitting to God in prayer, and through it, identifying with all of our spiritual needs.

The religious language behind "offered up (*prosenengkas*) prayers and petitions" in verse 7 looks at Jesus' sacrificial prayer life, considering Jesus' entreaties as sin offerings to bring us to God. The "fervent cries and tears" (v. 7) pictures his Gethsemane experience when he was "in anguish" and "his sweat was like drops of blood falling to the ground" (Luke 22:44). Moreover, his prayers, following the Gethsemane model, were for his own deliverance from suffering and death, for it adds they were offered "to the one who could save *him* from death" (Heb 5:7, emphasis added). It is probably better to translate it "saved him *out of* death" (*ek thanatou*) rather than "from death," for Jesus was not kept from dying but rather taken "out of" the grave so that death could not keep him captive.

The result was, of course, his resurrection and exaltation. "He was heard because of his reverent submission" (v. 7), again likely a reference to Gethsemane, where he prayed, "yet not my will but yours be done" (Luke 22:42). "Reverent submission" (*eulabeias*) is often translated "godly fear," but this is not fear of death but rather that reverence and awe that he felt for his Father and that was the essential core of his submission. The fact that God "heard" him means he granted his request. Jesus' vibrant prayer life is proof positive of his submission and dependence on his Father. In every area of his life (not just when suffering) he was in contact with and relying on his Father's presence. In this, too, Jesus is the perfect model for us in our obedience, submission, and dependence on God as expressed in regular prayer.

As the Son of God (1:1-2, 5, 8; 3:6; 4:14; 5:5), Jesus partook of his father's divinity and authority over all creation. So the author begins this central verse on Christ's obedience and submission with "Son though he was" (5:8) to show Christ's power and glory within his obedience. Though the perfect, omnipotent Son, he still had to "learn" (the main verb of verses 7-10) from his Father just as we do. The priests of the Aaronic line were fallible and filled with "weakness" (5:2), so they often failed to learn that critical lesson. It was the Son of God himself that provided the example of pure obedience, and it was lifelong and the result of his ministry of suffering. Jesus became incarnate so he could suffer and give his life to redeem us and atone for our sin. We learn in spite of our sinful tendencies, but he was without sin and pure before God in his suffering, so he learned "from what he suffered" (v. 8) and achieved perfect obedience as a result. No wonder he is so sympathetic to our dilemma and able to help us in our own fallibility (2:17-18; 4:15).

Third, as in verse 2, Jesus is appointed by his Father to his high priestly office (5:9-10). The author repeats the point he had made in 2:10, that God in bringing humanity salvation had made "the pioneer of their salvation perfect through what he suffered." We had discovered that this meant that Jesus' office as Savior and high priest was "brought to completion" (teleiōtheis) in his life of suffering and especially his death on the cross, leading to his heavenly exaltation and enthronement at the right hand of God. Now the author adds that this also meant Jesus "became the source of eternal salvation for all who obey him." This prepares for the meditation in 8:1-10:18 on Jesus' sacrificial death providing atonement for sins. The result of Christ's redeeming sacrifice is not just life but eternal life, a salvation that is efficacious forever, building on Isaiah 45:17: "Israel will be saved by the Lord with an everlasting salvation."

Those who receive this eternal salvation are "all who obey him." Jesus is the obedient servant of Yahweh and Son of God, and those who benefit emulate him in hearing and obeying his word of truth (Heb 4:12–13). The wilderness people perished due to disobedience (3:18; 4:6, 11), and the current generation were about to follow them into unbelief and failure, as will be exposed in 5:11–6:20. They must abandon the wilderness mistakes and follow the perfect model of Jesus in submitting and obeying God.

The second result of Jesus' completed office is that he is "designated by God to be high priest in the order of Melchizedek" (5:10), returning to verse 6 and Psalm 110:4. As stated earlier, the point is that he is not an earthly, temporal high priest like those of the Aaronic line but, as will be developed in Hebrews 7:3, he is "without beginning of days or end of life" and "remains a priest forever." With Jesus, there is no need for a continuing priesthood, for in him as "the source of eternal salvation" according to verse 9, death and finiteness, as well as sin, have been once for all overcome.

We have concluded the introductory material and now enter the central section of the entire letter. The emphasis on Christ as the divinely appointed eternal high priest and its implications carries through from here to 10:25. The first section (4:14–16) presents Jesus as the exalted high priest who resides and reigns in heaven as the Son of God and who is able to provide the help we need because he endured every temptation we face, yet never succumbed and was at all times victorious over sin and Satan's attacks. He not only won the victory for us but provides mercy and grace to us when we need it. This is why Paul could say that whenever we are bombarded with temptations and trials, God provides "a way out" so we can overcome them (1 Cor 10:13).

The rest of the material (5:1–10) compares Jesus with the high priests of the line of Aaron, showing us how he meets all their qualifications (vv. 1-4) but transcends them as the great heavenly high priest (vv. 5-10). The author wants us to know there is no longer a need for an earthly high priest, for Jesus meets all our needs and more from his throne in heaven.

Jesus' first qualification places him squarely in the line of the Aaronic priesthood. He not only was fully human but was selected from among the people to serve God and them (v. 1a). Second, Aaronic priests represented God's people in spiritual matters (v. 1b). Third (and this is a major area of contrast between Jesus and earthly high priests), they must recognize their own sins and deal "gently" with others since they know what people are going through (vv. 2-3). Needless to say, the sinless Jesus transcends this and helps us from a position of absolute strength. Fourth, like all high priests, Jesus is appointed by God to his office (v. 4). Yet again, there is contrast, for Jesus' appointment is made by an eternal divine oath (7:20-22).

In the rest of this section (5:5-10), we see how Jesus transcends the office and makes it uniquely his. First, in verses 5-6 his calling and appointment are as Son of God (Ps 2:7) and an appointment to be a "priest forever in the order of Melchizedek" (Ps 110:4), which becomes the central theme of the next few chapters (Heb 5-7). The two passages show that Jesus reigns as the priest-king and that the basis of his Melchizedekian priesthood is the fact that he is the eternal Son of God.

Second, he is characterized by perfect submission and obedience to his Father's call (5:7-8). Earthly high priests were often enamored with the power and prestige of their office, wearing long fancy robes with their ephod to show others how splendid they were. Jesus gave himself fully to his Father and to "learning" perfectly from his suffering so he could offer himself on the cross as an atoning sacrifice. In other words, he fulfilled his office perfectly.

Third and finally, as God's perfect high priest, he "became the source of eternal salvation" (v. 9). He was the eternal Son who was appointed to be "a priest forever" and thereby could provide "eternal salvation" to those who would come by faith. In 2:10, this perfect learning experience had made Jesus the "pioneer of our salvation," and this is shown to mean here that salvation and eternal life were the result. This becomes perfect proof that he indeed was designated the Melchizedekian high priest, fulfilling Psalm 110:4. The next three chapters are dedicated to unfolding the implications of this.

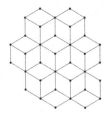

THE DANGER OF
SPIRITUAL LETHARGY
(5:11–6:20)

After quoting Psalm 110:4 and introducing the critical teaching that Jesus Christ is high priest "in the order of Melchizedek," the writer shockingly halts his presentation and accuses his readers of spiritual immaturity and laziness, leading to their inability to understand what he is saying about Jesus, and this even though they have been believers long enough to be teachers themselves. He then proceeds to provide the most detailed description of the danger of apostasy anywhere in the Bible. Clearly, he is frightened about the direction they are headed spiritually and deeply concerned that they do not realize the danger they are facing.

The key term is *nōthroi* ("lazy, sluggish"), which frames the main body with their basic problem: an unwillingness to put forth the effort to grow spiritually and in understanding. There are four parts to this section: (1) 5:11–6:3, calling them to quit being lazy and move on to Christian maturity; (2) 6:4–8, on the supreme danger of apostasy from the faith and the terrible consequences of doing so; (3) 6:9–12, encouraging them that he is confident they will heed the warning, cease their slide into spiritual oblivion, and overcome their spiritual weakness; (4) 6:13–20, encouraging them further regarding God's promises that provide a spiritual anchor that will give us hope.

SPIRITUAL IMMATURITY AND LAZINESS (5:11–14)

The author realizes he has gone too deep into Christian truth for these people, for they aren't mature enough to understand and are simply too lazy to try. He would love to say a great deal more (and, in fact, will do so in chapter 7), but they aren't ready to listen. "Hard to make it clear to you" (v. 11) is literally "difficult to explain," but that is not because the subject matter is too advanced but rather because these Christians are so dull both mentally and spiritually. He dare not continue with the Melchizedek theme because of their spiritual lethargy. The writer emphasizes throughout Hebrews the importance of the word of God as the purveyor of truth (1:1-2; 4:12-13) and the critical importance of listening and obeying (2:1-4; 3:7-19; 5:11-14; 8:10). These truths were revealed by Christ himself (1:1-2) and given through angels (2:1-4), but that is almost irrelevant when the people are not even listening. Until they are willing to yield to the penetrating power of biblical truth (4:12-13), all he can say will do no good.

He cannot "make it clear" to them because they are *nōthroi*, a term referring to an unwillingness to work at something because they are "sluggish" or "lazy," with the result that they are spiritually "dull."[1] Their shallow walk with the Lord is not the result of an inability to understand but rather a lack of desire to try to understand. They are hard of hearing as a result of this lethargy, as the text literally reads "lazy in understanding/hearing"

---

1. Some have recently argued that these readers are actually mature believers and that this negative cast is an attempt to shock them and move them to work even harder at their faith, but that is quite unlikely. Their weak stance for the Lord is systemic to the letter and at the heart of the argument. It must be the actual situation.

(*tais akoais*), meaning they aren't even trying to listen to the arguments. They are immature because they are completely inat-
tentive to anything being said. It is not irredeemable as yet, and
there is still hope, but they had better turn their lives around
while there is still time.

Sadly, they are not recent converts (5:12). In fact, they are
a second-generation church with a deeply mature and victorious heritage (10:32-34). With their background they should be
teachers in the church. In reality, they "need someone to teach
[them] the elementary truths of God's word all over again." That
is an incredibly sad commentary, for the "again" means they had
excellent spiritual mentors in the past. But the truths never stuck,
and they have regressed into spiritual and doctrinal ignorance
once more.

The "elementary truths of God's word" (v. 12) refers to the
basics, as will be explained in 6:1-3. They should be able to discuss advanced teachings like the Melchizedekian high priesthood of Christ but don't even know the ABCs of their faith. In the
new covenant passage from Jeremiah 31:31-34 (Heb 8:6-13), the
author prophesied that the people of Israel would no longer need
to "teach their neighbor" since they will "all know" God directly,
but that was not true of the audience of Hebrews. The Greek is
stoicheia tēs archēs, the "elementary principles of the beginning
truths of the words of God." This language was used of the "basic
elements" that make up the physical universe and here refers
to the beginning principles of the Christian faith as revealed in
God's "oracles" or spoken word. The author shouldn't even need
to mention this, for the people should have presupposed these
truths almost from the moment they first followed Christ.

Because of their shallowness, they "need milk, not solid
food" (v. 12). They are mentally challenged believers, infants in
an adult body, but it should not be this way. The sad truth is they
have stopped caring about their faith and have digressed back
to being babes in Christ (compare 1 Cor 3:1-2; Eph 4:14; 1 Pet 2:2).

Most recent commentators recognize the language of honor and shame. The writer wants to shame them into turning their life around and once again grow up as Christians—to stop drinking milk and start eating meat.

The shame of it all continues into Hebrews 5:13. The worst thing is that those who are babes in Christ and spiritual infants must live on milk and are unable to be "acquainted with the teaching about righteousness" (v. 13). They cannot digest adult fare and are unskilled in preparing gourmet meals. The pablum that is their daily fare leaves them unable to handle truly nourishing meals.

Some have interpreted "teaching about righteousness" as simply moral and ethical reasoning, since *dikaiosynē* ("righteousness") can have a primarily ethical connotation. However, it is certainly more in this context, as it is teaching about that righteousness that comes from God and his word. This is not the Pauline sense of justification as forensic righteousness—that is, God declaring the new convert to be righteous. Rather, it refers to the ethical side, living rightly before God. This refers to deep Christian principles for mature Christians who are able to discern right from wrong and forge a life that is pleasing to God. Such people are never lethargic but deeply care for theological and ethical truth and want to live by it.

While infants can drink only milk, "solid food is for the mature," with "mature" first in the sentence for emphasis (v. 14). "Mature" is *teleiōn*, recalling the perfection of Christ in 2:10 and 5:9, picturing Christ as the model we are to follow in our Christian walk. These Christlike followers have the discernment to understand the proper lifestyle and spiritual stance necessary to please God. This uses athletic imagery, as these spiritual adults "by constant use have trained themselves" (v. 14). with *gymnazō* depicting athletes in the "gymnasium" undergoing strenuous practice to hone their abilities.

Spiritual athletes learn the value of constant exercise and training in the faith and hone their strength and spiritual reaction timing. My wife and I enjoy watching the Tour de France in July and marveling at the incredible strength and reactions of these athletes. How they ride in a "peloton" of up to a hundred riders going forty+ miles an hour up and down those hills of the Alps and Pyrenees for nearly 200 miles a day for three weeks is beyond our imagination. It takes incredible ability and a lifetime of training to do such things. That is also true of the deep Christian life, and the picture here describes constant study of the word and growth in the life of the Spirit that will enable victorious Christian living.

The result is that these hardworking saints "have trained themselves to distinguish good from evil" (v. 14). The wilderness generation had failed to do that and so was overwhelmed by the pressure of being pursued by the Egyptian armies and the hardship of the exodus journey without sufficient food and drink. This inability to discern right from wrong destroyed them spiritually and led to them perishing in the wilderness, judged by God and found wanting. The people in these Hebrew churches were in danger of the same error. The pressure of persecution and suffering had eroded their ability to walk with Christ. They desperately needed to grow up and relearn the ability to discern biblical truth and make those moral and ethical decisions that would reinstate them with God. They needed to change their spiritual diets and eat "solid food" and also alter their practices and start building themselves up spiritually.

MOVING BEYOND THE ELEMENTARY TEACHINGS (6:1–3)

The theme is stated clearly at the outset, "let us move beyond the elementary teachings about Christ and be taken forward to maturity" (v. 1). Notice what is *not* being said, that because they are lazy, they can only be fed beginning elementary truths. No, the writer has decided to forgo the basic doctrines and force them to center on the solid truths that lead to maturity. If Jesus is truly "the apostle and high priest" (3:1) of their confession, they must build on the basics and go beyond to the deep truths.

"Let us move beyond" (pherōmetha) could be a divine passive, "Let God move us forward," and that would fit the "God permitting" of verse 3. The believers are asked to yield to the presence and power of God at this juncture of their lives. Some think this a set of Jewish doctrines that became a foundation for Christian teaching, others a prebaptismal catechetical list. Neither is quite correct. The Jewish parallels are definitely present, but these are Christian issues as well as Jewish. It is best to consider this list the theological juncture where Jewish background began to lead to Christian principles.

There are six items in three pairs listed: repentance from acts that lead to death that is made possible by faith in God; baptisms/instruction about cleansing rites that are connected to the laying on of hands; and the resurrection of the dead as linked to eternal judgment. The three pairs have a progressive feel to them, with the first two depicting the conversion process, the middle two Jewish and Christian ordinances, and the final pair the **eschatological** events that will draw history to a close.

1. "Repentance from acts that lead to death" (v. 1). This phrase proves the list is not Jewish, for these first two point to Christian conversion. While grounded in old covenant concepts (Num 23:19; Deut 4:30; Isa 6:10; Jer 26:3), the thrust here is distinctly new covenant and means to turn from sin to God. "Acts that led to death" is literally "dead works" (nekrōn ergōn) and has a double meaning, referring to human deeds that are empty, futile, and worthless and also "works righteousness," which is actually sinful and

leads to spiritual death. These refer to those actions that we must turn away from and repent, seeking forgiveness.

2. "Faith in God" (v. 1). This is the other side of turning from sin—namely, turning to God via faith in Christ and his atoning sacrifice, eschewing dead works, and embracing the living God. "Faith" occurs seventeen times in Romans 3:21–4:25 and connotes an essential belief and trust in the saving efficacy of Christ and the cross. Eternal life comes to sinners when they perform these first two actions here, and it is the foundation stone of the Christian doctrine of salvation.

3. "Instruction about cleansing rites" (v. 2). There is a difference of opinion about the meaning of this, as many have thought it a reference to Christian baptism; however, it is not the normal term used and is plural rather than singular (*baptismōn*), and in 9:10, this word is used for Jewish "ceremonial washings." Thus I prefer to see it as intended to describe teaching about the difference between Christian baptism and Jewish "washings," like the cleansing of priests, washing at **Qumran**, proselyte baptism, and ablutions in the pools of Jerusalem before offering sacrifices. So this is probably "teaching" about the superiority of Christian baptism over these Jewish rites.

4. "The laying on of hands" (v. 2). In the Old Testament this practice was used to authorize a person assuming an office (Num 27:18; Deut 34:9) or offering a sacrifice (Lev 3:2; 4:4). In the early church it was associated with healing the sick (Mark 1:41; 6:5; Acts 28:8), commissioning for service (Acts 6:6; 13:3;

1 Tim 4:14), or imparting the Holy Spirit (Acts 8:17; 9:17; 19:6). It is mentioned here as an initiating rite in the church and is probably mentioned here to sum up the passing on of these things in the corporate body of the church.

5. "The resurrection of the dead" (v. 2). We now turn from the beginning of the Christian life to the end events that will draw history to a close. The two here describe the destiny of believers (resurrection) and unbelievers (judgment). The direct revelation of this essential truth came fairly late in the Old Testament (Isa 26:19; Dan 12:2) but was still indirect and implicit much earlier, as with Enoch (Gen 5:24) and Elijah (2 Kgs 2:11) caught up to heaven. For Christians it was essential for a truly Christian theology (1 Cor 15:14–19). Death is the basic corollary to sin in this world (Rom 5:12–14), so it is essential that the sting of death be removed forever (1 Cor 15:54–57), and it is absolutely essential that they realize that this is only available to true believers.

6. "Eternal judgment" (v. 2). For the justice of God to be upheld, it is essential not only that the saved be resurrected but also that the unsaved receive their due punishment. In Daniel 12:2 the righteous receive "everlasting life" and the unrighteous "shame and everlasting contempt" (see Dan 7:9–14). Souls are created as eternal beings, so the enemies of God will continue to exist but will be cast into eternal hellfire (Mark 9:43, 45, 47; Rev 20:14–15).

In Hebrews 6:3 the author states his intention to provide the teaching that will move them "forward to maturity" (v. 1), but he recognizes that God will make the final decision as to the future of his readers and so feels he must add (literally), "If God permits." The next section (6:4-8) will discuss the tragic results of apostasy, and if that has taken place, there will be no teaching, for God will have rejected these people. Still, he is cautiously optimistic and prepares for the encouragement of 6:9-12 by saying, "we will do so," showing his expectation that God will indeed permit this mature teaching to take place. The first plural "we" is probably not a reference to multiple teachers but means "all of us," the author working with the people themselves to bring them to maturity.

THE TERRIBLE DANGER OF APOSTASY (6:4-8)

We now begin the key passage in terms of the problem behind this letter. These house churches are guilty of indifference to the things of the Lord and a resultant low spiritual commitment that has the author quite afraid that many of them may well fall into total spiritual ruin and commit apostasy. He does not think they will, in the end, do so (6:9-12) but feels serious warning is necessary since that is the direction they are moving at present. The stern warning of verses 4-8 is followed by cautious optimism in 9-12, and the two interact with one another to provide a balanced perspective on the two sides: God holds us responsible to maintain our commitment to him and, at the same time, gives us his strength to "fight the good fight" (see 2 Tim 3:7).

Needless to say, this passage has occasioned a great deal of debate and quite a bit of acrimony, and it is nearly impossible to be neutral and objective since it has produced such heated exchanges. I must try to be just that, but clearly I will be arguing one of the sides as well. To me the key is to develop a deep respect for the other side and welcome their challenges. You will have to decide whether I can achieve that openness, but I must try to do so. I do not want to force my opinion on you but rather to give you enough data to enable you to decide for yourself.

The structure of 6:4–6 is complex since it is composed of a series of parallel participles connected with the particles *te* and *kai*, both meaning "and." The best solution is to take *kai* as the major and *te* as the minor connective, yielding the following organization:

> having once been enlightened
> (and, *te*) having tasted the heavenly gift
>   and (*kai*)
> having shared in the Holy Spirit
>   and (*kai*)
> having tasted the goodness of the word of God
>   and (*te*) the powers of the coming age
>   and then (*kai*)
> having fallen away

The writer begins 6:4 with the two words *adynaton gar* ("for it is impossible"). The reason he wants these weak Christians to leave their shallowness behind and move on to maturity is the unbelievable danger they are facing. He wants to make starkly emphatic his major point: final apostasy cannot be redeemed. There is no hope whatsoever for anyone who follows this terrible path. The next two verses tell why, centering on the privileges of being a Christian. To throw all this away takes a coldness and contempt for the things of God that simply cannot be forgiven. Some have tried to water this down by taking it as hyperbole and translating, "It is quite difficult." That is a mistake—everywhere the term occurs it speaks of impossibility (6:18; 10:4; 11:6). Such a person cannot be brought back to faith.[2]

---

2. One type of apostasy, found in James 5:19–20, can be redeemed, but it is not final apostasy. This occurs when sin crowds Christ out and is not a cold, deliberate, calculated falling away but rather a surrender of one's life to sin. I would call the James 5 type "passive apostasy" and the Hebrews 6 type "active apostasy" due to its deliberate nature.

In 6:4b–5 five blessings are enumerated as resulting from conversion to Christ, and all are seen as gifts from the Triune Godhead to the believer. All are intended to enable the individual to grow in Christ and are seen as what takes place when we leave the "elementary principles" and move on to maturity in Christ. The sad story of the wilderness people, as discussed in Psalm 95 in 3:1–4:13 above, is certainly in the author's mind. The Christian life is a pilgrimage, and we wander through our lives in need of these gifts to enable us to complete our journey. These are the Christian blessings thrown away in the act of apostasy.

1. "Once been enlightened" (v. 4). Both terms are used of salvation and conversion in the New Testament. "Once" (*hapax*) is used in 9:26 and 28 of the complete, never-to-be-repeated sacrifice of Christ that has led to eternal salvation. The stress is on the complete, full experience of God's mercy and grace. "Enlightened" (*phōtisthentas*) is a divine passive signifying how God has shed his light on those who have come in faith and revealed his truths to them. There may be a reference back to Exodus 13:21 and the pillar of fire that "gave [the wilderness people] light" at night for their wanderings. Those who read baptism into this are mistaken, for there is no hint of that in this context. The light of God in the gospel has shone on his people.

2. "Tasted the heavenly gift" (v. 4). This does not mean a mere sip but instead pictures a full, complete experience of God and his gifts. Those who read baptism into the first blessing read the eucharist into this, but again, that is quite unlikely. This echoes Psalm 34:8: "Taste and see that the LORD is good," also cited in 1 Peter 2:3. The "heavenly gift" should not be narrowed to the Spirit or spiritual gifts but is a

comprehensive image for all the blessings God provides from heaven along with our salvation. Moreover, heaven is not just our future dwelling place, for we are already citizens of heaven (Phil 3:21) and aliens in this world (1 Pet 1:1, 17; 2:11). We are currently both earth-dwellers and citizens of heaven.

3. "Shared in the Holy Spirit" (v. 4). In 3:1 we are "sharers" (*metochoi*) in a heavenly calling, and in 3:14 we share in Christ. Building on these, we are now "sharers" in the Spirit, referring to the Spirit entering us at conversion (Rom 8:14–17) and endowing us with spiritual gifts (1 Cor 12:11–21), gifts that are "distributed according to his will" in Hebrews 2:4. This is thus a reference to the Spirit-filled life, as the Spirit guides and empowers us day by day.

4. "Tasted the goodness of the word of God" (v. 5). The word is often described as "good" to the taste (Pss 19:10; 34:8; 119:103; Ezek 3:1–3; 1 Pet 2:2–4) and is probably referring here to the proclaimed truth of Christian preaching (*theou rhēma*). The Bible often compares preaching to what we would call a gourmet meal—a wonderful way to think of it. Preachers should think of sermon preparation as readying a superb banquet for the church.

5. "Tasted … the powers of the coming age" (v. 5). This corresponds to the last two items in the list of verses 1–2 dealing with the end times events. The coming age is launched with the return of Christ and onset of eternity, and the powers would be the "signs, wonders, and various miracles" of 2:4 that were operative in the escape from Egypt and journey through the wilderness and are operative once more in the lives of the

readers of this letter. There is an already-and-not-yet
flavor to this as past, present, and future are intertwined in the experiences of God's people in every age.

These five privileges are meant to define what it means to be a
Christian. It is a marvelous list, and if it had occurred in Romans 8
in a positive context, it would be considered the most beautiful
set of blessings anywhere in terms of a brief, creedal-like presentation of Christian blessings. The purpose here, however, is to
add depth and detail to the warning of Hebrews 2:3: "How shall
we escape if we ignore so great a salvation?" Those who fall away
are giving up the greatest set of blessings ever made available to
mere mortals.

The final participle presents the tragic possibility of apostasy
in 6:6a: "and who have fallen away." This is not a conditional, as
some have interpreted it ("if they have fallen away"), but rather a
coordinate clause. They have experienced all these fantastic gifts
from God and then have ignored it all and fallen away from their
faith. This is why the author can say, "It is impossible ... [for them]
to be brought back to repentance." Virtually all recent commentators admit that this must be final apostasy, the absolute rejection of
Christ as Lord and Savior. The debate is over identifying the actual
state of those who commit this grievous sin. Many think they are
professing Christians but not actual believers, but the problem is
that they are called "holy brothers and sisters who share in a heavenly calling" in 3:1, and the five descriptives here in this paragraph
are such strong statements of actual Christian experience. You
will have to judge for yourself, but I feel I must reply in the affir-
mative. It is difficult to imagine the strong language used here if
apostasy was not possible for them. As we will see in verses 9–12,
none of them have done so yet, and the writer is convinced that
they will not do so, but the possibility remains.

If we return to the pilgrimage motif of this letter, this depicts
the wandering Christian pilgrim falling off the path to salvation, as

in 12:12–13 with the "lame" (another portrayal of the weak believer) becoming "disabled" and falling into the ditch. These people turn their backs on all God has done for them and "drift away" (2:1), then fall away completely from their salvation.

Is this the unpardonable sin of Mark 3:28–29? This is indeed possible, but it is not just that they can't be restored but that God will not be willing to restore such a one, as will also be stated in 10:26–31 and 12:15–17 later in this letter. Literally, this reads, "impossible to renew them to repentance," and the question is whether this means for the church to restore them or for God to do so. Likely both are included, but in light of God's action being central in 10:26–31 and 12:15–17, he is the primary actor here. This does not mean God will not be able to do so since nothing is impossible for God. Rather, it means God will refuse to bring them back, for they have gone beyond the pale.

In Jesus' ministry the unpardonable sin was blasphemy against the Holy Spirit (Mark 3:28–30), but in this context, Jesus is now the exalted Lord, and final apostasy is now also blasphemy against him. From "if God permits" (v. 3) to "it is impossible" (v. 4), the answer is clear: God will not allow them to return. However, the rest of this verse will add another nuance—they won't want to return. For the rest of their lies, they will hold everything Christian in contempt. In fact, this is how we tell a person who has committed the unpardonable sin—they laugh at any suggestion that Christianity could be true.

It is a growing consensus that the two participles of verse 6b ("crucifying" and "subjecting him to public disgrace") are causal, telling why they "cannot be brought back to repentance."[3] Both

---

3. Some take them as temporal participles and translate "as long as" they continue such things, seeing in this the possibility of repentance at a future time. But that does not fit the context here with its strong emphasis on the impossibility of such a thing.

are in the present tense—meaning that these apostates will stand for this for the rest of their lives. First, they have rejected Christ's work on the cross. It was a once-for-all event, but they are nailing him on the cross (*anastauroō*) "all over again" (*palin*) as they continually live a life opposed to his work of salvation. They are recrucifying not just Jesus the rabbi or even Messiah but the very Son of God (at the heart of this letter, 1:2, 5, 8; 3:6; 4:14; 7:3; 10:29), who is forced up on the cross all over again.

Moreover, he is held up to public ridicule (*paradeigmatizontas*). The mockery of Jesus on the cross will become the hallmark of these people for the rest of their lives. Here we have a pragmatic reason why these people will never be restored to faith. They will spend their remaining time on earth laughing at people who believe in Christ and at everything for which Christianity stands. They will spend so much time shaming him that they will never consider the possibility that they were right the first time and need to return to him.

In verses 7-8 the author uses an agricultural metaphor to portray the process of the blessings and cursings. Believers are compared to farmland and its productivity. The grace of God is likened to rain that falls on it and produces a crop. If the land is fruitful and fertile, producing a useful crop, it "receives the blessing of God" (v. 7). God is pouring his blessings enumerated in verses 4-5 on such maturing believers, and they will receive the "gifts of the Holy Spirit" (2:4) and be richly blessed. However, if the land/ Christian is unfruitful and "worthless," producing only "thorns and thistles" (v. 8)—an allusion to Genesis 3:17-18 ("Cursed is the ground because of you. ... It will produce thorns and thistles")— then the farmer will "curse" such land and burn it (v. 8; compare Isa 5:1-7; John 15:1-6). This is literally true, for burning up land places nutrients in the soil that help it to become fertile. The message, of course, is of fiery judgment that awaits the apostate.

ENCOURAGEMENT TO PERSEVERE (6:9–12)

They have been duly warned and in the kind of tone meant to terrify any reader. Now the author reverses himself and greatly encourages them, assuring them that "even though we speak like this" (v. 9)—that is, in severe tones meant to frighten the readers—he does so for their good because God has better plans for them. He has to wake them up to their dangerous spiritual slide and get them to change their course. Still, they must do their part— namely, to persevere diligently to the very end. He is asking for a total turnaround, for them to jettison their lazy, lackadaisical attitude toward the things of Christ and win through so they can inherit God's promised reward. Moreover, the language shifts from the "it" of the land to the direct "you" to make the promises here even more explicit.

Encouragement: God's Part (6:9–10)

He assures them that neither he nor God have turned against them and, in fact, they are "beloved" (v. 9, *agapētoi*; NIV: "dear friends"). The reason for this optimism is that even though he had to "speak like this" because of their poor spiritual situation, he is actually "convinced of better things in your case—the things that have to do with salvation." The reason for his confidence does not lie in them but in the God who loves them. His care and concern for them trumps their indifference. If he can only get them to wake up and realize what truly matters in life, they will be more than secure in God's enabling power.

The "better things" go back to that basic guiding concept that determines the organizational plan for 1:1–10:18, the "superiority" of Christ (*kreissona*; see on 1:4; 7:7, 19, 22; 8:6; 9:23; 10:34; 11:16, 35; 12:24) over everything Judaism or this world could offer. These superior things are the spiritual blessings enumerated in 6:4–5, 7, 13–20, and God has given them to his people. This is especially the case because these things "have to do with salvation" (v. 9), which is "so great" in 2:3 and eternal in force according to 5:9. It is *already* our experience in our present spiritual walk but *not yet* finalized, awaiting the return of Christ and the dawn of our eternity in heaven. Here and in most places in Hebrews, this refers primarily to the final salvation awaiting us in heaven (1:14; 5:9; 9:28). Our future is secure, and that gives us the strength to persevere. He is confident they are not descending to apostasy but ascending to their future inheritance, but they must continue to progress and endure. They are the good soil of verse 7 rather than the bad soil of verse 8. Still, the danger is very real, and some are giving signs of moving in the wrong direction.

The author is confident based on the character of God, not because of any inherent worth or spiritual maturity on their part. Using a double negative, he stresses the fact that "God is not unjust" (*adikos*)—that is, he is righteous and fair, faithful to his followers at all times. While they have indeed been spiritually sluggish (5:11; 6:12), at the same time, they have "worked" diligently and been faithful to him, showing "love" for God and their fellow believers. This demonstration of loving concern took place in the early days when they were a first-generation church ("you have helped his people," see 10:32-34; 13:1-3) and continues into the present (you "continue to help them" [v. 10]). Moreover, it is clear that this love for the fellow saints was prompted by love for God—namely, "the love you have shown him" (literally, "love for his name" [*eis to onoma autou*]). God is remembering their faithfulness and pouring out his blessings as a reward.

FURTHER EXHORTATION: THEIR PART (6:11-12)

Even though signs make him cautiously optimistic, the dangers are still very real, so the writer must continue to admonish (3:13) them to further perseverance. He demonstrates his deep love and concern with his opening "we want" (v. 11), actually a stronger verb better translated "deeply desire" or "yearn" (*epithymoumen*). He is greatly concerned that they take the positive steps necessary to put them on solid footing spiritually. "Diligence" (v. 11) is *spoudē*, connoting zealous action and eager, concerted effort. They must make growing in Christ the heart of their lives. Their goal (*pros*) must be to persevere until their hope in Christ is "fully realized" (*plērophoria*; also in 10:22). This must be done "to the very end" (*achri telous*), meaning that their entire lives must be dedicated to this goal. At that time, their hopes will indeed be complete, for they will enter their eternal destiny in heaven. As we persevere in the present, we must keep that hope alive to spur us on to ever greater effort.

This energetic "diligence" (v. 11) will keep them from becoming even more "lazy" (v. 12, the same *nōthroi* as in 5:11), the problem that has plagued them and kept them from maturing in the Lord. The way to do that is to "imitate those who through faith and patience inherit what has been promised"—namely, what has constituted their hope in Christ. "To imitate" (*mimētēs*) means both patterning your life after someone and also obeying what they teach and say. These are the models from the past, both the first-generation victors of 10:32–34 and the "heroes of the faith" in chapter 11. They are to avoid the anti-heroes of the exodus from 3:1–4:13 and emulate those who have successfully persevered. Their hope is tied up with their future inheritance (see on 1:4).

The means by which victory is achieved, with the end result being the reception of their inheritance, is "faith and patience" (v. 12). Many combine the two into a single idea (called "hendiadys") and translate this "persevering faith." These shallow believers have had short-term memory loss when it comes to the things of the Lord and desperately need the kind of trust in him that lasts and does not falter. Their biggest problem is not just the pressure of persecution but the good times when their thoughts turned not to Christ but to worldly pleasures. The author is calling them back to the priority of faithful living for Christ.

The final thought ("inherit what has been promised" [v. 12]) leads into the next section (6:13–20) about the promises of God. These promises provide an anchor for persevering faith and allow us to focus on him rather than ourselves. Abraham, Moses, David, and all the heroes of the Old Testament centered on the secure future God had provided for his people, and that gave them the strength to be faithful in hard times.

THE CERTAINTY OF GOD'S PROMISE (6:13-20)

THE PROMISE TO ABRAHAM (6:13-15)

Abraham is the archetype of the champion who trusted in God's promises and through many trials inherited the "promised land" for his progeny. These promises, of course, are the "Abrahamic covenant" of Genesis 12:1-3 and expanded in Genesis 15:1-21, becoming the foundation piece for all of Genesis (see also 18:18; 22:18; 26:4; 28:14). As a result, he became the father of the nation, and one of the major inheritances was called "Abraham's bosom" (Luke 16:22; NIV "Abraham's side") to depict the enclave of God's people in heaven as Abraham's family. He is the man whose faith was related to God's promises and persevered as a result, laying the foundation for the entire history of the nation as God's people.

The author cites Genesis 22:17, "I will surely bless you and give you many descendants" (Heb 6:14), part of that supreme test of Abraham's faith at the sacrifice of his promised son, Isaac. Emphasis is placed on the fact that this was a divine oath made because "there was no one greater for him to swear by" (v. 13). This divinely endorsed oath will become the main point in verses 16-18. The stress here is not on the countless descendants of Abraham but on the God-ordained certainty of the promise given to Abraham. The original of Genesis 22:17 has "I will surely bless you and make your descendants as numerous as the stars in the sky," but here it is worded "give you many descendants" (Heb 6:14), stressing the promise itself and leaving the idea of the innumerable progeny for later (11:12). God's sovereign control of salvation history is center stage. He is sovereign and in charge, and we are to follow Abraham's example and place our trust as well entirely in his promises.

So Abraham is the perfect exemplar of the hero who had "faith and patience" (v. 12) as he was "waiting patiently" (v. 15). This defines his entire life as described in 11:8–12, as he "went, even though he did not know where he was going" (v. 8) and then "made his home in the promised land like a stranger in a foreign country" (v. 9). Even the birth of his promised son Isaac demanded great faith and patience. The emphasis in verse 15 is on both God's faithfulness to his promises and on Abraham's faith in accepting those promises and living accordingly. This provides the model for us, giving us the strength to persevere amid the difficulties of life.

The concluding "Abraham received what was promised" (v. 15) could be taken to clash with 11:13 and 39, "They did not receive the things promised," but that simply means "during their lifetime." The promises were realized after they died and went to heaven, receiving the inheritance promised (v. 12b). That is the promise to us as well. Earth's tribulations and trials will continue, but in the final analysis, they are doomed to fail and will be replaced by God's promised eternal blessings. When we pass through "the valley of the shadow of death" (Ps 23:4 KJV), we must keep our eyes fixed on God and his future promises. Abraham is the great example to us that when we persevere in faith, God's promises will keep us on the straight and narrow, trusting him rather than the fleeting pleasures of this world.

THE IMMUTABLE OATH (6:16–18)

The author wants to make certain that readers know that God never goes back on his promises and so expands on the point he has just made about God's immutable oath. A major rule in oath-taking is that the person swear "by someone greater than themselves," for instance a parent, a powerful person, or the emperor himself. The ultimate oath thereby is to swear in the name of God, and so as verse 13 states above, God could only swear "by himself." The twofold purpose of all oaths is then made clear: to confirm what is said and put an end to all argument." With

God standing behind the assertion, there is nothing more to be said. When God anchors his covenant promise to Abraham with a divine oath, all possible debate is over, and the confirmation is iron-clad. At the Abrahamic covenant, the man himself swore by God (Genesis 14:22-23, 21:22-24) and made his entire household do the same (24:3-4).

In the next two verses (17-18), the attention shifts from Abraham and the ancient people to Abraham's "heirs"—namely, the believers of the first century (and our day). The Abrahamic covenant is an immutable promise that includes God's followers in every age. So the promise was not only clear but applicable to all who trust God throughout all history. As already affirmed in 1:2, 4; 6:12 (see also 9:15; 11:7-8; 12:17), Abraham's "heirs" were not based along genetic lines but along faith lines. They number those who have put their saving faith in God/Christ and persevered in faithful service to him throughout their lives. So the inheritance is established by God's immutable act and promise and then carried out on behalf of those who fulfilled their part by faithfully following God's mandate. God did not have to make an oath, for his word was more than enough. He did so to provide absolute confirmation of his intentions; there could be no doubt whatsoever that he would carry out his promises to the letter.

The writer sums up his point in verse 18, pointing out that "two unchangeable things" lay behind the salvation he had made available to Abraham's heirs, most likely referring to his promise made to Abraham and his confirmation of it by an oath (vv. 13, 17). In other words, God's promises are doubly secure and trustworthy. This is made even more emphatic when he adds, "in which it is impossible for God to lie" (v. 18), which stresses the fact that his covenant promise is absolutely trustworthy. The gods of the pagan nations could not be trusted and often tricked their followers, but not Yahweh.

He explains that the reason for saying what has just been said is so that "we who have fled to take hold of the hope set before us may be greatly encouraged" (v. 18). Several aspects of this need to be explained. The participle "fled" is *kataphygontes*, to flee from danger and take refuge in a place of safety. In a general sense, God's beleaguered people flee from the world's hatred and are finding safe refuge in their hope in God. Specifically, in this context, they are running from the spiritual dangers that lead to defeated Christian lives and apostasy and seeking safety in God's promises and the heavenly future they can have in him.

Hope is the antidote to spiritual defeat. In 2:1 the danger is "drifting away" and becoming shipwrecked on the shoals and rocks of sin. Here the answer is to "take hold of" (v. 18) hope and the promises of God that provide an anchor and safety from the dangers. The writer wants to make sure his readers are "greatly encouraged" in the midst of this struggle and give them the strength to persevere. They, like the wilderness generation, are part of a new exodus and refugees seeking asylum and finding it in the new hope that, in God's promises, is "set before" them in God's guaranteed future.

THE SPIRITUAL ANCHOR (6:19–20)

The dangers are nothing compared to the promises of God. The real problem is not in the "hope set before us" (v.18) but in the human tendency to lay back and do nothing about the situation—in other words, to become *nōthroi* (lazy, lethargic) about our relationship and duties with God. We have an absolutely secure future and refuge with him but sit back and do nothing with it. So in the final two verses of this section, the author once more tries to wake us up to all that the Lord has done for us.

Hope is meant to anchor us more deeply in Christ, and it is based on the unchangeable and immovable God of verses 15–18. So this new anchor is both objective (based on who God is) and subjective (how he is experienced by us) and, as a result, is both "firm and secure" (v. 19), a truly eternal security! We may not know how things are going to turn out in the near future, but we absolutely know how they will turn out in the deep future. So as I face serious health issues and economic troubles in the present, as people on whom I counted let me down and shocking down-turns in our society and economy threaten, I must turn to the God of the future.

Hope is not ephemeral and fleeting, for it is "anchored" in the one certain reality, my loving Father. As an "anchor for the soul" (v. 19), the spiritual side of our being (*psychē*) is firmly grounded in hope. Interestingly, this is the only place in Scripture *angkyra* (anchor) is used metaphorically (literally of a ship's anchor in Acts 27:29, 30, 40), though it was common in **Hellenistic** literature. The two descriptive additions, "firm and secure" (Heb 6:19), actually describe what an anchor does for a ship, keeping the vessel firmly grounded and secure from shipwreck (as in 2:1). We must remember that, for the believer, hope is not looking to an uncertain, merely possible wish but to a guaranteed future. This should spur every saint to greater effort in persevering, for what is hoped for is a completely certain destiny.

Now the author turns from the nautical metaphor to a pilgrimage metaphor, using one of his favorite images—that of "entering" the sanctuary in the temple, used of the wilderness pilgrims "entering God's rest" (*eiserchomai* in 3:11, 18–19; 4:1, 3, 5–6, 10–11) and here of Jesus as high priest entering "the inner sanctuary" (v. 19). We then follow him as our hope enables us to enter with him. "Behind the curtain" (v. 19) refers to the inner curtain of the sanctuary that leads into the most holy place. The picture is of Christ as high priest on the Day of Atonement entering into the holy of holies (9:12, 24–25) and of our hope enabling us to enter alongside him. This will be made more explicit in 7:19, which states that we have a "better hope ... by which we draw near to God."

Just in case readers are confused about what force makes our entrance into the holy of holies possible, he adds the means by which we are enabled to do so in 6:20. No mere human being had ever before been allowed into the holy of holies on the penalty of death (Lev 16:2). The high priest once a year on the Day of Atonement was allowed to enter because he represented the nation, and he did so after extensively cleansing himself of his sins (Lev 16:3–19). Christ offered himself as the atoning sacrifice for our sins, and he in his high priestly role became "our forerunner," once-for-all entering on our behalf and opening up the most holy place to us. The imagery switches to the race, and it echoes that of Jesus as our pioneer or champion in Hebrews 2:10. The picture is not of winning the race here but of Jesus as our champion and pioneer/forerunner who goes before us through the inner veil and leads us into God's holy sanctuary, enabling us to finish the race with him.

At the end of this section, the author reintroduces the theme that he broke off in 5:11 in order to give an extensive warning (5:11–6:20). This theme will now dominate the next four chapters (7:1–10:25)—namely, the eternal high priesthood of Jesus "in the order of Melchizedek." The citation of Psalm 110:4 unites Hebrews 7–10 with Hebrews 3–5 and with Psalm 110:1 (Heb 1:3, 13; 8:1; 10:12; 12:2) in providing an organizing structure for the entire letter. God's future promises have made our hope secure and forged a way for us into the very presence of God in his sanctuary.

———

Instead of proceeding with his message of 5:1–10, the author is so sufficiently alarmed with their spiritual state that he has to stop abruptly and address the danger that their spiritual lethargy has brought about. These people have not grown in the Lord for years, and now they have regressed and are close to committing apostasy. He has just introduced a topic that demands spiritual maturity to comprehend, the Melchizedekian priesthood of Christ, but they are incapable of understanding it and simply too lazy to make an effort to do so. He must tell them why and wake them up, lest they "drift away" and end up like the wilderness generation in the past.

The need was clear (5:11–14). They had fallen into a lackadaisical state where they had stopped caring about their faith and refused to work at their walk with Christ. They were a second-generation church with a stellar heritage but had failed to catch the spirit of their parents. They were spiritual infants, unable to care for themselves. They needed to wake up and start training themselves in the faith. They had to start growing in Christ, or there would be irreparable consequences.

It is time for them to quit being satisfied with the basics and move beyond them (6:1–3). These verses progress through the Christian life, showing how God has now moved from the Judaism of the old covenant and given them the new covenant, the Christian faith. First, they must build on the fact of their conversion, when they repented from their "dead works" and turned in faith to God, finding salvation. Second, they need to enter the Christian life—beginning with Christian baptism, which does so much more than its Jewish counterpart—and practice the laying on of hands, which imparts so much more as well. Finally, they desperately need to realize the privilege and warning that teaching about the end of this world represents. Resurrection is the greatest possible privilege, and eternal judgment is the greatest possible danger. This final pair directly introduces the next section on the danger of apostasy, for this final pair details the two options. Only the faithful will experience resurrection, and those who allow themselves to fall into apostasy will face eternal punishment.

The horrendous danger is described in 6:4–8. First, we are shown the unbelievable blessings God pours out on every believer (vv. 4–5). The list truly impresses us as we contemplate what is ours as believers: at conversion, God sheds his redemptive light on the new follower, pours his heavenly spiritual gifts into their lives, gives them the Holy Spirit, and enables them to experience fully both his revealed word and the eschatological powers that will be theirs in eternity. All this is what they are in danger of throwing away due to their indifference and growing worldliness (vv. 6–8). If they do so, they will be lost forever, for God will cast them out and never allow them to return. In fact, they will never want to do so, for the rest of their lives will be characterized by a studied contempt for everything Christian.

In 6:9–12 the writer turns from warning to encouragement, letting them know that neither God nor he has deserted them and that he is convinced they will respond to the danger by rededicating themselves to the things of the Lord. "Better things" await them (vv. 9–10) for, first of all, God is both faithful and just in his dealings with them, and second of all, despite their indifference, they have still shown they love him as well as their fellow saints. For their part, they must jettison their spiritual laziness and embrace a zeal for growing in Christ (vv. 11–12). In doing so, they need to center on their future hope, living their earthly lives with eyes fixed on the final prize, the eternal inheritance with him.

The rest of this section (vv. 13–20) tells the readers how they can find the strength to persevere, reminding them of God's promises and showing how they can place their trust in him, then using Abraham and the covenant promises of Genesis 12 and 15 as the example. God keeps his promises, and Abraham provides the archetype for discovering how we can faithfully learn to put our trust in him (vv. 13–15). In verses 16–18 the Abrahamic covenant is seen anchored in God's immutable oath. His beleaguered people must learn to place themselves solidly in his promises and realize that they can completely trust his unchangeable oath to protect his followers. Finally, his wake-up call draws this to a conclusion (vv. 19–20). Hope in the immovable God and his eternal promises provides our anchor, for it is based on God's immutable oath and provides an objective foundation for everything we do. The picture presented here is incredible. Christ as high priest enters the holy of holies, and for the first time in history, the new covenant followers enter alongside him and face an absolutely certain future. The writer is now able to go back to 5:10 and reintroduce the subject of the next several chapters (7–10), the high priestly ministry of Christ "in the order of Melchizedek."

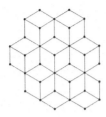

JESUS' ETERNAL
MELCHIZEDEKIAN PRIESTHOOD
(7:1–28)

This chapter has been awaited ever since its original introduction in 4:14; 5:5-6, but it was advanced material and above the heads of these shallow, indifferent people, so the writer had to challenge them to wake up spiritually and intellectually (5:11-6:20) before moving back and dealing with his main point. In 5:11 he had told us he had "much to say" about the Melchizedekian priesthood of Jesus, and now he turns to it. The purpose of this, as we know from 5:1-10, 11, is to support the superiority of Jesus over Aaron and the Aaronic priesthood by showing him as "a priest forever in the order of Melchizedek," who is a type of an eternal priesthood based on the fact that in the Genesis narrative he is "without beginning of days or end of life" (7:3). So 7:1-10 teaches the superiority of Melchizedek based on Genesis 14:17-10, while 7:11-28 centers on the superiority of Christ based on Psalm 110:4.

THE SUPERIORITY OF MELCHIZEDEK (7:1-10)

DESCRIPTION OF MELCHIZEDEK (7:1-3)

In this opening paragraph, the writer rehearses the salient details from the biblical account (Gen 14:17-20) that are behind Psalm 110:4

and that he will develop to make his point in Hebrews 7:4-10. In actuality, this begins with "for" (*gar*), omitted in NIV. It shows that verses 1-3 are meant to tell why Jesus was high priest "in the order of Melchizedek" according to 6:20. As a result, the Melchizedek **typology** will be explained in several stages, with verses 1-3 explaining 5:6, 10 and 6:20, then 6:4-10 explaining 6:1-3, and finally 6:11-28 developing 6-10. The immediate purpose is to demonstrate Melchizedek's superiority to Abraham and Aaron, therefore to the Aaronic priesthood of the Jews.

In Genesis 14:17-20 Abraham returns from his defeat of the kings of Sodom and Gomorrah and their allies, giving a tithe of the spoils to Melchizedek, "king of Salem" and "priest of God Most High." The author lifts three things from the first part of this (1-2a): (1) "King of Salem" may be mentioned because of the traditional connection of Salem with Jerusalem, with the name meaning "city of Salem." Though the fact is debated (many think Salem was ancient Shechem), that may well have been the first-century view. "Salem" means "peace," as we will see below. (2) Abraham gave this priest-king a tithe or "tenth of everything" (v. 2) as his thank offering to the "God Most High" both Melchizedek and Abraham served. Melchizedek is the first priest mentioned in the Old Testament and becomes a figure of legend in Judaism. (3) As a priest of God, Melchizedek "blessed him" (v. 1), significant not just because it shows God was pleased with Abraham's victory but also for the argument of this letter that Melchizedek was thereby superior to Abraham since the greater blessed the lesser (see verse 6).

The author now explains that the very name Melchizedek demonstrates his importance (6:2b), meaning "king of righteousness," while his throne as "king of Salem" means "king of peace." This clearly has messianic significance, which scholars have linked to Isaiah 9:6-7; 11:1-9; 32:16-18; Jeremiah 23:5; 33:15; and Zech 9:9-10. He is thus saying that as messianic typology, Melchizedek also transcends both Abraham and the Aaronic priesthood.

Then in 7:3 four further points are made, all essential to the author's argument. The rhythm and high theological content lead some to call this an early hymn, but that is unlikely here. This is an excellent writer who often uses such beautiful wording.

1. "Without father or mother"—In Judaism the ancestral tree was considered very important to show family lines, especially important figures like royalty and priesthood. The absence of such information in Genesis 14 is highly unusual. Two erroneous interpretations have been made: some think Melchizedek is a Christophany—an appearance of Christ in the Old Testament—but there is no evidence for that, and throughout the Bible, he is treated as a human figure. Others take a similar tack and think he is a heavenly being like one of the gods. However, once again, it is clear that he is never regarded anywhere as a mythological figure but always as a human being like Abraham. The author treats this typologically to show he is a "type of Christ." It is Jesus Messiah who is the divine figure, not Melchizedek.

2. "Without genealogy"—No major figure appears in Genesis without genealogical roots. This is especially true of the priestly line, for each one had to prove he came from the line of Aaron. So this detail showed that Melchizedek was transcendent above the Aaronic priesthood and directly aligned with the God he served. Of course, this does not mean Melchizedek literally had no parents or ancestors. It draws a typological conclusion from the absence of such in the Genesis account, something rabbis did frequently.

3. "Without beginning of days or end of life"—Like the previous point, this is not meant to label Melchizedek

as an eternal, uncreated being but rather for typological purposes. He did not stem from any priestly
line, and we know of no ancestral heritage. Rather,
he points beyond himself to the One who truly fulfills
his office, Jesus the Christ. Since Melchizedek had no
beginning or end in Genesis 14, his priesthood also was
without origin or conclusion and again was perfect as
a type of Christ and his eternal priesthood.

4. "Resembling the Son of God"—Finally, he is "made
   like (aphōmoiōmenos) the Son of God," meaning that
   Melchizedek as a historical person prefigured Jesus
   as Son of God, the primary christological title thus far
   (on which see 1:2, 5, 8; 2:6, 10; 3:6; 4:14). God fashioned
   him (made like) as a Christ-figure to foreshadow who
   and what was to come in salvation history. His priesthood had eternal significance as pointing forward to
   Christ, high priest forever.

5. I will present the conclusion as a fifth and final point:
   therefore, "he remains a priest forever," not in reality
   but as a Christ-figure. As we stated above, he was not
   a heavenly being or a Christophany, but he did foreshadow Christ himself, so he had an eternal priesthood in terms of its significance. For the author, this
   proves his superiority over the Levitical Priesthood
   and, therefore, the superiority of Christianity over
   Judaism.

GREATER THAN ABRAHAM AND THE
LEVITICAL PRIESTHOOD (7:4-10)

The greatness of Melchizedek was a problem for Jewish exegetes.
The group at **Qumran** thought him an archangel (11QMelchizedek),
and many connected him to Shem, so born in Abraham's line. The

author now moves into the second reason for the superiority of Melchizedek over Abraham—namely, the thank offering of the tithe of the spoils of the battle. He cites from Genesis 14:20 that this constituted "a tenth of the plunder" (Heb 7: 4) taken from the victorious battle. He emphasizes that it is "the patriarch Abraham" (v. 4) who gives the tithe in order to highlight the transcendent greatness of Melchizedek and the fact that this was indeed an offering to God of the firstfruits of the battle. "Patriarch" is placed at the end to stress the importance of Abraham and, therefore, the even greater status of Melchizedek.

Having shown the greatness of Melchizedek vis-à-vis Abraham, he turns his attention to the Levites and the Levitical priesthood. He begins with the laws of tithing. There were two levels, building on the original tithe in Genesis 14:19, which consisted of a tenth of the spoils of war, a practice common among the Greeks, as well as many others. In the Torah, agricultural products and other offerings were tithed and collected by the Levites (Lev 18:21), who then gave a tithe of that to the priests (Num 18:26). By the first century, the tithe itself was collected by the priests. The point is that these same Levites who represented God and stood above all other Israelites were descended from Abraham and were in his loins when he gave the tithe to Melchizedek. Therefore, the latter was doubly superior to the Levites, who were in Abraham's loins. The writer adds that Melchizedek (and Christ, like him) "did not trace his descent from Levi" (Heb 7:6) and so stood above both the Levites and the Levitical priesthood.

As we already saw in verse 1, when Melchizedek met Abraham after the battle, he showed him that God was pleased by "blessing him" as "priest of God Most High" (Gen 14:18-19). Abraham is described here as the one "who had the promises" (Heb 7:6), showing that he, not the Aaronic priests, is the central figure. The priesthood is two stages removed from Melchizedek in importance. They are merely tools, while Abraham is the source of God's promises to Israel. Still, Melchizedek is superior, and he prefigures Christ.

The writer now explains, "without doubt the lesser is blessed by the greater" (v. 7). Of course, there are numerous times when the lesser blesses the greater (Job 31:20; 1 Kings 1:47; 8:66), and we praise and bless God in worship all the time. The author means "*in this instance* this is the case." In fact, Abraham followed this principle when he accepted the blessing.

A further demonstration of Melchizedek's superiority stems from the tithe episode—namely because even though both the priests and Melchizedek "collected" tithes to God, the former were finite figures and died, while in the Genesis story, the latter did not but rather "is declared to be living" (v. 8). This is why he foreshadowed Jesus as "a priest forever" (5:6; 6:20; 7:17, 21). The contrast is highlighted with two strong phrases, "in the one case ... in the other case" (v. 8), which stress this essential difference.

The Greek behind "declared to be" in verse 8 is much stronger than the translation; *martyroumenos* is better read as "witnessed to be," as the biblical story becomes a divine witness to the everlasting nature of Melchizedek's ministry. Of course, his eternality is entirely in the person of Jesus, the Son of God, as we will see in 7:15-17 below. The ongoing nature of his office comes through the high priestly ministry of Jesus, especially in terms of his sacrificial atoning death on the cross (see 9:12-14).

The final proof of Melchizedekian superiority comes from the simple fact that every priest descended from Abraham, and therefore, when Abraham gave Melchizedek the tithe, the priests were in his loins giving the tithe with him. Of course, at the same time, Levi had not yet been born, so the writer begins verse 9, "One might even say," meaning he recognized it was not literally so yet was a valid surmise. Abraham acted for his descendants when he acknowledged Melchizedek's relationship to God and himself with the gift of the tithe. He more than any other figure maintains this corporate solidarity with his progeny, for as father of the nation and the originating patriarch, every future descendant stems from him.

So verse 10 is a proper conclusion to this important first section. In every sense of the statement, "when Melchizedek met Abraham, Levi was still in the body of his ancestor." Levi's relation to the Melchizedek figure came "through Abraham" and the divine choice behind the entire episode. In other words, the superiority of Melchizedek is part of the Abrahamic covenant and promise as fulfilled in Jesus, the "priest forever in the order of Melchizedek." Jesus' high priestly ministry, as eternally efficacious for salvation, is anchored in this critical event.

THE SUPERIORITY OF JESUS
AS HIGH PRIEST (7:11-28)

Psalm 110:4 returns to the center of the argument cited multiple times (11, 15, 17, 21, 28) as it interprets the significance of Genesis 14 for salvation history. This section argues its point based on Jewish typology—that is, the view that earlier events and figures in the biblical account foreshadowed later accounts, which fulfilled and completed their meaning. Therefore, Melchizedek was a "type" of Christ in the sense that his story was connected to it in salvation history and completed by it. Jesus thereby becomes a later-day Melchizedek, a high priest with an eternal ministry.

There are three sections to the argument here: verses 11-19, centering on the perfection attained through Jesus rather than Levi; 20-25, centering on the divine oath that lay behind Jesus' coming to earth; and 26-28, centering on the character of Jesus' high priestly ministry.

The Perfection of Jesus' Priesthood (7:11-19)

The imperfection of the Aaronic priesthood (7:11-12)
The simple fact, the writer argues, is that the Aaronic order was never meant to introduce the age of perfection. The theme of this section is stated right in this opening verse. This is an imperfect world, and the Levitical priesthood has been unable to solve the

dilemma. God's sense of order demanded "perfection," and the Levitical system was unable to provide it (7:19; 8:7; 10:1). He begins with a contrary-to-fact conditional—"if perfection could have been attained [but it wasn't]." In fact, this is the case even though the priesthood was given under the Mosaic law. The Torah itself has not solved the sin problem. The priesthood was supposed to be the perfect mediator that brought sinners to God and made access to him possible. It failed to do so adequately. The problem was that priests were finite creatures with the same sin problem as the people they were trying to help.

The only solution was for "another priest to come," not an Aaronic priest but instead one "in the order of Melchizedek" (v. 11). This proved that the original Levitical priesthood had failed and had to be replaced. "Another" (*heteron*) means a priest of a different type, and this draws together all the contrasts from verses 4–10. This is not just a different kind of priest but a brand-new priestly order, "the order of Melchizedek," as we have seen. The "coming" or arrival of this new priest is likely a reference both to the incarnation and to his exaltation in heaven, for it is an arrival with "eternal" implications.

A key implication is noted in verse 12. If the new eternal priest has radically "changed the priesthood," then the law has been changed as well. The laws of clean and unclean, as well as the sacrificial system, dealt with sins one at a time and could never solve the sin problem. Only Jesus could do that, and the next four chapters in Hebrews will be devoted to telling how he had done so. This new stage is God's move to the law of Christ and the eternal salvation achieved as a result. The new law involves the high priestly ministry of Christ, the subject of these chapters. In Galatians 3:24, we are told that the law was "our guardian (or custodian) until Christ came," so from the start, it was intended as a temporary institution preparing for its replacement at the coming of Christ. It was able to make people aware of sin but could never remove sin or bring salvation. Only Christ could do that.

Christ from the wrong tribe (7:13-14)

The opening "He of whom these things are said" (v. 13) looks to the person fulfilling the Melchizedekian expectations—namely, Jesus, stressing the connection between the two figures. Priests could only come from the tribe of Levi (Exod 28:1-4; Num 1:47-54), while Jesus was born of the tribe of Judah. So by the Mosaic law, he could not be a priest. This is further evidence that a "different" kind of priest (v. 12) from a "different" tribe (v. 13, also using *heteros*) necessitated a new law, as verse 12 has just stated. The proof of this claim is that in the history of Judaism, no member of the tribe of Judah has ever performed the central task of a priest, to "serve at the altar" (v. 13) and present sacrifices to God. So in the old order, he could not have been a priest. It demanded a new order, and God established that when he arrived and instituted the new covenant age.

This is made all the more clear in verse 14, which explicitly tells us "that our Lord descended from Judah"—that is, not stemming from Levi or Aaron. He is not interested at this point to emphasize the royal descent from David but the tribal descent from Judah. This thrust is made evident in the last part of this verse, telling us that when Moses gave Israel the law and its ordinances, "in regard to that tribe [he] said nothing about priests." There was no link whatsoever between the Levitical priesthood and the tribe of Judah, so Jesus in the old order could never have been a priest.

Moreover, he does not use the normal term for ancestral descent but rather *anatetalken*, meaning he "has arisen from Judah," a term used in Numbers 24:17 of the rising of a star from Jacob, part of the messianic expectation in the Old Testament. This, connected with the designation of him as "our Lord" (v. 14) gives great stress to the fact that this man is much more than a priest and demands a wholesale change in the expectations surrounding his arrival. He is priest-king and Messiah, with all the glory of the Melchizedekian figure from Psalm 110:4.

The superiority of the Son as priest (7:15–17)

One point was "cleared up" in 7:14 (the tribal ramifications), and another becomes "even more clear" (v. 15). There the non-Levitical nature of the new priesthood was clarified, but now the salvation-historical Melchizedekian nature of the eternal priesthood is established. This is the main point of everything he has been saying—that is, that "another priest like Melchizedek" in Genesis 14:17–20 and Psalm 110:4 has now "appeared" (Heb 7:15) and, therefore, the entire Old Testament has now been fulfilled or brought to completion. There is a deliberate change of wording from "in the order of" (5:6, 10; 6:20; 7:11) to "in the likeness of" (*kata tēn homoiotēta*) in verse 16, as the emphasis has moved from descent to the nature of the new office. This new priest is not "like" Aaron but "like" Melchizedek in that he is eternal and exalted.

Aaron's importance was finite and temporary, for he effected only the priestly line, which developed on the basis of ancestry—and all the Mosaic regulations centered on that (7:16). Still, every Jewish priest became so only via their alignment with the Levitical line. So ancestry was everything. The Melchizedekian line was superior because it was based not on human ancestry but on "the power of an indestructible life" (v. 16). When we translate literally, the contrast is clear: "the law of a fleshly regulation" versus "the power of an indestructible life" (v. 16). It is the greatness of the infinite versus the partial value of the finite, the power of the eternal God versus the weakness of a mortal priesthood. The combined might of the Jewish leadership, the Roman military, and Satan himself could not take the life of Jesus, and the ignominy of the cross led to the wonder of Jesus' exaltation and enthronement in heaven. While his mortal body was killed on the cross and laid in a grave, in reality, his life was indestructible and could not be held in the grave. By its very nature, Jesus' life concluded with resurrection and exaltation.

There is some debate as to whether this "indestructible life" includes Jesus' preincarnate glory or whether he is pictured as entering into this state after the cross at his resurrection and exaltation to glory. Several see this as something that had a beginning, but that clashes with the emphasis throughout the New Testament on his preexistent splendor (for instance, John 1:1–14; Phil 2:6; Col 1:15–16; Heb 11:27). Likely, the author was thinking of his eternality as a whole in this. Jesus, like Melchizedek, would be "without beginning of days or end of life" (7:3).

Everything said in chapter 7 so far leads in 7:17 to another citation of Psalm 110:4. "For" (*gar*) tells us why this different priest led an "indestructible life" (v. 16). As "a priest forever" (v. 17), he would indeed be both indestructible and triumphant. Moreover, "it is declared" should actually be translated "it is witnessed" or "testified" (*martyreitai*). Psalm 110:4 is shown to be Scripture's witness to the significance of the true end of Jesus' life. It goes beyond David and beyond even its messianic significance to attest to the **eschatological** and **soteriological** truth and relevance of the death and resurrection of Jesus as the "priest forever," who makes salvation possible for sinful humankind. This is further evidence that Psalm 110:1 and 110:4 provide the organizational core of this letter. As the indestructible Melchizedekian priest, the next chapters (7–10) will unfold why the world has been changed forever by his arrival.

Replaced by a better hope (7:18–19)

The writer ends this section (vv. 11–19) with its proper conclusion, that the "former regulation" (v. 18) brought by Moses has therefore been replaced by a "better hope (v. 19)—namely, Christ as the "priest forever, in the order of Melchizedek," who has made salvation possible for sinful humankind. The law was shown to be "weak and useless" in 7:1–10, and so it had to be "set aside" (v. 18) or "abolished, annulled." The term *athetesis* refers to the cancellation and replacement of a legal decree, and so the law here is annulled and replaced by the new law of Jesus. The "perfect" means of redemption could only come via the "different priest" (v. 11) whose "indestructible life" (v. 16) could lead to eternal salvation. The old was "weak" because it was carried out by finite, sinful human beings and "useless" because it could never solve the sin problem but could only deal with sins one at a time.

This is spelled out negatively and positively in what follows (7:19). Negatively, "the law made nothing perfect." The "perfect" (*eteleiōsen*) means not just sinless perfection but also the "completion" or "fulfillment" of God's redemptive plan (see further 7:11)—in fact, primarily the latter here. The old system could accomplish neither goal, and so God's plan of salvation had to culminate with his sending his Son to be the perfect high priest as well as the atoning sacrifice for sins. Since the Aaronic priesthood was unable to attain God's goal of bringing his plan to completion, he had to annul it and bring a new plan into operation.

Positively, this new system introduced a "better hope ... by which we draw near to God" (v. 19). This actually becomes a very important summary statement that will be unpacked carefully in the chapters to come. The idea behind "introducing a better hope" prepares for the arrival of the new covenant, seen as "better" in 7:22 (see also 8:6). The Mosaic law dealt only with present sins committed and could not provide future hope nor gain its adherents access to the presence of God. Christ went beyond the veil (6:19; 9:3; 10:20) and opened the holy of holies to his followers. We have accompanied Christ into the very presence of God. With this, both the present and the future are transformed forever.

There is much more meaning than we think in "by which we draw near to God." In the old covenant system, only the high priest could truly "draw near," and then only once a year on the Day of Atonement, when he sprinkled blood in the holy of holies for the sins of the nation (Lev 23:26–32). However, as a metaphor, it meant to draw near in worship, and the entire system was developed to make that possible. Yet it was an imperfect system and could attain that only partially since it was corrupted by the sinfulness of both the priests and the people.

When Adam and Eve fell in the garden, a schism was established, and both the old and new covenants were dedicated to bridging that gap and bringing humanity back to God. The law was a stopgap measure intended from the start to prepare for the coming of Christ, for only he could remove the schism entirely. The result is that a brand-new era came into being, and through Christ, we have a level of access that draws us nearer to God than even the high priest could ever have imagined for, in Christ, sin has been conquered. We enjoy an intimacy and nearness to God not seen since Adam and Eve before the fall.

The original readers needed to understand the implications of this: they could only enjoy this new access once they followed God and left the old system so they could enjoy the new. They were trying to enjoy both, which could only end in disaster, namely apostasy and the jettisoning of their faith. For us today, this is also a crucial point: we cannot hold onto the world and its ways as Christians. Conversion is an all-or-nothing move from the world to becoming a Christ-follower.

The Benefits of the New Covenant (7:20–28)

The basic message of this central section (5:1–7:28) has now been established: the old system has been replaced by the new law of Jesus, the Son and high priest, who has introduced a permanent solution for sin and salvation. Now, in the rest of this chapter (7:20–28), we will be told what this new covenant reality will do for us. First, in verses 20–22 Jesus will be placed in office by an eternal divine oath, which will enable him to be the "guarantor of a better covenant." Second, in verses 23–25 he has become a "permanent" priest who is able to save us completely. Third, in verses 26–28 we learn we have a perfect, eternal high priest who has completely met our every need.

Guarantor of a better covenant (7:20–22)

In actuality, the Levitical priesthood began with a command (see Exod 28:1; 29:35), not an oath; but the Melchizedekian high priest was confirmed with an eternal oath in Psalm 110:4, "The Lord has sworn and will not change his mind," and this immutable oath lay behind Jesus' high priestly office. This is a new point added to 5:6, as the unchangeable nature of the oath demonstrates the eternal trustworthiness of the office.

Once more, the Levitical system was based on finite, temporary legalities and sinful creatures who often failed in their duties. The Melchizedekian order was built on an eternal oath and a perfect high priest, "a priest forever." The Aaronic order has already ended, while the Melchizedekian order will never cease, for Jesus will forever be both Son and high priest. Interestingly, the name "Melchizedek" does not appear again in Hebrews; in fact, 7:17 was its last appearance in the letter. The writer apparently wants to center on Jesus as the priest forever rather than the one who prefigures him. The emphasis, too, is on the fulfillment in Jesus more than in the promise itself. He will be center stage from this point forward.

This divine oath builds on 6:13–18, and in this context, has authorized and empowered Jesus to be "the guarantor of a better covenant" (v. 22). It is difficult to overstate the importance of the term "covenant" for all of Scripture. It unites the two Testaments. Indeed, "testament" is another word for "covenant," and we think of the biblical systems as the old covenant and the new covenant, which itself is associated with the coming of Jesus into this world and the new age of salvation he has introduced. He becomes the "mediator" of this new entity his Father has given his people in 8:6.

The "covenant" is designated as "better," linked with the superiority of Jesus over the Levitical system, indeed all of Judaism (1:4; 6:9; 7:7, 9). This joins the list of such descriptives, as the covenant is "better" in 7:22 and in 8:6; "new" in 8:8, 9:15, and 12:24; "eternal" in 13:20; and "second" in 8:7. This all prepares for the lengthy citation of Jeremiah 31:31–34 in 8:6–13, where the covenant concept will be explained fully. A covenant is a promise or treaty that binds two groups together and gives each certain responsibilities for maintaining the relationship. Christ is the One who binds together the new covenant relationship between his Father and those who come to him in faith.

As the "guarantor" (*engyos*) of this new relationship, Jesus provides "surety" or certainty that a promise will be kept and a debt will be paid. If a person was unable to fulfill the debt, the "guarantor" would do so on her behalf. So Christ guarantees that God will be faithful in his covenant promises. He has done so with his sacrificial death on the cross, and he will continue to do so based on his exaltation to the throne of God in heaven. So this new covenant is "better" because it is erected on an eternal foundation. No wonder this produces the "better hope" of 7:19. It is centered on the eternal, omnipotent Godhead and is completely reliable.

The completeness of our salvation (7:23–25)

The basic difference between the two priestly orders is now applied. The writer uses a **chiasm** to do so, with A = the result and B = the reason:

> A   Need for many priests (v. 23a)
> > B   Aaronic priests died in office (v. 23b)
> > B'   Jesus the Melchizedekian priest lives forever (v. 24a)
> A'   Need for just one permanent priest (v. 24b)

The Levitical priests died and could not continue in office, while Jesus is "a priest forever" (Ps 110:4) and therefore "lives forever" and "has a permanent priesthood" (v. 24). Once again we have the antithesis between "the many" and "the One." As a result of the mortality of every priest, Judaism needed a vast number of them down through the centuries as current ones died and had to be replaced. Josephus wrote that eighty-three high priests held office from Aaron to the destruction of the temple in AD 70 (*Antiquities* 20.227). However, in the new covenant, only one is needed, for he "lives forever" and is available at all times in every age. Moreover, since he is God of very God, omnipotent and omnipresent, he is always able to "intercede" for each one of the saints.

It is imperative that all readers understand the implications of Jesus as the everlasting high priest, for it underlies everything being said in chapters 5–10. Our own reception of eternal life is the natural outgrowth of his eternality shared with his followers. Moreover, as we face our own struggles (1 Cor 10:13), we find strength to persevere by throwing ourselves in dependence on him who provides a "permanent priesthood" (Heb 7:24) on our behalf. It is not just that Jesus as high priest "lives forever" but that he does so on our behalf and is permanently present in our lives to strengthen and undergird us in our struggles. "Permanent" is *aparabatos*, "inviolable, unchangeable,"[1] and continues the emphasis on Jesus' immutable, indestructible personhood and office.

The wondrous conclusion (*hothen*; "therefore") is Jesus' power ("able to" is *dynatai*, connoting his power to accomplish what he wills, as also in 5:7) to "save completely those who come to God through him" (7:25). "Completely" is *eis to panteles*, which could be temporal ("forever, for all time") or stress degree ("completely, absolutely"). It is unnecessary to choose, for likely both aspects are intended here. Jesus has the power as the eternal high priest to save completely and for all time, one of the great passages on the security of the believer. His power is absolute and everlasting; the way to God is always open, and he is with us every moment to supply strength and help when we need it (1 Cor 10:13). What an incredible promise this provides as we contemplate the importance of persevering in our faith.

---

1. Some have given it the active sense of "untransferable," referring to the passing of his office on to successors, but that does not fit the thrust here and is quite unlikely.

The means by which we participate in this full salvation is to "come to God through him," a present tense verb stressing the ongoing nature of our perseverance. Christ has the power and never forsakes his people (Gen 28:15; Deut 1:5, 9; 31:6, 8). This is not just the moment of conversion but speaks more of the daily walk with the Lord, as we "come to" (v. 25) him in worship and dependence. "Come to" is virtually synonymous with "draw near" and is an important concept in Hebrews (7:19; 10:25).

The basis for this powerful ministry in the lives of his followers is that "he always lives to intercede for them" (v. 25). The "always lives" stems from Psalm 110:4 and again refers both to Christ's person and his office as being eternal, meaning he is present every minute for all time. "Intercession" (Isa 53:12; Luke 12:8; Rom 8:33–34) is the basic ministry of a priest who mediates God's people before God and stands for them. Primarily, this intercession was accomplished once-for-all on the cross, and Christ is in heaven as our mediator based on his atoning sacrifice on the cross. This doesn't mean that God is reluctant to grant our needs and that Jesus needs to be ever interceding or asking him to act on our behalf. His redemptive work is finished, so this intercession means not the work of salvation but the distribution of its daily benefits in our lives. Christ is ever-present to strengthen us in time of need, guide us in our daily walk, and enable us to overcome our daily struggles and difficulties.

Our perfect, exalted high priest (7:26–28)

Many take this small paragraph as concluding the first half of this central section (3:1–7:28). While it does sum up several ideas, I prefer to see it as the final of the three sections describing the privileges of living in the new covenant age (7:20–22, 23–25, 26–28). There is a beautiful progression of thought moving from Jesus as high priest guaranteeing our new covenant experience (vv. 20–22) to saving us completely (vv. 23–25) to becoming the perfect high priest on our behalf (vv. 26–28). Many have commented on the beautiful rhetoric employed in these verses, and it is another passage that is quite hymnodic in its style.

"Such a high priest" (v. 26) means one like that described in recent chapters, and the rest of the verse sums up what has been said. The point is that he "truly meets our need" (v. 26) far more than any other option like the Levitical priesthood (or secular society today) ever could. That "need" is not referring to leisure or comfort but to a right relationship with God. It is the spiritual need in light of eternity, not the personal desires in light of the things of this world, that is in mind. This is especially so in light of the Greek, which is *hēmin eprepen*, "such a high priest is *fitting or proper for us*," pointing to the spiritual side of life in this context. What we truly "need" is forgiveness and eternal life, not temporary earthly pleasures.

Christ is the only one suited to be this perfect high priest, for he alone is without sin and able to give himself as the paschal sacrifice for sin, and he alone has been exalted to the right hand of God to reign over God's kingdom. What follows in verse 26 is a list of five characteristics that effectively sum up what has been said thus far in the letter about Jesus, Son and high priest. The first three are personal attributes, and the latter two show his state of being and status.

1. "Holy." This is not the usual term (*hagios*) but is *hosios* (only here in Hebrews), a term that adds the concept of covenant faithfulness and absolute purity. He is devout in the way human high priests could never attain, for he is without sin and completely faithful to God and his covenant obligations.

2. "Blameless" (*akakos*). This too refers to the purity of his flawless character, meaning "innocent" or one whom evil cannot corrupt. His moral uprightness is absolutely in control of his being, and he is at all times

obedient to his Father, remaining free from temptation and sin.

3. "Pure" (*amiantos*). This is usually used for things (for instance, the temple) rather than people, describing that which will not defile God's followers. When used of the saints, it depicts ritual or moral purity. Here it would define the results of the first two terms, the life of purity lived for God, especially the sinless nature of Christ as eternal high priest.

4. "Set apart from sinners." The first three terms centered on Jesus' sinless nature, and this then sums up this theme, as he is "separate from" (*kechōrismenos*)— more than a difference in kind but actual local separation, a life apart from sin and sinners. This is connected to what follows, where after his death, he was separated and exalted to heaven. He lived a life set apart from the evil of this world and, after death, assumed the ultimate separation from sin in heaven.

5. "Exalted above the heavens." There has been a natural progression in these five terms, moving further and further from the sinful nature of the Aaronic high priests to the sinless nature of Jesus' being and now finally his exaltation "higher than" (*hypsēloteros*) the heavens themselves. He is not only with God in heaven; he is God himself, and heaven is where his throne is. The writer seeks language that will help his readers understand just how "high" this "high priest" really is. We cannot truly understand this fully, and the truly wondrous thing is that this incredibly exalted high priest is involved in our lives and loves us.

The next two verses (7:27–28) set up another contrast, this time between the priests of Aaron and Christ. Unlike the Aaronic priests, Jesus did not need to make daily sacrifices for his sins, for he was sinless (4:15; 7:26; 9:14). Nor did he need to do so for the sins of the people, for his was a one-time sacrifice for sins on the cross, which never needed to be repeated. As the perfect, sinless high priest, his is a "once-for-all" ministry (*ephapax*), used five times in chapter 9 for emphasis (9:7, 12, 26, 27, 28). His salvific act was eternally sufficient. In the author's mind was the Day of Atonement, when the high priest would annually sacrifice first for his own sins and then for the nation (see also 5:3). "Day after day" does not mean the Day of Atonement occurred every day, for it was an annual celebration. But he did participate in the sacrificial system "day by day." Several believe the author here is linking together the Day of Atonement with the daily sacrifices theologically to show the inadequacy of the whole system. This makes a great deal of sense here.

Jesus, on the other hand, made a one-time sacrifice for sin when he "offered himself" on the cross. He did not do so for himself, for he was without sin, completely unlike the priests of Aaron. His was a voluntary sacrifice "*of* himself" (not "for" himself) so that our sins might be forgiven and the power of sin might be broken. The point is that true atonement could not come through the priesthood but only through Christ.

Verse 28 concludes not only this small section but also the chapter as a whole. The law, as a finite system, was able only to appoint "men in all their weakness" as high priests. It dealt with human commands, while the appointment of Christ stemmed from the divine oath (7:20–22). The Aaronic order proceeded carefully and in detail based on human ancestry—as each high priest died, he was replaced by another finite high priest. God, however, with a powerful oath, appointed a once-for-all high priest who offered himself as a once-for-all atoning sacrifice, the "eternally perfect" high priest.

The office of high priest is characterized by weakness, imperfection, and sin that must be forgiven before each one can do his duty to his office. Jesus, however, has been "perfected" (2:10; 5:9) in his office and person, but not by being forgiven, for he was at all times in his earthly life sinless (4:15; 7:26; 9:15). This is the key contrast—weakness versus perfection. Jesus alone can suffice, for his high priestly work is "perfect forever" in its power and effect. Salvation alone can come through him. Through him the Day of Atonement has become an eternal "Today." This truth is as relevant today as back then. All the so-called religious solutions people come up with to justify their Christ-less lifestyle flounder, for all human mediation fails to provide lasting answers, and only Christ has eternally satisfied humankind's need for a meaningful salvation.

In 1:1–4 the writer showed the superiority of the new revelation in Jesus, the Son of God, and in 1:5–2:18 he stresses his superiority over the angels. In 3:1–4:13 he shows why there is such emphasis on Jesus' superiority. The second-generation Jewish Christian churches he is addressing (probably in Rome) have been falling away from their heritage (the strong and dedicated first generation church; see 10:32–34) and resemble the wilderness generation during the exodus from Egypt who failed in the wilderness and were rejected from experiencing God's "rest," perishing in the wilderness. In 5:1–10 he began to get into his next point—Christ as a "priest in the order of Melchizedek"—but had to stop because his readers weren't mature enough to understand it or take it to heart. So he paused for a lengthy excursus, warning them of the dangers of apostasy and encouraging them by asserting he didn't think they would do so because of the presence of God and Christ in their midst (5:11–6:20).

So now, in chapter 7, he can get into his material, beginning with the superiority of Melchizedek over the Aaronic priesthood (vv. 1-10) and then turning to the superiority of Christ over the Aaronic high priests (vv. 11-28). In verses 1-3 he looks into the historical record behind Psalm 110:4—namely, Genesis 14:7-10—showing that Melchizedek was a type of Christ, prefiguring him as an eternal high priest and superior to Abraham and, therefore, at the same time, above the Levitical priesthood. Then in Hebrews 7:4-10 this is explained in more detail, as Melchizedek's superiority over Abraham is applied to the Levitical priesthood since Levi was in Abraham's loins when three things took place: giving the tithe (vv. 4-6a), receiving the blessing (vv. 6b-7), and failing to die (vv. 8-10). The point is that the readers (and us) should never fall away from Christ, the infinitely superior one, and return to the former inferior belief system.

The rest of the chapter (vv. 11-28) centers on Psalm 110:4, cited several times (vv. 11, 15, 17, 21, 28) to prove Jesus was the figure prefigured by Melchizedek as "the priest forever." The first point developed is the absolute perfection of Christ as the eternal high priest (vv. 11-19). The Levitical order was imperfect (vv. 11-12) because it was unable to solve the sin problem and bring God's order to the chaos of this world. Levis were sinful, just like those they served, and so were insufficient to fulfill God's purposes.

Two further reasons are attested for the superiority of Jesus as the Melchizedekian priest. First, he comes from the tribe of Judah and so could never be an Aaronic priest, who must descend from the tribe of Levi (vv. 13-14). Second, his eternal nature and office as high priest gave him an "indestructible life" (v. 16), and as the exalted high priest, he could only be fit as a "priest forever in the line of Melchizedek" (vv. 15-16). He alone could suffice in the eternal heavenly high priestly ministry to which God called him.

The conclusion of this segment is that Christ, therefore, has brought about a "better hope" (vv. 18-19) that has led to the removal of the Mosaic order and its replacement by the new covenant established by Jesus. The old order could not bridge the gap and provide a perfect completion for the plan of God. It sufficed for the interim period and enabled God's people to maintain a relationship with him, but it was never a long-term solution and simply prepared the way for its fulfillment in the coming of Christ.

The author's message has been completed, and he is ready to draw 4:14–7:28 and the Melchizedekian high priesthood of Jesus to its completion. He does so with verses 20-28, which makes its point in three stages. First, as a result of his atoning sacrifice, he is the "guarantor of a better covenant" (vv. 20-22). Christ is the perfect One to guarantee this new system, for he is sinless and the eternal high priest of the heavenly sanctuary and so affirms God's faithfulness to his plan of salvation and the new order by which it will be enacted. A covenant is a "testament," and he testifies not only verbally but by his actions that it is built on better promises and provides a better hope. This applies to us every bit as deeply as it did to these Hebrew Christians; our future will never be secure from a this-earthly perspective, but in Christ, our better hope provides an "eternal security."

Second, he is an eternal, "permanent" high priest who is able to save "completely" (vv. 23-25). Two wondrous truths emerge from this concept. First, "completely" is both temporal and degree in its focus. The salvation we receive in Christ is permanent and intense, as his divine strength is poured into us to meet the constant challenges life brings. Second, the basis for his strengthening activity on our behalf is that "he always lives to intercede" (v. 25) for us, meaning that he works in our lives so that we experience the full benefits of our salvation.

Third, and finally, we have a perfect, eternal high priest who guarantees God's presence and work in our lives (vv. 26-28). Only Christ could provide this, for he was exalted and enthroned at the right hand of God, assuming the office of the eternal high priest offering final salvation to those who put their trust in him. In his personhood, he is morally upright and pure, and in his state of

being, he lives a life separate from the sins of the Aaronic priesthood. As a result, he is exalted even above the splendor of his heavenly home. His high priestly work is vastly superior to the Levitical
priesthood, which demanded endless repetition of its religious
acts since they never sufficed to remove sin. Jesus' one-time sacrifice of his own blood was eternally sufficient. So Christ as the
only eternally perfect mediator alone can suffice for making people
right with God.

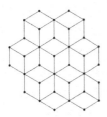

PRIESTHOOD AND COVENANT
(8:1–13)

We now enter a section (8:1–10:18) moving from the superiority of Christ's person and office to the superiority of the results of his work as the Melchizedekian high priest in three areas—covenant, sanctuary, and sacrifices. The remarkable story of Jesus continues. He is the preincarnate glorified Son who entered this world as the God-man, living a perfect life as the Son of God and yielding his life as the atoning sacrifice on the cross to bring eternal salvation to us sinners so we could enter eternity with him through faith and obedience. As the heavenly high priest, Jesus ushers in the new covenant age (8:1–13), fulfilling the promise of Jeremiah 31:31–34, and fulfills the **typology** of the sacrificial system, bringing about a new era of salvation and worship (9:1–10:18).

MINISTER OF THE SUPERIOR SANCTUARY (8:1–5)

THE MINISTRY OF THE EXALTED HIGH PRIEST (8:1–2)

This critical new section begins with a general statement of his high priestly work, reintroducing several key themes to prepare for the connection between Psalm 110:1, 4 with the new covenant promise of Jeremiah 31:31–34. Hebrews 8:1 summarizes chapters

1–7, and verse 2 introduces the new theme. The exalted Lord and eternal high priest is now the minister of the new covenant. The author considers this the "main point" of his argument, for the inadequacy and finiteness of the old mandates a new era of salvation. "What we are saying" (v. 1) is literally "the things being said" and has in mind everything said thus far, summed up in Psalm 110:1, cited at critical points as the central core of the letter (1:3, 13; 8:1; 10:12; 12:2): the enthronement and exaltation of the Son and Messiah after his high priestly sacrifice of himself on the cross was accomplished.

Here it is presented as the culmination of what has gone before. The "right hand of the throne of the Majesty in heaven" (v. 1) is the basis of all that transpires. He is the eternal, enthroned Lord of all, and this anchors his work as high priest forever, and when he "offered himself" (7:27), he brought "eternal salvation" (5:9) to those who react with faith. His is now a heavenly ministry, vastly superior to the earthly ministry of the Levitical priesthood. The idea of the "throne" is added to stress the royal aspect of the scene. In Jesus the union of the priestly and the royal are forged forever. The "Majesty in heaven" is a reverential title for God (1:3) and pictures the **Shekinah** glory that rested on the mercy seat in the holy of holies (Lev 16:2), bathing every aspect in the glory of God.

There has been some debate as to the connotation of "true tabernacle" (v. 2) in this context and 9:11. Let us note four options: (1) Jesus' body (many church fathers, Calvin)—but this would be his glorified body rather than his incarnate form, and this doesn't fit well here. (2) The church (some recent scholars)—but Christ didn't enter the heavenly sanctuary through the church, and God's people are never called a "tabernacle." (3) The heavens as the holy place—there is no hint in Hebrews that the heavens are ever seen as the path to God. (4) Heaven / the heavenly reality—this is the most likely and sees heavenly worship in the heavenly sanctuary as the new covenant reality.

As high priest of the heavenly temple, Jesus "serves in the sanctuary, the true tabernacle set up by the Lord, not by a mere human being" (8:2). His is an eternal ministry in the heavenly sanctuary, not a temporary ministry in an earthbound temple. We must define "true tabernacle" carefully. This does not mean the Jerusalem temple was false and Old Testament Judaism a false religion. Both were "true" for their times, but when one rejects the eternal and goes back to the temporary, it becomes false in the sense that it was fulfilled and replaced by the new eternal reality of new covenant religion. Both Judaism and the earthly temple have been brought to completion in Christ, and the argument of this letter is that they now take their place as past preparation for the "true" or final approach to God. The contrast in the fact that the Lord pitched the heavenly tent, not any human being, stems from Numbers 24:6, where the tents of Israel were divinely established rather than human places of worship.

The Inadequacy of the Earthly (8:3–5)

"Is appointed" (v. 3) is a divine passive and means, "God appoints every high priest" to participate in the sacrificial system (5:1). Thus the Son, as the heavenly high priest, was obligated to offer himself (7:27; 9:11–14) as a "gift and sacrifice" on the cross to complete his earthly ministry. If "gifts" and "sacrifices" are meant to have separate meanings, the first refers to meal offerings and the second to blood-offerings. However, they are meant together here to sum up the sacrificial system as a whole. "It was necessary" (v. 3) means the system itself demands the high priest participate. But it also means that for Christ, everything prepared for the absolute necessity of the cross. He was sent to earth and became incarnate for the express purpose of becoming the atoning sacrifice for our sins.

Verse 4 begins with a contrary-to-fact clause ("If he were on earth [which he isn't]") and adds the point that his had to be a heavenly ministry, for he was of the wrong tribe and family to be an Aaronic priest (7:13–14). As an earth-dweller, he could not be a priest and had to leave earthly sacrifices for those who were of Aaron and could "offer the gifts prescribed by law" (v. 4). Yet God had indeed appointed him to be the Melchizedekian high priest and had also elevated him to his right hand in heaven. Therefore, Jesus had to fulfill his office and high priestly ministry in the heavenly sanctuary. As a result, his ministry is as superior to earthly priests as heaven is superior to this earth. The Levitical order, along with its ministry, was ineffective and inferior and had to be replaced when the new covenant era was instituted.

What was true of the Levitical order was equally true of the earthly sanctuary that "is a copy and shadow of what is in heaven" (v. 5). On earth, the temple came first; but in reality, the heavenly sanctuary was the prototype from which the earthly was constructed. The "sanctuary, the true tabernacle" in verse 2 was the "pattern" (*hypodeigma*) behind the Jerusalem temple, which was "copied" (v. 5) from it under Moses' direction. As a "shadow" (v. 5: *skia*) of the original, it was transitory and ephemeral, for the true reality behind the earthly sanctuary was at all times in heaven, and it awaited its future fulfillment under Jesus. Thus Jesus, in his heavenly high priestly ministry, was actually reinstating the original eternal worship of heaven that lay behind the Mosaic order, which was never more than a shadowy imitation.

To prove the extent to which the Mosaic worship was a "copy and shadow" (v. 5), the author uses Exodus 25:40, introducing it as a warning or "solemn command/instruction" (*kechrēmatistai*) given to Moses. This is a divine passive, meaning the instructions came from God according to the heavenly blueprint, and the design for this "copy and shadow" was revealed to Moses in Exodus 25–30. Exodus 25:40 provides the command that lay behind it all: "See to it that you make them according to the pattern shown you on the mountain."

Both the sanctuary and the Levitical order that flowed from it were earthly copies of the heavenly reality to which Christ returned when he sat at the right hand of God (Ps 110:1). Every detail of the building and of the system was fulfilled in the new covenant ministry and revelation of Jesus. The entire purpose of the Mosaic plan was to foreshadow and prefigure—as well as prepare for—the full reality that came with Jesus. Therefore, as an institution, it no longer had relevance or usefulness for these Jewish readers, whose hope and trust must wholly be placed in Jesus.

MEDIATOR OF THE SUPERIOR COVENANT (8:6-13)

THE NECESSITY OF THE NEW COVENANT (8:6-8A)

The ministry as well as the sanctuary and covenant behind Jesus demand a new form, which we have just seen (8:3-5) is the original heavenly form reinstated by Jesus' high priestly ministry in heaven. The superior ministry noted here is his high priesthood, proven "better" or superior based on its heavenly origin and eternal relevance. "But in fact" (v. 6) is actually "but now" (*nyni de*) and refers to the "last days" when Jesus fulfilled God's promises and established the new covenant. The contrast with verses 4-5 continues the emphasis on the new order brought about by the superior ministry Christ "received" (v. 6) or "obtained" from God.

Two reasons for its superiority are provided. First, in verse 6 Christ is "mediator" (*mesitēs*) of a superior covenant, referring to a go-between, a person who brings together two parties in conflict and establishes a treaty between them. In commerce, it describes a middle person in a contract. A covenant is a contract or treaty that binds the two sides to one another. Moses mediated the old covenant (9:16-22), Jesus the new. In every respect, Christ was the New Moses, who mediated a new and better covenant that brought the old to completion.

Second, this new covenant "is established on better promises." These promises include entering God's eternal rest (4:1), receiving our final eternal inheritance (6:12, 17; 9:15), the Abrahamic covenant (6:15; 7:6), and our heavenly reward (10:36; 11:13, 33, 39), as well as what will be told us in the Jeremiah prophecy of the next several verses. Not only is ministry and covenant superior in the new order but the promises behind them are also much better.

Another contrary-to-fact conditional begins Hebrews 8:7: "If there had been nothing wrong with that first covenant [but there was]." Something seriously wrong lay behind the old covenant (8:7-8a), and so the Triune Godhead was forced to find a "place ... for another" and search for it (v. 7) by sending his Son. The problems that have been enumerated regarding the Mosaic order led God to find fault (v. 8) and seek a new system that would prove superior and replace the fallible old ways. The fault lay especially with the priesthood, who were not able to meet the needs of those under their care. The people have fallen into the sins of the wilderness generation (3:1-4:13), and a new system was necessary to turn them around. This system was prophesied in Jeremiah 31:31-34, and the author cites this passage from the **Septuagint** in Hebrews 8:8b-13.

THE REVELATION OF THE NEW COVENANT (8:8B-13)

Jeremiah 31:31-34 is based on Israel breaking the old covenant made in Exodus 24 (see Heb 9:18-22). The covenant conditions are repeated in Jeremiah 7:23 ("Obey me, and I will be your God"), but they are broken again in 7:24-26. The speaker throughout 31:31-34 is God. This is the only place it is quoted directly, but it is alluded to in Matthew 26:28; 1 Corinthians 11:25; and 2 Corinthians 3:2, 6, 14. In Jeremiah, this passage is part of a major section on the future restoration of the nation (chapters 30-33) with the coming of the Messiah and the onset of the day of the Lord. The condemnation and judgment of the first twenty-nine chapters are reversed, when an undeserving people experience God's mercy. Here we are told it will come when God reveals a new covenant for his people, a new age of salvation that is coming.

The covenant promise (8:8b-9)

"The days are coming" (v. 8) refers to the arrival of the Messiah and the "day of the Lord" that will introduce that central event of history. Here the "days," in keeping with Jeremiah 30–33 (see above), are the time of restoration when the judgment will be reversed. Both the northern nation (Israel) and the southern (Judah) of the divided monarchy are included, therefore designating the whole people of God. Their "ancestors" (v. 9) is literally "their fathers" (*patrasin*) and are to be identified with the recipients of the new revelation given through the Son of God in 1:1-2. Jesus the Son at his "coming" has "revealed" the new covenant and made it available through his atoning sacrifice on the cross.

The wilderness generation (3:1-4:13) failed to keep the old covenant (Exod 24:4-8; see Heb 9:18-22) with its stipulations and lost their place, perishing in the wilderness. Now the new generation has a new covenant and a new opportunity to reclaim that place as God's people but is in danger of failing to persevere. The fathers of old "did not remain faithful to my [Mosaic] covenant," and the result is a devastating indictment and even more devastating judgment—"I turned away from them" (actually "I ignored them," with *ēmelēsa*, found also in 2:3). There they "ignored" God's great salvation, so here God in retaliation "ignores"[1] their restoration as his people. Their terrible error is in danger of being replicated by the current generation, and the writer is trying to call them back to their walk with the Lord. God has done his part and given them the new covenant to provide the strength they need. Now they must put it into practice and experience a revival.

The new covenant benefits (8:10-12)

Four new privileges are presented, replacing the inadequacies of the old with a new relationship with God and a new presence of

---

1. While the author does not insert this term here, since it is part of the Jeremiah quote, he still would have likely seen this connection with 2:3.

promise and hope in their lives. Here the "people of Israel" (v. 10) are both the nations of Israel and Judah from verse 8, the whole people of God. "After that time" (v. 10) refers to the days following the arrival of the Messiah and start of the new era he was to institute.

1. The laws written on their minds and hearts—This goes beyond the mere intellectual side, for memorizing and remembering the laws was an essential part of Deuteronomy, as in 6:6–8; 11:18–20. But hearing did not lead to obedience, and the law could not solve the sin problem. The promise here centers on a new heart, for obedience must proceed from the heart. Moreover, the Mosaic ordinances involved the performance of religious rites—eating the right foods, making the correct sin offerings, and so on. In the new order, God took over—"I will put … and [I will] write" (v. 10), as in Ezekiel 36:26: "I will give you a new heart and put a new spirit in you."

2. "I will be their God, and they will be my people"—In a sense, this becomes the new covenant formula, with an already/not yet perspective. It was initiated and experienced in embryonic form in the old covenant.[2] It will be renewed and enter a new sphere of intimacy with Jesus and the Spirit indwelling hearts and will culminate in the new heavens and new earth of Revelation 21, when it will be said, "Look! God's dwelling place is now among his people, and he will dwell with them. They will be his people, and God himself will be with them and be their God" (v. 3). In the here and now, the new heart will be filled with the literal presence of the Triune Godhead.

---

2. Exod 6:7; Lev 26:12; Deut 26:18; Jer 24:7; Ezek 11:20; Zech 8:8, 13:9.

3. Knowledge of God on a personal level (v. 11)—Israel, of course, knew Yahweh but in an external rather than internal fashion (a religious experience). In its frequent apostate state, it did not know him at all. With a new depth of spiritual experience, it would enter a period of personal depth never before even imagined. Before, knowing God was connected with covenant loyalty, but now it enters a new plane, the individual and experiential level that begins a direct awareness of God in one's life. Moreover, this knowledge will become universal among the faithful: "they will all know me, from the least of them to the greatest." It is important to note that "no longer will they teach their neighbor" does not mean the church would not need "teachers." The teaching office was critical from the start (see Acts 2:42, where it is the first of the church's "pillars"). This means there will be no need for rabbinic-style intermediaries between God and his people.

4. Forgiveness of sins (v. 12)—This climaxes Jeremiah 31 and the list here, for until sin is eradicated, there can be no full relationship with God. Again, the people of the old covenant knew this (Exod 34:6-7; Isa 43:25; Mic 7:18-19), but they experienced it mainly at the ritualistic level through the daily sacrifices, culminating in the Day of Atonement festival, which constituted "an annual reminder of sins" (Heb 10:3). In Exodus 34:6-7, at the giving of the law on Sinai, God describes himself as "The LORD, the compassionate and gracious God ... forgiving wickedness, rebellion, and sin." However, the prophets developed a theme, due to the severity of national sin, disparaging sacrifices, and ritual. This new theme began with 1 Samuel 15:22-23 at the

rejection of Saul as king: "To obey is better than sacrifices, and to heed is better than the fat of rams," a motif
continuing in passages like Psalm 50:8-10; 51:15-17;
Hosea 6:6; and Amos 5:21-22. Since the sacrifices dealt
with sins only one at a time and could never solve the
sin problem, full and complete forgiveness had to
await Jesus' atoning sacrifice and the arrival of the new
covenant. Only then would God "remember their sins
no more" (Heb 8:12). Only Christ's once-for-all sacrifice made that possible.

Conclusion (8:13)

Now the writer goes one step further: the new covenant is not only
superior to the old but supersedes it, proving it to be "obsolete and
outdated" (v. 13). This is the strongest statement in Hebrews about
the Mosaic law, indeed, in the New Testament as a whole. Yet we
must remember that he is not saying something that the prophets never before realized. He is attempting to interpret Jeremiah's
message, and so we can paraphrase, "When Jeremiah calls this covenant 'new,' he (that is, Jeremiah) means the first one is obsolete
and outdated." The implications of God inspiring Jeremiah to call it
a "new" covenant are explored, and this means that it was always
God's intention and not a spur-of-the-moment realization. The
purpose of the law given to Moses was, from the start, meant to
prepare the people for the coming of the Christ, the Son of God.

Now that the event has taken place and the "new" has come,
the old system by divine intent has become "obsolete" (palaioō), a
verb that means "to make old and no longer valid or viable." The
writer adds that as obsolete, it is also "outdated" (gēraskon), old and
needing to be retired and replaced. This is the case also with the
Mosaic order. The new has replaced the old, and it is "soon to disappear" (engus aphanismou). The term is stronger than "disappear"
and often connotes a violent destruction. For this reason, some
believe this is speaking of the Jerusalem temple here, prophesying

its soon destruction. However, there is no hint of that, and it is quite unlikely. He is simply using a strong metaphor for the "passing away" of the old system.

————

In chapter 7 we learned what it meant for Jesus to be "high priest forever." Now in chapter 8, we see what his high priestly ministry accomplished in terms of the new era Christ established—a new covenant, new sanctuary, and new sacrifices. He became the high priest of heaven when he offered himself as the atoning sacrifice on the cross, and he was exalted to heaven and enthroned as both the sovereign Son and high priest. In his priestly ministry, he entered the "true tabernacle" and opened up the sanctuary of heaven, making complete access to God available to all believers (vv. 1–2).

The earthly sanctuary and ministry in it were inadequate vehicles for the new covenant ministry, and so Christ's was a heavenly ministry in the heavenly sanctuary (vv. 3–5), where his exalted service opened heaven up to the people of God and brought an eternal significance to Jesus' priestly ministry. The earthly sanctuary was a mere copy of the heavenly, so Christ's ministry fulfilled and brought completion to the old Mosaic system and introduced God's true purpose of salvation for sinful humankind.

Jesus' high priestly ministry in the heavenly sanctuary made necessary a new covenant reality, and so Christ became mediator of a superior covenant, establishing it on his eternal work as high priest, and overcoming the inadequacies of the old covenant, which was unable to solve the sin problem and find an eternal solution (vv. 6–8a). In doing so, Christ fulfilled the new covenant prophecy of Jeremiah 31:31–34 (Heb 8:8b–12).

The new covenant was to replace the old and bring four benefits to God's people (vv. 10–12): (1) God gives them a new mind and a new heart with which to understand and apply the new laws of the kingdom. (2) These new hearts will be filled with the actual presence of the Godhead and will live this new covenant reality. (3) With this new heart filled with God, his people would finally come to know him on a personal level. (4) A true and final forgiveness of sins was the result of Christ's atoning sacrifice and was at the heart of the new covenant.

In conclusion, the writer states (v. 13) that Jeremiah, in calling this the "new" covenant, meant that the old had lived its purpose, becoming obsolete and outdated in light of Christ's coming, and needing to be replaced. The old era passed on and was replaced by the new covenant age and the eternal salvation it brought into reality.

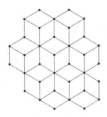

THE SANCTUARY AND
THE NEW COVENANT
(9:1–28)

F urther defining the superiority of the new covenant, the writer
now turns to the sanctuary and its place in God's plan, building
on 8:1-2 (the true tabernacle) and 7-13 (the new covenant prophecy of Jeremiah). In chapter 9 he discusses the place of "sanctuary"
(9:1-10) and "sacrifice" (9:11-28) in this new plan of salvation and
demonstrates how here, too, the place of the sacrificial system is
fulfilled or brought to completion and replaced by Christ's once-
for-all sacrifice of himself.

The sacrificial blood of Christ is superior to the blood of bulls
and goats. The latter suffices for only one sin at a time and leads
to merely temporary forgiveness. It demands continual repetition.
Only Christ has eternal results.

THE TEMPORARY SUFFICIENCY OF THE
EARTHLY SANCTUARY (9:1-10)

FURNISHINGS AND ARRANGEMENT (9:1-5)

The tabernacle, and later the Jerusalem temple, were constructed
of temporary earthly materials guaranteed to wear out in time.

Moreover, the ministry conducted in it only sufficed for a brief
period, for it covered only one sin at a time. The material covered
in 7:1–8:13 centered on the arrival of the new covenant and Jesus'
high priestly ministry within it. This chapter's discussion continues that theme, introducing the new sanctuary that replaces the
"tabernacle" of the Mosaic system. At the outset, the contribution
of the old sanctuary is traced, moving from the organizational
plan (9:2–5) to the ritual and service in the tabernacle (vv. 6–7)
and finally demonstrating the inadequate temporary nature of its
contribution (vv. 8–10). The purpose is to underline the absolute
necessity of the new order established by the sacrifice of Christ.

The two themes are noted in the introductory 9:1—the old covenant system had "regulations for worship" (the arrangement) and
"also an earthly sanctuary" (the furnishings needed for that worship). "Had" is actually the imperfect *eiche*, "was having," emphasizing the continuous nature of the system. There was never a
final closure because it could not solve the dilemma of sin. It was
an external system enacted in an "earthly sanctuary" (see also
8:2). Only Christ could provide the final solution, and the Mosaic
regulations were meant to prepare for his coming, fulfilled in the
events of verse 11. The particles "Now ... but" introducing verses
1 and 11 (*men ... de*) show the two sections (1–10, 11–28) are deliberately placed side by side in contrast with one another.

The two compartments of the sanctuary are the key to its
arrangement. The holy place contains the lampstand and table of
showbread (v. 2). The most holy place contains the golden altar of
incense and the ark of the covenant (v. 4), itself containing the gold
jar of manna, Aaron's staff that budded, and the stone tablets of
the covenant (vv. 3–4), and then above the ark the mercy seat and
the cherubim of glory (v. 5). The tabernacle, rather than temple, is
being described because the entire emphasis is on the Mosaic con-
trasted with the things of Christ. This is the tabernacle that traveled with the wilderness people in their wanderings. However, the

order of this was followed assiduously in the Solomonic temple, so this applies to the later period as well.

The writer calls the two rooms the "first" and "second," definitely not in terms of importance but probably the order in which the high priest entered them for ministry, having to pass through the first as well as the "second curtain" or veil to get to the second. The furnishings listed depict the ministry of each room. So the "first" compartment, the holy place, contains on its south side the seven-branched golden "lampstand" (three on each side of the main stem) that was "kept burning continually" with lamps that were to be "tended continually" (Lev 24:1–4; see also Exod 25:31–40; 37:17–24). On the north side was the table of showbread ("the table with its consecrated bread," Heb 9:2), a five-foot by two-and-a-half-foot table of acacia wood covered with gold plating, with twelve loaves of bread placed on it every Sabbath (Lev 24:5–9). The old bread was consumed by the priests who served there.

Now the attention shifts (Heb 9:3–5) to the most holy place, commonly called "the holy of holies." The "second curtain" (v. 3) or veil (the first was the outer curtain at the entrance of the sanctuary) separated the holy place from the most holy place, constructed of fine linen embroidered with purple, scarlet, and blue yarn with designs of cherubim. No Israelite had access, and even the high priest entered just once a year on the Day of Atonement, and then only because he represented the nation and had undergone a week of ritual cleansing from sin. It was the most sacred spot in the world because Yahweh dwelt there. Of course, he is omnipresent and everywhere at all times, but the most holy place was his special dwelling place. In the first century, it was an empty room, as the Babylonians and others had long before cleaned it out of its furnishings. Still, it symbolized all it had previously meant to the Jewish people.

The first piece mentioned is "the golden altar of incense" (9:4). It stood in the holy place next to the curtain, but it is mentioned here because it stood in the same relation to the most holy place as the altar of burnt offering did to the holy place—that is, it was the means of access to the holy of holies. Since the Greek word for "altar" can also mean "censer" (*thymiatērion*), some think it refers to the censer or bowl the high priest used to carry the fiery coals from the altar (Lev 16:12). But that is not as likely, for the incense altar is far more important and would fit the imagery much better.

Just as the ark signified the presence of God, the incense altar signified humanity's worship of God. The high priest never entered the holy of holies without incense from the altar, and on the Day of Atonement, he sprinkled blood on both the altar and the ark. Both the altar and the ark are described as "golden" to stress the beauty and glory of these pieces.

The only major piece of furniture in the most holy place in both the tabernacle and temple was the ark of the covenant, and all the other articles mentioned here were kept in the ark. It was taken from the temple at its destruction by the Babylonians in 587 BC (Jer 3:16) and never seen again, though many legends sprang up about its preservation, perhaps hidden by an angel (2 Bar 6:7). It was never replaced, and the holy of holies remained an empty room, as the Roman general Pompey discovered to his surprise when he entered it in 67 BC (Josephus, *War* 1.152–53). In place of the ark, a small stone slab was placed in the room, called "the stone of the foundation."

The ark was the most sacred article of furniture in the tabernacle, indeed in the world, and when it was transported from place to place, no one dare touch it on penalty of death (2 Sam 6:6–7). It was 3.75 feet long and 2.25 feet in width and height, constructed of acacia wood covered inside and out with gold leaf (Exod 25:10–16). The writer notes three items placed in the ark. The "gold jar of manna" (Heb 9:4) signified God's care and protection of his people during the wilderness wanderings (Exod 16:33–35). It was "golden" to continue the glory and sacred nature of each item. Then "Aaron's staff that had budded" (Heb 9:4) was in the ark to signify the way in which God provided for the spiritual needs of his people, as his staff budded to show the nation God's choice of Aaron (and the Levites) to lead the priestly line (Num 17:1–13).

The most important item in the ark was "the stone tablets of the covenant" (Heb 9:4), the slabs with the Ten Commandments that were broken due to Israel's idolatry, replaced, and then deposited in the ark (Exod 25:16; Deut 9:10, 10:1–5). This signified the centrality of the covenant for God-Israel relationships.

Now the writer turns to that "above the ark" (9:5) to stress its covering and segue into its primary purpose, namely atonement for sins. At the top, "overshadowing the atonement cover," are "the cherubim of the Glory," two gold statuettes above the mercy seat, believed to support Yahweh's invisible presence. They stood at the ends of the mercy seat, facing each other with their wings touching above the midpoint of the ark (thus "overshadow"). They stood for the **Shekinah** "glory" of God dwelling among his people (*shakan* is the Hebrew term for "dwelling").

The mercy seat was the throne of God (1 Sam 4:4; Ps 80:2), and it was believed God sat on this *bēma*, or throne of justice, to make his legal decisions. The "atonement cover" is *hilastērion*, the term for "propitiation" or "make atonement" (Heb 2:17; see also Rom 3:25). When the high priest on the Day of Atonement sprinkled blood on the mercy seat (Lev 16:1–19), he was atoning for the sins of the nation the previous year. To "atone" means to "cover," and it was believed God placed the sins of the people under the mercy seat and "covered" or forgave them. When the order of the text moves from the altar of incense in 9:4 to the mercy seat in verse 5, he is preparing for this path of the high priest on the Day of Atonement, imagery that will dominate Jesus' path as well from 9:1–10:18.

The author has said all he needs to discuss at this point and so concludes by remarking, "We cannot discuss these things in detail now" (v. 5) because that would go beyond his intentions. Enough has been communicated on the actual furnishings, and now it is time to turn to the actual service taking place in the sanctuary.

The readers are now able to understand the way the ancient pieces prefigured Christ and now the author wants to move into the way their rituals prepared for the work of Christ in his ministry.

RITUAL AND SERVICE IN THE TABERNACLE (9:6-7)

The inadequacy of the earthly system is seen in the fact that the priests performed their rituals "regularly" (v. 6) or continuously, and the high priests once a year, but neither sufficed to remove the sin problem. Only Christ's once-for-all sacrifice of atonement could do that. "When everything had been arranged" (v. 6) referred to Sinai and the beginning of the Mosaic era. The keynote for this time is the endless repetition of the priestly "rituals"—namely, the sacrificial system, involving both the holy place (the priests in the "outer room"[1]) and the most holy place (the high priest in the "inner room").

The regular rituals in the holy place included the daily trimming of the lamps (Exod 27:20-21) and incense offerings (Exod 30:8), as well as the weekly replacing of the showbread (Exod 25:30). Sacrifices took place every day, early in the morning and at twilight (Exod 29:38-41). The emphasis is on the regularity of the rituals, and that demonstrated clearly their insufficiency. They could only deal with one sin at a time and did make it possible for Israelites to enter the presence of God, but it never took away sins, and the forgiveness only lasted until the next sin. Thus it was a never-ending set of rituals. At this stage, this more than sufficed for the Old Testament saints and satisfied their need to draw near to God, but it was still insufficient because it could never be a permanent solution. Still, it was perfect for its time and a gift from God to his people.

---

1. The holy place is the "outer" because it is the room entered from the outside. The most holy place is the "inner" because it is entered after passing through the holy place.

The high priest ministered in the "inner room," the holy of
holies (v. 7) but only once a year and under strict regulations
(Lev 16). The limitations of the ritual are stressed—only the high
priest enters and only once a year and only with a blood sacrifice.
It clearly could never suffice and had to be repeated every year
in perpetuity, with separate sacrifices for the high priest himself
and for the nation.

Yet of all the priestly religious rituals, it had the greatest relevance, for it presaged the once-for-all atoning sacrifice of Christ.
The contrasts will be drawn out in the rest of this chapter: Christ,
the "priest forever" (5:6; 7:17), would offer himself on the final
Day of Atonement as the once-for-all sacrifice "for the sins of the
people." No atoning sacrifice would ever again be needed, and salvation is now made available for all humanity.

THE INADEQUACIES OF THE RITUALS (9:8–10)

The Holy Spirit now discloses the true significance of the two
covenants and the reasons for the movement to the deeper reality of the new era and its Christ-centered salvation. As the Spirit
inspires Scripture (3:7; 4:12–13; 10:15), he clarifies the unfolding
divine truths behind the covenants. In doing so, the Spirit reveals
the deficiencies of the old system and why it had to be replaced.
This is more than inspiring the biblical writers as they developed
canon—it is the illumination of the church so they can understand
the significance of those truths. The Spirit is here disclosing how
direct access to God and his presence could not be made available
"as long as the first tabernacle was still functioning" (9:8).

There is a significant debate as to whether verse 8 should be
translated "the way into the most holy place ... as long as the first
tabernacle" or whether it is better seen as, "the way into the sanctuary ... so long as the first room (the holy place)." The question
is whether the language is meant to be understood temporally or
geographically. Is the idea that of having access to the most holy

place by passing through the holy place, or is it of moving from
the old era to the new? The NIV translation is definitely superior,
for it is meant temporally of the movement from the era of "the
first tabernacle" to that of the heavenly sanctuary in which Christ
functioned as high priest.

The message is that God's people had no access to the direct
presence of God in his most holy place under the old dispensa-
tion, for they had to approach God through the priestly sacrificial
system centered on the holy place. Only with Christ was direct
access made possible, as Jeremiah 31 in Hebrews 8:8–12 made clear.
Both the holy place and the most holy place were barriers—only
the priests had access to the one, and only the high priest had
access to the other. The people were kept out of both and so were
doubly removed from direct access to God. As we will see in 9:11–15,
Christ entered through the curtains and opened complete access
to God for us all. As in 8:10–11 from Jeremiah 31:34, they will never
again need a priestly mediator. So only Christ could suffice to make
that a reality.

In verse 9 the writer clarifies his point. What he has just said
is actually an "illustration" or "parable" (*parabolē*) intended "for
the present time." In other words, the sanctuary with its two compartments symbolically represent the old covenant system, which
actually became an impenetrable wall between God's people and
his direct presence. Each compartment represented a further step
removed from God. It is Christ's high priestly act of offering himself for sin that alone will open up the way to God.

Moreover, "the gifts and sacrifices being offered were not
able to clear the conscience of the worshiper" (v. 9). As in 5:1 and
8:3, "gifts and sacrifices" sum up the entire sacrificial system.
They dealt only with external sins one at a time, not the internal reality of sin. "Not able to clear" (v. 9) is literally "could not
perfect the conscience" (*teleiōsai*), meaning they could not "complete" their actual purpose of cleansing people from sin. The conscience was never clear, for sin was ever-present and continued its

stranglehold on the individual. Worship was indeed made possible by the sacrifice, but it only was sufficient for the present time until the next sin mired the person in guilt. The external rituals were unable to rid the heart of sin or transform the conscience because they were human acts devoid of divine power.

These "external regulations" are enumerated in verse 10—"food and drink and various ceremonial washings," which dealt with the things of this earthly life only and did not make the conscience right with God. Not only the sacrifices but the food laws ("food and drink"; see Lev 11) were based on human ceremony rather than internal cleansing. They were adequate for the previous era of the Mosaic law, but Christ had fulfilled them and brought them to completion. That age was now over—finished—and had given way to the new order.

There is some question about the relation between "the present time" (v. 9) and "the time of the new order," with *diorthōsis* meaning, "time of reformation/correction" (v. 10). There is general agreement that the contrast is between the two covenant ages. The "present time" is the time of change, when the work of Christ completed and ended the old covenant age and introduced the new era, the "time of correction," when the imagery and purpose of the old order was fulfilled and the new order brought final salvation into this world. To the author, the "time of (spiritual) reformation" is not in the future, for Christ has already come, fulfilled the old in his suffering and death, and ushered in the new. So the "present time" is the time of change, and the "time of correction" can take over and bring eternal salvation to the readers.

THE COMING OF ETERNAL REDEMPTION (9:11–14)

The author has now proven the weaknesses of the old order and the necessity of the coming of the new order with Christ (Heb 9:1–10) and now turns to the arrival of this great gift from God, the new covenant with eternal redemption (vv. 11–22). The "first tabernacle" sufficed for the Mosaic period but was inadequate for cleansing the sinner internally, and the new had to come with Christ. The fleshly sacrifices had to be never-ending because they dealt with sins only one at a time. Only Christ's high priestly ministry and his once-for-all sacrifice (they are interconnected) could lead to eternal forgiveness and the solving of the sin problem. This is the primary theme for the rest of this chapter and, in fact, is the culmination of the material from 4:14 to this point (see 4:14; 5:1, 9; 7:25–27; 8:3, 6).

When this "time of the new order" had arrived, Christ "came as high priest of the good things that are now already here" (9:11). There is a textual debate as to whether we should read this in a realized sense, "the good things that have come,"[2] or in a futuristic sense, "the good things that are about to come."[3] While the textual evidence is almost equal, the context strongly favors the first option, and the NIV's "things that are now already here" is a good translation, highlighting the new covenant reality that has come with Christ, as we will see also in 10:1, "the good things that are coming"—that is, all the blessings of the kingdom age that are in the process of being realized by God's people.

The emphasis is on the arrival of Christ and his entrance into the true heavenly sanctuary "through (dia) the greater and more perfect tabernacle" (9:11). The imagery is Christ, by his atoning sacrifice, passing through the outer compartment, the holy place, in order to enter the holy of holies, the sanctuary in heaven (as also in 6:19–20; 8:1–2). The earthly priests could serve only in the former and could have no lasting effect. Christ's ministry was "greater and more perfect" (v. 11), achieving eternal redemption and a final inheritance in heaven. The earthly tabernacle/temple is earthly, while the heavenly is "not made with human hands" and thus "is not a part of this creation." This repeats 8:2, "set up by the Lord, not by a mere human being," and reemphasizes the fact that true

---

2. *genomenōm,* as in 𝔓⁴⁶ B D* Origen.

3. *mellontōn,* as in ℵ A Byz.

believers are citizens of heaven (Phil 3:20) and aliens in this world (1 Pet 1:1, 17; 2:11). Christ has brought his followers into the heavenly reality.

This does not say Jesus passed through the earthly heavens (the sky) to enter heaven. That is not hinted here. His entrance was directly into heaven at the moment of his death. The only "heaven" here is where God and Christ dwell and where we will have our home for eternity. Moreover, this "perfect tabernacle" is not a metaphor for Christ's body, with Christ "passing through" by means of his blood. This must be understood elsewhere in Hebrews (see 8:1–2) as the heavenly sanctuary where Christ performs his high priestly ministry.

Verse 12 adds that his entrance into heaven was not "by means of the blood of goats and calves." Jesus did not need to perform a two-stage sacrifice (first for himself and then for the nation) like the high priest on the Day of Atonement. He was sinless. Moreover, there was no longer a need for "the blood of goats and calves," the required sacrifices for the atonement rituals (Lev 16:3–16). He shed "his own blood" as the atoning sacrifice for our sins. This enabled him to enter the heavenly sanctuary, having won the victory not just over individual sins but over sin itself and Satan. During the old covenant age, the blood of the ritual had to be sprinkled on the mercy seat of the ark every year and had no force in removing future sins not yet committed.

The result is the attainment of "eternal redemption" for those who will turn to him in faith. Christ entered his eternal glory on the victorious note of having redeemed, or rescued, his followers from sin and death and giving them their eternal inheritance in heaven. To be "redeemed" is to be ransomed or purchased in order to obtain our freedom from bondage and pay for our release. Christ's blood was the ransom payment, and the reward was eternal life. God redeemed Israel from bondage in Egypt (Deut 7:8; 13:5), and Christ redeemed us (Mark 10:45) on the cross (Gal 3:13).

So the saints share his eternal glory by joining the family of
the Godhead and belonging to him from the moment of their conversion. The "old order" could never do this and dealt only on the
temporary, earthly level. Contrary to the RSV, NRSV, NJB, and TEV,
this does not say that Christ entered the heavenly sanctuary "with
his own blood" but rather that he entered "through" or "by means
of" his redeeming sacrifice. His blood was shed on the cross and
did not need to follow the Mosaic ritual of being carried and sprinkled in the holy of holies. It remained at the cross and sufficed as
a once-for-all sacrifice.

The rest of this section (9:13-14) consists of a single sentence
and spells out the complete contrast between the blood of the
Mosaic system (v. 13) and the blood of Christ (v. 14). The earthly
rites were ceremonial and could only "sanctify" or "render holy"
by making them "outwardly clean." They could never cleanse the
conscience or the heart (9:9-10). People could enter the tabernacle and engage in worship, but it was all external, never internal
with true worship. Only Christ could bring internal cleansing and
sanctification.

The "goats and calves" of verse 12 and "goats and bulls" here
in verse 13 looked to the Day of Atonement ritual when the high
priest first offered a bull for himself and then a goat for the nation
(Lev 16:3, 5-16). At the same time, these form a metaphor that
stands for the entire Levitical system. The "ashes of a heifer" were
mingled with water and sprinkled on the worshipers (Num 19:1-10)
to cleanse and purify them. But again, it achieved only an external cleansing and was ineffective in the long run.

So the blood of Christ (Heb 9:14) provided the far greater effects
because he "through the eternal Spirit offered himself unblemished to God." There has been a lot of discussion as to whether
the "eternal Spirit" is the Holy Spirit or the Spirit of Christ. Either
is possible, but as in 2:4, 3:7, 6:4, and 9:8, it is better to see the
Holy Spirit here. The emphasis on the eternal nature of Christ
and his work has dominated recent chapters, and it continues
here. The Spirit's work in relation to Christ is eternal in its results

and highlights his eternal nature as part of the Triune Godhead. This could be an echo of the suffering servant of Isaiah, who in Isaiah 42:1 was promised, "I will put my Spirit on him." The Spirit indwelt and worked with Jesus throughout his life of servanthood.

The "unblemished" sacrifice of Christ made it the perfect offering for sin. He was the perfect lamb (Exod 29:1; Lev 1:3, 22:22–24; Num 19:2) offered to God as the perfect sacrifice. This is one of the greatest contrasts, as high priests were fully human and, in the first century, were especially evil and pawns of Rome. Christ's perfect obedience and sinless life made him the perfect sin offering.

The results are spectacular, as his sacrifice was able to "cleanse our consciences" (in contrast to Heb 9:9) from dead works (v. 14, "acts that lead to death"). What the Mosaic law could not do (vv. 9–10) is now accomplished by Christ's perfect sacrifice, and the effects are eternal rather than temporary. The "dead works" here refer to sinful actions rather than the rituals themselves. The fleshly actions of human beings have no power to bring life, only death. The law was unable to solve the dilemma, but Christ by shedding his blood has done so.

The twofold purpose of Jesus' sacrifice is our own cleansing from sin and our liberation that enables us to "serve the living God" (v. 14). Note the antithesis between "dead works" and the "living God." Death is replaced by life, and our works are removed and replaced by serving or obeying God. Also, the sacrifices cleansed externally and allowed the individuals to worship, but it was an external, religious worship in the temple rituals. Christ has brought a new age and a new depth of worship, as we worship or "serve the living God."

MEDIATOR OF THE NEW COVENANT (9:15–22)

THESIS: RECEIVING THE ETERNAL INHERITANCE (9:15)

The previous passage (9:11–14) dealt with Jesus' entrance into the heavenly sanctuary, and now the writer turns to the eternal results of the new covenant. Since Christ, the heavenly high priest, has

offered himself as the perfect sacrifice for sin, he is "the mediator of a new covenant," reintroducing this theme from 8:6, 8–13
(see also 12:24). As we saw there, he is the go-between who has
brought the two sides, God and humanity, together under a new
order, established by his incarnation and atoning sacrifice and
confirmed by the signing of a new covenant that has brought eternal salvation for those who come in faith. In this chapter the basis
of Christ's mediation comes to the fore—his sacrificial death.

There is a predestinarian air in "those who are called," echoing
the theme from 3:1, "holy brothers and sisters, who share in the
heavenly calling." Here the calling is seen in terms of its accompa-
nying benefit, receiving "the promised eternal inheritance" (9:15).
The promises of God are frequently stressed (4:1; 6:12, 15, 17; 7:6;
8:6; 10:36; 11:9, 13, 17, 33, 39) as an essential component of the new
order in Christ. They are connected with the hope that we have
realized in Christ and the certain future he has guaranteed. In
the old covenant, the inheritance was the "promised" land, and
now it is an eternal inheritance in heaven, with "inheritance"
(klēronomia) another dominant theme (1:2, 4, 14; 6:12, 17; 11:7–8;
12:17) describing the privileges received from becoming God's children—namely, the eternal promises realized (10:36; 11:39). Here
the promise is seen in terms of its final reality, the inheritance of
eternal life and reward.

What has brought it all about is Christ's mediatorial work, his
high priestly offering of himself—"he has died as a ransom to set
them free from the sins committed under the first covenant" (v. 15).
He has supervised and effected the removal of the inadequate old
system and turned condemnation into forgiveness. In doing so
he has provided redemption (9:12) from transgressions committed under the first covenant, as in 8:12 (= Jer 31:34). Once more,
redemption is achieved when Christ through his death on the cross
pays the ransom price that "sets his followers free" from the guilt
those sins have produced. The faithful are called to persevere in
Christ and find spiritual victory in his blood sacrifice.

THE NECESSITY OF DEATH (9:16–17)

There is a significant debate over the use of *diathēkē* in 9:16, as the
NIV follows the traditional understanding and translates it, "in
the case of a will." The term was used both of a covenant and of
a last will and testament in the **Hellenistic** world, and as is the
case with most final wills, the latter use demanded the death of the
one making the will. However, this has been challenged by many
recent interpreters because the emphasis is on covenant throughout and that, in actuality, a will was placed into effect when it was
made and signed rather than when the testator died. So the author
is drawing on the imagery of the Old Testament, that covenants
were ratified with animal sacrifice, and we would paraphrase, "In
the case of a covenant, it demands death by sacrifice." So the thrust
is that the new covenant had to be ratified by the sacrificial death
of Jesus as a covenant-making sacrifice.

We are now told how the removal of the old covenant has taken
place. It is Christ's death that both cleanses the repentant sinner
and brings about the new covenant salvation. Christ took both our
sins and their penalty on himself and died on our behalf so that
we could live. In this sense, he is both the high priest who offers
the sacrifice and the sacrifice itself that launches the "time of the
new order" (9:10). He is also both mediator and testator, the one
who forged the new covenant reality and, at the same time, produced its effects, the reception of the final inheritance by those
who repent and come to Christ in faith.

In verse 17 as well, we must change "will" into "covenant," and
it will read, "because a covenant comes into force only when some-
body has died." Like the sacrifice of the heifer, goat, and ram at
the ratification of the Abrahamic covenant in Genesis 15:9 and
the sacrifice of young bulls at the ratification of the Mosaic covenant in Exodus 24:5, the new covenant was brought into being
with the sacrifice of Jesus the Christ. Several have added here that
Jesus' death not only brought into being the new covenant but also
brought an end to the old covenant and broke the curse that lay on

humanity, producing the new era of salvation. Jesus' death was not only necessary for the sake of our salvation; it was also a legal necessity for removing the old, inadequate covenant and launching the new covenant age.

THE LAUNCHING OF THE FIRST COVENANT (9:18–22)

Pretty much everything in this paragraph has been covered before, but this turns all the details into a single package and relates it as helpful background to Jesus' high priestly ministry. Here he presents how the "first covenant" was inaugurated and shows that blood sacrifice was the essential ingredient, thereby explaining why the second or new covenant had to be launched with blood as well. The verb *engkainizō* ("put into effect") connotes "bringing something new (*kainos*) into effect" and is a legal term denoting the "inauguration" or "ratifying" of a covenant/treaty relationship. Verses 16–17 demonstrated that such a covenant could not be launched without a sacrificial death, and 18–22 develops that legal principle further. A blood sacrifice was necessary.

The covenant ceremony itself is drawn from Exodus 24:3–8 and explicated in Hebrews 9:19–21. Still, there are significant differences with the Exodus account:

In Exodus 24	In Hebrews 9
Sacrificed oxen	Sacrificed goats and calves
Sprinkled on altar and people	Sprinkled on scroll and people
Sprinkled blood	Blood with water, scarlet wool, and hyssop

The "goats and calves" are added here in assimilation to 9:12–13, and as there they are symbolic of the entire sacrificial system. Having "the scroll and all the people" (v. 19) instead of "the altar and the people" actually changes very little for, in both readings, they emphasize God and the people, the two figures signing the covenant agreement. The blood from the sacrifices was placed in a bowl and sprinkled on the altar, dedicating the ceremony to God. Then there was a reading from the covenant scroll followed by using the hyssop branch to sprinkle the people, signifying their cleansing. The addition of water, scarlet wool, and hyssop simply brings out various details in the covenant ceremony. Water was added to the blood to prevent coagulation and to symbolize spiritual cleansing.

The scarlet string and the hyssop, a lengthy stalk of the marjoram plant used to sprinkle the blood, were connected in the ceremony for purifying a leper (Lev 14:4-6). The scarlet string was used to tie a clean bird to the hyssop. A second bird was sacrificed, with its blood placed in a vessel. Then the first bird was dipped in the blood, sprinkled onto the former leper, and set free to fly away, symbolizing the liberation from uncleanness. All in all, the entire scene of Hebrews 9:18-21 is used to demonstrate the failure of the sacrificial system to truly cleanse from sin.

The material in 9:21 was not mentioned in Exodus 24, the ceremony for inaugurating the covenant, though some think it was anyway because it is part of a separate tradition found in Josephus (*Antiquities* 3.206). Either way, it is added to make this a comprehensive comment on the sacrificial system as a whole. The sprinkling of blood was essential for every part of Jewish ritual, as made clear in verse 22, where the writer stresses that "the law requires that nearly everything be cleansed with blood." Of course, this is slight hyperbole, for the meal offering (Lev 5:11), for various water ceremonies (Lev 15:10), or for purifying by fire (Num 31:22-23) are exceptions. However, these are simply the old adage—the exception proves the rule. Blood was the central element for everything.

The primary use of sacrificial blood is mentioned to conclude this section, "without the shedding of blood there is no forgiveness" (9:22b). It is also the author's primary point, for the forgiveness effected in the old covenant sacrifices prepared for and was fulfilled in the once-for-all sacrifice of Jesus. The sacrifices were insufficient for bringing about true forgiveness because they only dealt with sins one at a time and could never achieve lasting forgiveness. Only Jesus could do that. Still, the thrust here is that blood played a significant and critical role in the old covenant, initiating the covenant, cleansing the conscience, and bringing about access to God. It was a positive force and met its purpose for the needs of the old covenant. But it was not a long-term solution and simply led up to the final answer provided by Jesus' atoning sacrifice.

THE PERFECT SACRIFICE (9:23-28)

THESIS: THE BETTER SACRIFICES (9:23)

This section begins by reiterating the earlier point from 8:5 that the Mosaic system was a copy of the heavenly things and then drawing a crucial contrast between the copies and "the heavenly things themselves." Earlier the inadequacy of the sanctuary and covenant in the old order was developed, and now the author turns to the sacrifices themselves, the third component of 8:1–10:18. The previous section to this one (9:18-22) showed how these "copies" were indeed "purified with these sacrifices" (v. 23). "Purified" (*katharizō*) is the key here and shows how even the religious vessels of the tabernacle had to be cleansed in order to fulfill their sacred purpose.

Using a "lesser and greater" hermeneutic, the writer establishes the superiority of the new covenant, which centered on the "heavenly things" (v. 23) and not the earthly copies. Since the blood sacrifices of the Mosaic system were insufficient for producing eternal results, the true heavenly sanctuary needed "better sacrifices than these" (v. 23). Animal sacrifices could no longer suffice, for they produced only temporary cleansing and functioned on an earthly plane. Again, this lesser function was adequate for the old order, for it enabled worship and a relationship with God and prepared for the final reality to come with Christ. But now Christ has inaugurated the new covenant order, and that needed a superior sacrifice—namely, the atoning sacrifice of Christ.

There is some difference in opinion about why the "heavenly" reality needed to be purified, with some thinking it implicitly points to the purifying of heaven, the inauguration of the heavenly sanctuary (building on Exodus 24), or the spiritual cleansing of the people of God. The problem with the first two options is why heaven itself would need either cleansing or covenant inauguration since it is already perfect. So the best option is the cleansing of the saints. The emphasis is on the spiritual cleansing and the clear conscience (9:14) produced by the sacrifice of Christ. The sacrificial blood of the old covenant could not produce this; only the blood of Christ was adequate.

The Two Systems: Sanctuary and Sacrifices (9:24–28)

The contrasts between the two systems are developed further here. Hebrews 9:24–28 deals first with the heavenly sanctuary itself and then with the sacrifice that inaugurates it. The imagery used to explain it continues to build on the Day of Atonement, as Jesus Christ, the high priest, enters the sanctuary. He did not enter the earthly sanctuary "made with human hands" (see 8:2) and a mere copy of the true heavenly sanctuary, nor did he need to cleanse himself and sacrifice for himself. Rather, he ascended from the dead and entered "heaven itself" as the "high priest forever" (5:5). For all eternity, he will "appear for us in God's presence" (v. 24).

Even more remarkable is that he is doing so "for us" or "on our behalf" (hyper hēmōn). It is part of his high priestly ministry and heavenly intercession (7:25) to render the help we so desperately need. Christ's presence in heaven mediates God's presence in our lives.

From the sanctuary the attention turns to the sacrifices, beginning with the old covenant (9:25–26a). The Day of Atonement ritual was an annual festival, with the earthly high priest "offering himself again and again," meaning his blood sacrifice could never take away sin and bring lasting forgiveness. It dealt only with past sins, and so every year, another atonement ritual was necessary to bring about remission for the sins committed during that year. There are two contrasts in this verse—first, the necessary repetitive nature of the earthly high priest's entry into the holy of holies and then the fact that the blood he sacrificed was "not his own." To enter the holy of holies on that sacred day, he had first to offer a young bull as a sin offering for himself and his household (Lev 16:3, 6).

The contrast with Christ takes place in Hebrews 9:26a. Christ did not have to sacrifice for himself, for he was "without sin" (4:15). His was a "once for all" sacrifice, and this means that if he had been an earthly high priest, he would have had to "suffer many times since the creation of the world." Since Adam had introduced sin into the world, that malignant force had dominated humanity. That means that Jesus would by necessity have died on the cross again and again, just as the Mosaic law mandated. That also means he would have had to enter the heavenly sanctuary to offer that sacrifice to God time and again. That would make no sense whatsoever. Christ's sacrificial death on the cross would no longer be needed, for the high priest already was doing that on the Day of Atonement.

So the answer is provided in 9:26b–28. Rather than repeated sacrifices with the blood of "goats and calves" (9:12–13), Christ "has appeared once for all at the culmination of the ages to do away with sin by the sacrifice of himself" (v. 26). Rather than needing to be offered in perpetuity, the eternal sacrifice of Christ sufficed for the rest of eternity and solved the sin problem for all time (*hapax* and *ephapax*, also in 7:27; 9:12; 10:10). Moreover, he appeared "at the culmination of the ages" (also in 1 Cor 10:11) also called "the fullness of time" (Gal 4:4 ESV), "the end of the age" (Matt 13:38–39; 24:3; 28:20; 1 Cor 10:11), and "these last times" (1 Pet 1:20). All of time is divided into that which precedes and prepares for the incarnation of Christ, and that which follows and is the aftermath of his coming.

The purpose of his arrival is to "do away with sin" (Heb 9:26) —
that is, remove its effect on fallen humanity and provide eternal salvation for those who repent and come to him in faith. "Do
away" is *athetēsis*, translated in 7:18 as to "set aside" the Mosaic
regulations by the actions of the Melchizedekian high priest. Sin
is annulled or removed, taken away, and rendered powerless by
the once-for-all sacrifice of Christ. This could never have been
done by the Aaronic ritual, which, as said earlier, only dealt with
sins one at a time.

Christ's sacrifice is in utter contrast with that of the rest of
human beings, who are appointed by God "to die once, and after
that to face judgment" (9:27). Sinful human beings cannot find forgiveness for themselves, for they are at all times under the power
of sin and unable to get right with God on their own merits. When
Christ died once, he brought salvation to humanity. When fallible human beings die, it is their destiny immediately to face God
in judgment for their sins, the final one of the four "elementary
teachings" in 6:2 (see also 12:26–29), for they have never ceased
being sinners. Finite, fallible humanity lives in "the fear of death"
(2:15), and Christ's atoning sacrifice alone can bring hope and victory over sin and death (2:14–18).

Only Christ could do that, for all humanity is under sin and
unable to rise above it (9:28). The word "once" is *hapax* and in
complete parallel with Christ's "once for all" death. Christ's "once"
achieved salvation, while humanity's "once" leads to judgment.
Every person faces a one-time death and judgment, and at the
same time, Christ's one-time sacrifice enables converts to avoid
that judgment. As painful as it was to the Triune Godhead, the
Father offered the Son so that salvation could come and abrogate
the power and effects of sin in this world.

The verb translated "take away" here is actually *anenengkein*
and is better translated as "offered to *bear* the sins of many," as
it is an important indicator that is the one allusion in Hebrews
to the vicarious sacrifice of the Suffering Servant in Isaiah 53:12,

"For he bore the sin of many, and made intercession for the trans-
gressors." The "many" in Isaiah and here refers to the innumerable number of those who will turn to Christ for forgiveness. He
"bore their sins" by making himself the substitute for them and
taking their sins upon himself.

The great promise is provided in verse 28b, "he will appear a
second time, not to bear sin, but to bring salvation to those who
are waiting for him." Christ's first appearance culminated in his
"bearing our sins," an unrepeatable one-time event. This second
appearance will mean victory and ultimate salvation for the faithful "many." The idea of a second coming is a fitting euphemism
for this event, and the saints are depicted as those "waiting for
him," with *apekdechomenois* describing an excited expectancy for
his arrival. This has been true down through the ages, and several Christian movements (like dispensationalism) have centered
on this expectation. How can any true believer fail to be utterly
thrilled with the prospect of final victory, the defeat of sin, and the
onset of eternal reward that will attend his return? The two comings of Christ are the true center points in the history of our world,
bringing salvation and then eternal joy and reward in their wake.

———

This section turns to the sanctuary that was the centerpiece of
Levitical ministry in the old covenant system and contrasts that
ministry (vv. 1–10) with the new covenant ministry of Christ
(vv. 1–28). The purpose is to continue to stress the superiority of
the new by showing the inadequacies of the old and how much
more the new reality provided for the people of God, to encourage these many weak Christians not to fall away back to Judaism
but remain with Christ.

First, this details the furnishings of the Mosaic tabernacle
(vv. 1–5), a plan also followed by the temple. There were two compartments, the holy place, where daily worship and sacrifice were

conducted, and the most holy place, where the high priest entered on the Day of Atonement once a year. The primary pieces of furniture in the holy place (vv. 1–2) were used for the daily worship and offerings made to the Lord. The lampstand, or seven-tiered candelabra, was kept lit at all times to signify the light of God that permeated throughout the rituals. Then the table of showbread contained the sacred loaves dedicated to the Lord and then consumed by the priests and replaced a week later.

The most holy place / holy of holies (vv. 3–5) was too sacred to be entered by sinful human beings, and only once a year did the high priest enter on the Day of Atonement to receive forgiveness and atone for the sins of the nation. The golden altar of incense was actually in the holy place at the entrance and provided access to the holy of holies. The most sacred piece of all was the ark of the covenant, with the mercy seat that became the throne of God and place of atonement. In the ark was placed the gold jar of manna, signifying God's provision for his people; Aaron's staff that budded, signifying God's chosen leadership for his people; and the stone tablets of the covenant, signifying the Mosaic injunctions by which God led his people. The cherubim of glory were the angelic forces that oversaw it all.

Then the rituals themselves are presented (vv. 6–7), first the daily sacrifices performed by the priests in the holy place and then the annual Day of Atonement service performed by the high priest in the most holy place. The first provided for individual sins one at a time, the second for the sins of the nation in a given year. While this was sufficient for the Mosaic era, it is inadequate for the present (vv. 8–10) because it demanded continuous sacrifices and offerings that were never fulfilled or completed in terms of the divine intention to provide final payment for sin and direct access to God. It needed constant repetition and could never prove adequate to the task.

So the second half of the chapter (vv. 11–28) centers on the only thing that can suffice: Jesus' high priestly work on the cross and in heaven. The superiority of his work as high priest of heaven is breathtaking, making "eternal redemption" available (vv. 11-14). The Levitical system was an incredible gift for its day, enabling Israelites to maintain a covenant relationship with God, but it was never adequate in the long run. A sanctuary "made with human hands" (v. 11) and the blood of goats and calves could never remove sin, for it could only deal with one sin at a time. Earth-centered sacrifices made a person externally clean but not internally undefiled. On the other hand, the eternal Spirit was at work in the new covenant, and the effects last forever. While this was meant for these Jewish Christians in the first century, it is invaluable for us as well, and we would all do well to meditate on the glorious reality of what Christ has accomplished on our behalf.

So Christ has entered the heavenly sanctuary (vv. 11-14), and in his exalted, enthroned state, he mediates the new covenant for us (vv. 15-22), and his ransom payment has not only redeemed us but given us an eternal inheritance (v. 15) and liberated us from sin. Moreover, the death of Jesus has not only cleansed us from sin, it has also brought about the new covenant. For a covenant to come into force, a sacrificial death is necessary to seal it (vv. 16-17), so Christ's death welcomed the new covenant age and the new era of salvation into this world. He has inaugurated the new covenant, mediated it for humanity, and oversaw its effects for the new covenant age. He did all this for us, and we should be filled with awe at the depth of the divine love to do all this for such unworthy rascals as us!

The description of the covenant ceremony (vv. 18-22) both demonstrated the necessity of a blood sacrifice and the inadequacy of the old sacrificial system, for it had to be repeated again and again and was never sufficient, while Christ's once-for-all sacrifice had eternal effects. In the covenant ceremony as well, Christ's work was vastly superior and alone could solve the sin problem.

The superiority of the new covenant and the sacrifice that initiated it continues in verses 23-28. Both the cleansing of the saints

(v. 23) and the entrance into the heavenly sanctuary (v. 24) were only possible because of Christ's perfect sacrifice. Earthly sacrifices like those on the Day of Atonement were never-ending, for they could only deal with transgressions for the year preceding (vv. 25-26a). Only Christ's sacrifice could end the mind-numbing repetition of the old system, for it was eternal in scope and did away with sin forever (26b-28). On its own, humanity had only one destiny—death and then final judgment. Christ's sacrificial death alone could break that bondage, and through it, the repentant could find forgiveness and salvation.

The one-time first "coming" of Christ not only achieved eternal redemption for all who put their trust in him for salvation, but it will also culminate in a "second coming" (v. 28b), which will bring victory and eternal glory to the faithful. At that time, our eternal salvation will be finalized.

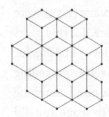

THE LEVITICAL SYSTEM
AND THE NEW ORDER
(10:1–18)

This passage culminates the first ten chapters of this letter and its emphasis on the superiority of the person and work of Christ over everything Judaism has to offer. The writer wants his readers to know what they will be giving up if they fall away from Christ and go back to their old covenant ways. This concludes those arguments by summarizing the meaning and purpose of the new covenant and Christ as high priest of the new order. This passage is also intimately related to 8:1–9:28, which serves as the concluding element of the emphasis on the superiority of the covenant, sanctuary, and sacrifices Christ has offered in his high priestly work.

There are four movements by which the writer concludes his thoughts: the old order prefiguring the new (Heb 10:1-4); the incarnation and obedience of Christ seen in his offering of himself (vv. 5-10); the sufficiency and glory of the one sacrifice (vv. 11-14); and the superiority and sufficiency of the new covenant (vv. 15-18).

THE OLD FORESHADOWS THE NEW (10:1-4)

Once again the many versus the one sacrifice anchors the point being made. The thesis is found in the first verse—"The law is only a shadow of the good things that are coming—not the realities themselves." The emphasis in "law" is not the Written Torah so much as the old system that lay behind and is expressed in it. Only Christ's atoning sacrifice was able to provide a "once for all" solution for sin (7:27; 9:12, 26, 28); all the repeated sacrifices of the Mosaic order could only "foreshadow" their fulfillment in Christ by continually reminding God's people of their sinfulness and need for spiritual cleansing. It is the many versus the one, the never-ending nature of the Levitical order versus the one-time, eternal act of Christ.

The contrast is between "shadow" (*skia*) and "reality" (*eikōn*). The shadow is not a "copy" (as in Platonic thinking) but an incomplete essence or insubstantial pattern that foreshadows or prefigures the greater reality to come. The "reality" or true "image" the old system looked forward to can be found only in Christ.

The "good things that are coming" (10:1) is not still a future event but is looked at from the perspective of the old covenant and has replaced it. It comes in two stages—namely, the two comings of Christ (the new covenant introduced by Jesus' arrival and the final order that will come with his second coming). Especially in mind are cleansing and forgiveness of sin and a new and complete access to God, both promised in the new covenant passage of Jeremiah 31:31–34 (see Heb 8:8–12). The insufficiency of the old system is stated succinctly and well here—"the same sacrifices repeated endlessly year after year" (Heb 10:1). Proof of inadequacy is evident, as final absolution is impossible to attain.

"Make perfect" in verse 1 does not mean sinless perfection but rather perfect access to God. It is the "perfect" salvation Christ brings. If this had been attained by the law, there would be no need for further sacrifices (10:2). For these first-century believers, the repetition of sacrifices in the Jerusalem temple would be proof of the point made here. The Levitical sacrifices cannot cease, for the sinful nature of people continues. If the old order had completely worked and eliminated sin altogether, "the worshipers (in the temple) would have been cleansed once for all, and would no longer have felt guilty for their sins" (v. 2).

From verse 3, we know the writer has the Day of Atonement in particular in mind, with the notation that it provides "an annual reminder of sins." The emphasis is that while partial worship is allowed, full and complete worship is not, for every year the sacrifices must be continued, and perfect access to God never results. Their conscience has not been cleansed (9:9, 14), and they must come back again and again. In fact, the very sacrifices featured on that "day" provide "an annual reminder" that their sins have continued and they still need to be cleansed. The entire sacrificial system provides perpetual proof that they remain bound to sin and need to be liberated. That will not occur under the law and must await the arrival of Christ and his atoning blood sacrifice. Only then will God's people have free access, for they will have entered with Christ behind the curtain into the inner sanctuary (9:11–15). Sin will no longer be uppermost in their minds, for final forgiveness will have been secured by Christ.

The conclusion comes in 10:4, "It is impossible for the blood of bulls and goats to take away sins." In verse 1 they could "never" do so, and now in verse 4 it is "impossible," echoing 9:13, where these Levitical sacrifices provided only outward cleansing and were unable to cleanse the conscience. The sentence begins with "impossible" (*adynaton*, see 6:4) to stress the absolute inability of the blood of animals to solve the human dilemma and remove the effects of sin. All the old system could do was remind people of their dilemma; it could never solve it. It did cleanse, but only one sin at a time, and perfect and final forgiveness was never attained.

THE NEW ORDER: THE INCARNATION AND OBEDIENCE OF CHRIST (10:5–10)

THE BASIS: THE OBEDIENCE OF THE SON (10:5–7)

Interestingly, Christ is presented as the virtual author of Psalm 40:6–8, singing it at his incarnation ("when Christ came into the world, he said"). He begins his earthly sojourn with surrender to the Father and promises to obey the Father's will. This is a Davidic psalm, and his promise of fealty is fulfilled in the son of David, the royal Messiah, at the same time the Son of God.

In the opening of the psalm (v. 5), a contrast is drawn between the "sacrifices and offerings" of the Mosaic system and "the body you prepared for me." This is likely why the writer picked this psalm, as the body of Christ replaced the Levitical sacrifices as the vehicle of redemption. The actual Masoretic Text (the Hebrew Old Testament) has "you have given me an open ear," but the author used the **Septuagint** for the emphasis on the "body," thus a reference to the incarnation of Christ. He and the other New Testament writers considered the Septuagint not more inspired than the Hebrew but a Spirit-led paraphrase interpreting the Hebrew text and adding nuances God was approving, here extending the ear to encompass the whole body. The body given Jesus at the incarnation became the means of a superior sacrifice to that of the animal sacrifices. His incarnate body is given back to the Father as a living sacrifice.

This is expanded in verses 6–7, stating that God was not pleased with "burnt offerings and sin offerings." Four terms are used for the sacrificial system, each denoting a possible different sacrifice—sacrifice (the peace offering or thanksgiving vow), offering (the meal offering as a gift to God), burnt offering (thanksgiving and the expiation of sin), and sin offering (for ceremonial defilement). Primarily, they are meant to be together and summarize the entire sacrificial system.

God was not displeased with the system as a whole. After all, he had given it to Moses, and it was God's will for the interim period until he sent his Son. However, the sacrifice he truly wants is total obedience to his will and complete access to his presence, and sacrificial offerings were only of true value when they were outward expressions of inward piety and obedience. Jesus fulfilled these intentions perfectly, for his was an absolute surrender to the will of God throughout his earthly life.

For David in Psalm 40:6-8, these verses expressed his realization that keeping the law was not enough. God was not pleased with his surface obedience to the legal requirements of the law. He demanded more. Several commentaries think "it is written about me in the scroll" (Heb 10:7) refers to the law itself, specifically to Deuteronomy's demands for the relationship of the chosen leaders of Israel to Yahweh himself—namely, for total surrender and obedience. Jesus, as the Davidic Messiah, applies this to himself and fulfills it perfectly by saying and living out in his life the proper response—"I have come to do your will, my God" (10:7). Jesus was the perfect embodiment of the ideal king, completely subservient to his Father in every respect.

COMMENTARY: OBEDIENCE AND SACRIFICE (10:8-10)

The author now comments on the two major aspects of Psalm 40:8 (Heb 10:8-9a) that are relevant to his basic point—namely, what has been set aside and what has been established. Then he shows its relevance for his argument (vv. 9b-10). First, God's displeasure with the "sacrifices and offerings" (v. 8) is noted and applied to the end of the Levitical order. All four terms for sacrifices are present from the Psalm (vv. 5-6), but now they all are plural to stress the repeated nature of them in the Jewish system. As a result, God was "not pleased" (v. 6), drawn from 8:8 and Jeremiah's prophecy in 8:8-9, reporting that the Lord had "found fault with the people" (Heb 8:8). Since the old sacrifices never sufficed (9:8-10, 23) and God neither desired nor was pleased (vv. 5-6) with them, he set them aside. They had to be replaced, and their true purpose was to provide temporary forgiveness for the period of the Mosaic law and prepare for the coming of Christ.

Second, Christ's affirmation and sacred promise that "I have come to do your will" (v. 7) in fulfillment of Psalm 40:8 is established by him (Heb 10:9b). The perfect tense "I have come" (ēkō) in verse 7 looks at his life of obedience as a single complete whole and shows he was always characterized by his faithful reflection of his Father's will. In the incarnation and life of obedience of Christ, the old covenant system ended and the new order was inaugurated to replace it. The Levitical sacrifices could not take away sin, so it was taken away by the obedient atoning sacrifice of Christ. "Establish" is a legal term for "causing to stand" as law, and the two terms ("set aside," "establish") picture one law removed and another put in place to supersede it. The new law of Christ has brought final salvation and will carry though into eternity. This provides a proper close to the legal discussion and prepares the way for 10:19-25, which will challenge the readers to live out this new reality in their daily lives and segue into the exhortation (10:26-13:19) that will end this letter.

The will of God lived out in Jesus' life has not only led to the new covenant reality. It has also anchored a life of holiness for those of us who, like Jesus, have been obedient to that will (10:10). The results of the once-for-all (see 7:27; 9:7, 12, 26-28) sacrifice of the body of Jesus Christ are wondrous—both salvation and sanctification. The "we" shows that all believers are included. The Triune Godhead has given every single one of us the inner strength and spiritual power to live the life of victory exemplified in Christ himself.

Christ's surrender to the will of God is seen in its ultimate form: giving himself over to die on the cross. Not only is it the final proof of his life of obedience, but it provided atonement for sin and spiritual power to live for God never before seen. Through Jesus' self-sacrifice, we have true obedience exemplified, as well as salvation won. "Made holy" (vv. 10, 14, 29) refers to the consecration of the self to a life of service to God and a completely obedient lifestyle in which we live to please God in everything we do. The offering of the blood of Christ both provides the archetypal example of such sacrifice and becomes the source of spiritual strength by which we are enabled to follow that example.

THE ENTHRONED HIGH PRIEST (10:11–18)

THE EXALTED HIGH PRIEST (10:11–14)

The inadequacy of the old sacrificial system has dominated the last three chapters, been summarized once in 10:1–4, and now is encapsulated in a single powerful statement (10:11). The constant repetition demanded of the system (v. 11) is set in contrast with the "for all time" nature of Jesus' high priestly work (v. 12). The emphasis is on the "day after day" nature of the earthly priest's "religious duties" and the "again and again" quality of the "same sacrifices" (v. 11) needed to effect forgiveness and a relationship with God. It is never-ending and tedious, for no person ever experienced final results. The statement "stands and performs" (v. 11) is literally true. The priest never sat down while performing his religious duties (Deut 17:12; 18:5). The problem is that none of the sacred rites were truly effective in "taking away sins" (Heb 10:11). None lasted beyond the next sin. The priests served continuously for insufficient results.

Not so Jesus. He, as the high priest of heaven, has offered himself as a single sacrifice "for all time," and when his atoning sacrifice was finished, he "sat down (contra v. 11) at the right hand of God" (v. 12). To "sit" is to finish his work, and at the close, Jesus was exalted and enthroned in heaven, predicted in Psalm 110:1 and a key verse in the letter (see also 1:1, 13; 8:1; 12:2). There is an interesting contrast here in the Greek phrase *eis to diēnekes*, which in verse 1 means "endless repetition," and here in verse 12 means "offered for all time." The strong antithesis is quite cleverly done. The earthly priest never stopped, while Jesus, the heavenly high priest, sat down in exalted glory for all eternity. Here the cross, the empty tomb, and the exaltation in glory become a single event in salvation history, and its effects last throughout eternity.

The writer cites Psalm 110:1 once more (see 1:4, 13) in verse 13, "and since that time he waits for his enemies to be made his footstool." Yet in the time indicated in this short paragraph, this refers to the one event yet to arrive—namely, the cosmic victory of Christ over his (and our) enemies. The *single event* of verse 12 is past, and we are currently awaiting the event predicted in the last part of Psalm 110:1, "until I make your enemies a footstool for your feet." That will take place at the **eschaton**—second coming and last judgment. Now God's Son and high priest sits at his right hand, drawing history to a close. He (with us) "waits" (*ekdecho-menos*, referring to eager expectation of the event) for this final destruction of evil.

This is the moment every true follower of Christ longs for, when the powers of evil are brought to their knees, and the dark kingdom is destroyed. The "enemies" are all the purveyors of sin and debauchery in this world, beginning with Satan and the cosmic forces of darkness. The picture in Psalm 110:1 depicts Christ sitting on the heavenly throne at God's right hand, but it also includes him sitting on the white horse as conquering King (Rev 19:11–21). As this segues into the warning against apostasy (10:26–31), the weak believers are challenged to recognize that they, too, could become enemies of Christ.

Now the author returns to the holiness of verse 10 and shows how the enthroned Christ is at work in the lives of the faithful (10:14)—namely, the further effects of the "one sacrifice" that "has made perfect forever those who are being made holy." The previous two verses centered on Christ fulfilling Psalm 110:1, and now the author turns his attention to its effects on the faithful. Every term in this sentence is significant. The means "by" which God's people are perfected is the "one sacrifice—Jesus' high priestly fulfillment of the Day of Atonement and the atoning death of Jesus on the cross—and its effects last "forever" (v. 14; the same "for all time" language as in v. 12). There will never need be another sacrifice or offering, for those who come to Christ in faith and experience his atoning work are brought to perfection for all eternity.

The perfect tense "has made perfect" in verse 14 (*teteleiōken*) stresses the eternal state of being that results from Christ's work on the cross. The law could never do so (10:1a), and only Christ could "complete" the work of God in us and provide "perfect" access to him (10:1b). Christ has provided final forgiveness, and eternity is God's gift to us as a result. The emphasis again (as in 10:1) is not on sinless perfection so much as on total access to the Lord as we come to him in worship and prayer.

This perfect access and worship is part of the process[1] of sanctification, as we "are being made holy" (v. 14) with the present tense participle *hagiozomenous* stressing the ongoing nature of the process of holiness at work in our lives. We never cease growing in Christ. In Ephesians 4:13 Paul beautifully describes this as the process of "attaining to the whole measure of the fullness of Christ." Sanctification is the process by which we step by step become more like Christ, and this is a "perfect process" and goal for the Christian life.

LIBERATION UNDER THE NEW COVENANT (10:15–18)

The writer goes back to 8:7–13 and cites once more a portion of the new covenant prediction from Jeremiah 31:31–34 in order to draw everything together and culminate the deep theology of the last few chapters on the new covenant (8:1–10:18). Together, the two form an **inclusio** that frames these three chapters under the new covenant reality. In particular, he chooses that portion promising a deep inward knowledge of God and the forgiveness of sins (8:10, 12 from Jer 31:33b, 34c). In Hebrews 8 the author quoted the Jeremiah passage to indicate the end of the old covenant, and here uses it to show the perfection of the new covenant as fulfilled in Christ.

At the outset, the true Author—the Holy Spirit who penned this by inspiring Jeremiah—is highlighted as the divine witness

---

1. Some speak of this as a finished act and believe it describes not a process but the finished result of the believer's consecration to Christ. I prefer to give the present tense its full due and see this as the continual growth of the believer in Christ.

who "testifies to us about this" (v. 15). The content of his witness is undoubtedly the high priestly ministry and atoning sacrifice of Jesus as presented throughout this section. The emphasis is upon the Triune Godhead affirming the truth of this. The Father, Son, and Holy Spirit have intervened and solved the human dilemma, taking it upon themselves to lovingly bring forgiveness and salvation to fallen humanity. Christ's witness and intercession have been stressed throughout (10:5-7, 16a), and now the Spirit joins him in a symphony of attestation.

The finality and reality of the new covenant is seen here (10:16) as a gift from the Lord for the faithful. The stress throughout is on the personal pronoun "I." God is acting on their behalf, and his activity is personalized by substituting "with them" here for the impersonal "with the people of Israel" in 8:10. "After that time" means at the end of the old covenant age when the Mosaic system would be abolished and replaced by the new covenant in Christ. The readers (and us) are the recipients of these promises and now must live out that privileged existence day by day.

The author has chosen the beginning and the end of Jeremiah's four promised benefits to encapsulate them all. The internal nature of the new system (in their hearts, on their minds) contrasts greatly with the external nature and ritualistic forms in the old system. The new "laws" center on salvation and sanctification and involve an eternal state of forgiveness and being right with God. Following the pattern established by Christ, the resulting lifestyle will be one of obedience and faithfulness to God. The order of the two is reversed, with "heart" first, probably because a hardened heart was the primary cause of the failure of the wilderness generation (see 3:8, 10; 4:7).

The promise of forgiveness in verse 17 is especially stressed when the author comments, "Then he adds" to highlight it. The Levitical practices centered on a "reminder of sin" (10:3), while in the new order, God would "remember (their sins and lawless acts) no more." Here the writer adds "and lawless deeds" to the

Jeremiah quote to stress that God has forgiven all sins and sinful acts as a result of Christ's one-time atoning sacrifice. Forgiveness is universal and complete for those who repent and come in faith. They will not just be remitted—they will be stricken from God's memory; they will be no more.

This has all led to the final verse of the central section of 4:14–10:18, and it draws everything together. If all sins are forgiven for those who come to Christ, the conclusion is clear: "sacrifice for sin is no longer necessary." The Levitical regulations are no longer needed, for everyone relates completely to Christ and the cross in all salvific matters. Christ-followers have been decisively cleansed from sin, and thus no offerings will ever again be necessary.

————

This is the culminating section for the book so far and closes the emphasis on the superiority of Christ over the old covenant system (1:5–10:18). The first part demonstrates how the final purpose of the Levitical order was to prefigure the arrival of Christ and the new covenant era he would bring (vv. 1–4). The problem with the old, as we have seen, is that it did accomplish its purpose and enabled God's people to worship him and enjoy his presence, but it could not do away with sin. It dealt with one sin at a time and had to be reenacted every time a person committed another sin. It thus could not provide complete access to God; only Christ could do that. The sacrificial blood of the ceremonies had to be endlessly repeated, and still the sin problem would not go away.

In his commentary on the psalm, the writer first discusses what Christ has set aside (vv. 8–9a)—namely, the "sacrifices and offerings" of the Mosaic system, which have been inadequate for achieving lasting forgiveness for sins. Then he discusses what Christ has established (vv. 9b–10)—namely, his perfect obedience to the will of God that led him to give his life as a sacrifice for sin and inaugurated the new covenant age of salvation. This has also enabled the Christ-followers to live holy lives and consecrate themselves to God.

Finally, Jesus has become enthroned as the exalted high priest of heaven (vv. 11–14), and repentant sinners are liberated under the new covenant system he inaugurates (vv. 15–18). The purpose of the incarnation was for God's Son to enter this world and become the eternal high priest ("high priest forever" of Ps 110:4; see Heb 5:6). The Mosaic system proceeded by endless repetition and thus could never suffice, but Christ came and provided the once-for-all sacrifice that took away sin and brought eternal salvation. Moreover, he was enthroned in heaven as sovereign and high priest, awaiting that final victory when all the evil powers would become "footstools for his feet" (Ps 110:1). In so doing, he has "perfected," or completed, God's work among us and gave us perfect access to God so that we can grow in holiness.

Then, in Hebrews 10:15–18, the writer returns to Jeremiah 31:31–34 (see 8:7–13) to stress that it was the Triune Godhead who gave us the new covenant. He restates the first and last of Jeremiah's four promises to help us realize anew that in Christ, God's laws have been internalized (in our hearts and minds) and have become part of our very being and, as a result, our sins are forgiven and gone forever. The final verse (18) culminates, in a sense, all of chapters 5–10 when it concludes, "sacrifice for sin is no longer necessary." The one atoning sacrifice of Jesus on the cross has been an eternal act, and we are finally free from sin's evil tentacles.

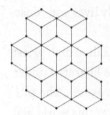

EXHORTATION TO WORSHIP
AND PERSEVERE
(10:19–39)

We are at the turning point of this magnificent letter. The theological presentation—an incredible contribution to our understanding of early church theology—is finished. The superiority of Jesus over the Mosaic law and the new covenant over the Old is now complete. Thus the writer turns to exhortation, challenging the readers to persevere and remain faithful to Christ in their daily lives. This will be the theme for the rest of the letter (10:19–13:21).

The opening paragraph (10:19–25) provides the second great transition passage of the letter, after 4:14–16. The material in between (5:1–10:18) carries the central message: Jesus as the heavenly high priest offering himself as the atoning sacrifice for sins and launching the new covenant era. The goal is to bring those among fallen humanity who repent to God's salvation and enable them to find redemption. So the rest of the letter will apply the theology of this middle section and seek to spur the readers to act and remain faithful to the Triune Godhead who provided all this.

CALL TO PERSEVERE IN WORSHIP (10:19-25)
The next two sections could be labeled the yin and yang of faithful perseverance, with verses 19-25 providing the positive side, the

blessings attendant on drawing near to God, and verses 26–31 the negative counterpart, the terrible consequences of apostatizing from the faith. For years this first passage (vv. 19–25) has been one of my favorite choices when I want to preach on the benefits of giving our all to Christ. The middle chapters have proven completely that Jesus the Christ is indeed the Son of God and high priest of our faith and that we are living in the new covenant age and experience all the benefits of being Christ-followers. Now we see what kind of difference those blessings entail for our daily lives.

This paragraph is actually a single sentence of continuous admonition, applying the truths developed in the letter and with all this in mind. The first part (vv. 19–21) is causal ("since"), summing up God's great gift from 5:1–10:18 with two privileges—first, what Christ has done for us (vv. 19–20, the bold entrance he has effected into the most holy place in the heavenly sanctuary); and second, what Christ has become for us (v. 21: "a great priest over the house of God"). The author informs us what we have in Christ and then what we should do with it. This latter comes to us via commands (vv. 22–25), a string of three hortatory subjunctives ("let us" commands), which enumerate our responsibility. Interestingly, the three center on the three main blessings—draw near in faith (v. 22), hold firmly onto hope (v. 23), and spur one another to love (vv. 24–25).

The Basis for Life under the New Covenant (10:19–21)

The first of the two privileges (namely, what benefits we have in Christ) is found in verses 19–20 and relates our newfound confidence (*parrēsia*), which can subjectively mean "boldness" and objectively mean "authorization." The boldness aspect is primary, though both are likely part of the thrust. Christ as high priest has "authorized" our entry into the sanctuary of heaven, and that leads to our confidence as we enter.

Still, the new access to God was beyond the ability of all Jewish believers to comprehend. Lay people could not get beyond the court of Israel in the sanctuary, priests beyond the outer courts, while once in their lifetime (like Zechariah in Luke 1), they may be chosen to minister in the holy place. Once a year, the high priest could enter the holy of holies, but only because he represented the nation rather than himself when he did so. So the thought that in the new covenant believers had constant access into the very presence of God was almost too much to accept. The confidence and boldness was ultimate in every way.

On the basis of Christ's blood sacrifice, our boldness is "to enter" (*eisodon*) the holy of holies directly. There is quite a bit of background to this earlier in the letter. In 6:19-20 our new hope in Christ affords our "entry" into "the inner sanctuary behind the curtain." Then in 8:1-2 it is Christ as heavenly high priest who is enthroned and "serves in the sanctuary, the true tabernacle," thereby affording us our place there as well. In 9:11-12 it is Christ's blood that has brought about our "eternal redemption" by enabling him to pass through "the greater and more perfect tabernacle." Finally, in 9:24 Christ never entered the earthly temple after his death on the cross but rather the true temple in heaven itself, appearing in God's presence on our behalf.

As we accompany Jesus, our "high priest forever" (5:5), into the most holy place, we enter via "a new and living way opened for us through the curtain, that is, his body" (10:20). As I said above, no person on their own authority was ever allowed to enter the holy of holies.[1] Christ's high priestly act of offering his own blood as a substitute for each one of us has afforded "a new and living way" into the very presence of God that enables us to enter with him. This entryway is "new" because it is the heart of the new covenant age he has brought into this world. It is "living" because it means we have eternal "life" in him through it. This way, we are told, has been "opened for us," employing the verb *enkainizō*, which is seen

---

1. Only the high priest could enter the holy of holies once a year, and then only because he represented the nation.

in NIV and many expositions as meaning a way "opened" and providing access to God (see 6:19–20; 9:12). However, in 9:18 this same verb speaks of the "inauguration" or "putting into effect" of the Mosaic covenant, and it might refer to the dedication or consecration here of the new covenant. Both nuances may be present here.

This new opening is effected "through the curtain, that is, his body." The picture is of the veil separating the holy place from the most holy place, with the high priest passing through it on the Day of Atonement. Christ has fulfilled that imagery via his atoning sacrifice for sin, and when he ascends to his heavenly sanctuary, he effects a once-for-all entry that produces eternal salvation (5:9; 9:12, 15). Eternal access to our loving Father is the result. Moreover, he further defines this curtain as "his body" (tēs sarkos autou; literally, "his flesh").

A major question is whether "his flesh" modifies "way" (he entered via his blood sacrifice) or "curtain" (seen as the barrier preventing access to the holy of holies and presence of God). In the latter sense, Christ would be removing that separation forever. In actuality, both make much the same sense, but grammatically the curtain or veil is primary, and Christ via his bodily sacrifice has caused the veil to in a sense be torn in two (the imagery at the crucifixion, Matthew 27:51), making access to God permanent for believers. Thereby God's people are strengthened and enabled to persevere on their pilgrimage through this life.

The second of the two privileges we have in Christ (vv. 19–21) summarizes the main christological truth of Hebrews, in which Christ is presented in 10:21 as "the exalted or great (Ps 110:1 in Heb 1:3, 13; 8:1; 10:12; 12:2) priest over the house of God (Ps 110:4 in Heb 5:6; 6:20; 7:17, 21)." The very Son of God became incarnate and gave himself as the atoning sacrifice that cleansed sins and brought forgiveness. "Great priest" was a common appellation for the high priest as the greatest of all God's priests. Here it looks to Christ's sovereign authority and power as the high priest of heaven who has finally nullified the power of sin.

In a sense, this recapitulates 3:1–6, where Moses is seen as honored for serving over God's house, and Christ has the greater honor as the builder of that house. In 3:6 Christ is "faithful as the Son over God's house." In the Old Testament, God's household is the people of Israel, and now it is the church as the followers of Christ. God's people in both covenants are his family, and Christ is sovereign over them as they remain faithful to him.

THE VICTORIOUS LIFE OF PERSEVERANCE (10:22–25)

All three commands are present tense here, stressing the ongoing nature of the reactions to our bold access to God that Christ has effected. They are in perfect synchrony, with the first the vertical or Godward side of the Christian life, the second a blend of the vertical and horizontal or fellowship-oriented side of the Christian life, and the third the horizontal. Together they powerfully describe what it means to be a Christ-follower.

A life of pure worship (10:22)

The first is to "draw near" in worship, detailing our response to the new access to God Christ has made possible. Obviously, worship and prayer (4:16; 7:25; 11:6; 12:22) are upmost in the writer's mind. The "how-to" is then presented in four parts, two prepositional phrases followed by two participial clauses, all of them showing what constitutes a God-centered lifestyle:

1. "A sincere heart"—This is, first of all, a pure or true heart and second, a single-minded heart, focused entirely on the Lord. The "sincere or true heart" (*alēthinēs*) is the polar opposite of the "hardened" heart that is "always going astray" as with the wilderness people of 3:8, 10; the "sinful, unbelieving heart that turns away from the living God" in 3:12. This is the new heart of Jeremiah 31:33 (Heb 8:10) in which God has written his new laws of the kingdom and that thereby lives in obedience to those truths.

2. "The full assurance that faith brings"—This flows out of the single-minded heart and describes "the fullness (*plērophoria*) of faith," likely meaning in a general sense the full or complete life that faith in Christ produces as well as the specific "full assurance" (also 6:11) of certainty that realization of Christ's sovereignty over this world provides. The future is no longer uncertain regarding things that truly matter, for the Godhead supervises their world and guarantees the demise of evil. With this, we can truly know that "all things work together for good" (Rom 8:28 ESV).

3. "Our hearts sprinkled to cleanse us from a guilty conscience"—Employing imagery from the sacrificial system, this becomes a powerful metaphor for conversion and consecration to ministry. When Aaron and his sons were consecrated into their priestly office, they were washed with water and sprinkled with blood and anointing oil (Exod 29:4, 21; 30:30; Lev 8:6, 30; Num 8:7). Moreover, at the covenant ceremony of Exodus 24:8, Moses sprinkled the people with the blood of the sacrificed young bulls. So this pictures believers brought into a new covenant relation with God at conversion and inaugurated as priests to serve God all their lives (Exod 19:5, 6; Isa 61:6; Rev 1:6; 5:10). "Sprinkling from an evil conscience" especially stresses the forgiveness of sins that is a prerequisite for the Christian life. This cleansing is not external and incomplete like in the sacrificial system but is internal and final, true conversion from a life of sin.

4. "Bodies washed with pure water"—This is virtually synonymous with the previous, representing the outward sign for the internal cleansing just discussed. It is debated whether this is speaking of Christian baptism, for many think it is simply referring to the Old

Testament imagery of ritual cleansings. However, it is
hard to think of a first-century believer reading this
without thinking of baptism. Still, the emphasis is on
the imagery of cleansing rather than the act itself. As
1 Peter 3:21 makes clear, baptism is not a salvific event
but a "pledge" made by a "good conscience" to serve
God, exactly the meaning here. In Ezekiel 36:25-26,
the sprinkling and cleansing provides a new heart
and puts a new spirit in the people to serve God.

The confession of our hope (10:23)

"Hold unswervingly" (*katechōmen*) is a major verb used for persevering in the faith and remaining true to the traditional truths of
Christianity (see also 3:6, 14; 4:14). This, in effect, tells how we draw
near to God and serve him boldly (v. 22). This is strengthened by
the addition of *aklinē*, "firmly, unswervingly," which demands all
our effort in remaining true to Christ. In the author's mind is both
true doctrine and true Christian practice, the heart and the mind.
The rapid growth of Christian creeds like 1 Corinthians 15:3-8,
Colossians 1:15-20, and Philippians 2:6-11 was for this purpose, providing official statements of doctrinal truth to help the saints persevere. It could be said that virtually everything written in the New
Testament relates to this: reaching the lost and strengthening the
faithful. We remain "firm" in Christ by holding fast to these truths
and allowing them to guide our beliefs and our conduct. This is
why I am producing these commentaries: to help Christians to
understand what God has done and requires of us and to enable
them to be as excited as I am about the privilege of studying and
applying these truths to my life.

The content behind our perseverance is "the hope we profess."
For us as believers, "hope" is not an uncertain quest with few guarantees. For the unbeliever, hope is always ephemeral and without
an anchor in reality. However, for the child of God, hope looks to
a certain future that has not yet unfolded but has been grounded

in God's sovereignty over his creation. So for us hope is very real and concrete, for our future ends in an eternity in heaven with the Lord, the angels, and all the saints. This is the same command as in Hebrews 3:6 ("hold firmly ... [to] the hope in which we glory"), 6:11, 18 ("what you hope for may be fully realized"), 6:19 ("hope as an anchor for the soul"), and 7:19 ("a better hope ... by which we draw near to God"). This term sums up the meaning of perseverance in Hebrews. A great Bible study would be to take these passages on hope and put them together, deriving the message.

This hope is "professed" or "confessed" (*homologian*), an act that is both upward (the worship of God) and outward (the corporate witness of the church). The early church cared deeply about dogmatic truth and rehearsed it often. In recent years, that love for truth has somehow been lost, and feelings have taken over the church. It has gotten easier and easier for false teachers to flourish in the pulpit, for so long as they work the emotions, people will flock after them. We must learn that biblical truth and living the Christian life to please God are exciting and necessary goals for church worship and life.

The reason for centering on our hope in Christ is that "he who promised is faithful." Christin hope is based on taking God's promises seriously. When we realize the truth of this, it is easy to get excited about our future. Our sovereign Lord is absolutely trustworthy and faithful, and he always keeps his promises. That is at the heart of the doctrine of the security of the believer. The future is in his hands, and he will not leave you or forsake you (Gen 28:15; Deut 31:6, 8; Josh 1:5). We can be faithful to him because he is eternally faithful to us.

Spur one another to love and good deeds (10:24-25)

We have now come to the purely horizontal side of the Christian life: corporate fellowship. As we will see in Hebrews chapter 12, this is a primary antidote to apostasy, as the members of God's family continue to challenge each other to cast off their prevailing sins and remain faithful to the Lord. This is not just your average exhortation to good works. It goes two steps beyond that, commanding the saints first to stimulate each other to do so and second to look for ways to do so. The church is to become a manufacturing center, and the major product to transport far and wide is good deeds.

"Consider how" (v. 24) is *katanoōmen,* "pay close attention," transliterated as "look for ways to" do a thing. We are not to be passive, waiting for opportunities, but active, creating opportunities not only to show love but to teach others how to do so as well. This is especially seen in the verb that follows, "spur one another on" *(paroxysmon),* which could be translated, "incite one another to a riot" of love and good works. The author wants visible expressions of the deep love that binds the church together to explode and shock everyone. One of the best witnesses and evangelistic tools for God's people is this sense of love and the gift of helping. When people are going through hard times, they need to know that there is one group that will always be there for them— their fellow brothers and sisters in Christ.

"Love and good works"[2] are two sides of the same coin. Love is the supercharged feeling of selfless caring and giving that molds us into the body of Christ, and good works are the visible sign of that love in the church. This is the polar opposite of the way society works in our secular world. There the mood is that of entitlement and self-gratification, of taking rather than giving. In Christ, the other is placed first. Rather than "What can you do for me?" it is, "What can I do for you?"

Verse 24 tells *what* needs to be done, and verse 25 centers on *how* it can be done. In times of trouble, it is easy to dig a hole and crawl in to lose yourself in it. Christ has established a community of love in which we turn to each other. The weak Christians in these house churches had lost the sense of identity and were

---

2. The term often used is hendiadys, when two words flow together and translate each other. Good deeds are the practical expression of love in the church.

retreating into themselves. So they had to refuse to "give up meeting together" and seek each other out for encouragement and help. Literally, they were abandoning "the assembling of yourselves,"[3] first of all referring to the weekly worship service, but at the same time, including the regular times of fellowship as a group. The saints are a family and must live like one, maintaining a oneness and the need for one another. Scholars often realize that the writer has in mind the community of the last days, the "church of the firstborn, whose names are written in heaven" (12:22–24). The end times have begun (see below on "the Day approaching"), and we are the people who will usher in eternity. As such, we must live like this now. Our church services are a touch of heaven and are meant to lead us home!

Those "in the habit of doing" so—namely, separating themselves off from the rest of the church—are the *nōthroi* Christians (lazy, sluggish) of 5:11–6:12 (the term occurs in 5:11 and 6:12), those in serious danger of apostatizing. They had become worldly and were abandoning each other and thinking about returning to their former Jewish roots. This is the problem behind the whole letter. These people thought they were strong enough to go it alone but actually displayed their weakness to all.

Our task as God's community of the last days is to encourage one another, which draws together material from many places on the need to be involved in each other's lives (3:13; 12:5; 13:22). Every one of us goes through periods of discouragement and defeat, and we need our brothers and sisters in Christ to jolt us awake at such times and help us realize we are not, nor dare we be, alone at such times. The basic meaning of *parakaleō* is "to exhort," and this includes both negative admonition (3:13) and positive encouragement (here). Clearly, both are essential ministry tools for the saints.

---

3. The Greek is *tēn episynagōgēn heautōn*, which literally is "synagoguing together" and connotes an atmosphere of togetherness and sharing as the people of God.

In fact, the author concludes that this becomes all the more critical "as you see the Day approaching" (10:25). This is the day of the Lord when Christ returns and this world as we know it ends. There is both a positive and a negative aspect to this. Positively, this evil world is going to end and faithful believers receive their eternal reward. This encourages us to live in light of the certain knowledge that all wrongs will be righted and all our sacrifices rewarded. Negatively, as we will see in 13:17, we will "give account" to the Lord at the **parousia** and final judgment. The question is, do we want to stand before the throne in joy, knowing we have "fought the good fight" and are receiving "the crown of righteousness" (2 Tim 2:7, 8), or in shame, knowing we have mishandled "the word of truth" (2 Tim 2:15)? We must get serious about our obligations to the Lord.

FURTHER WARNING AGAINST APOSTASY (10:26-31)

THE DEADLY PROGRESSION OF SIN (10:26-27)

The logic here follows closely that of 6:4-6. These are second-generation Christians who grew up in the church and had enough teaching behind them to be teachers in the church (5:12). However, many of them were following the pattern of the wilderness generation in the exodus (3:1-4:13) and falling into serious error. The theme of receiving biblical truth is often in the Pastoral Letters (1 Tim 2:4; 4:3; 2 Tim 2:25; 3:7; Titus 1:1) and John (John 8:32; 1 John 2:21) and highlights the salvific force of God's revelation. This is not just intellectual awareness but embraces real knowledge. These are members of the church, and "truth" here is a semi-technical word for the gospel of Christ.

We have spent the last several chapters centering on all that Christ has accomplished with his incarnation as Son of God and his high priestly ministry that brings atonement and forgiveness to sinful humanity. This is an unbelievable privilege, but it also places a great obligation on us to live lives worthy of all he has done for us. When those who have grown up in the church (like these have) fail to live by it, they are in grave trouble. The warning here is very much needed.

Two factors make the sin particularly heinous. It is continuous, and it is deliberate (called sinning "defiantly" in Num 15:22–31; see Prov 2:13–14) in direct defiance of God. They obviously delight in thwarting God and persist, turning it from an act into a lifestyle. They know it is wrong, and that just makes them enjoy it all the more. It should not be surmised that persistence in sin is always apostasy, for that is untrue. Apostasy includes willful sin but goes a critical step beyond in consciously repudiating God and Christ. The person caught in ongoing sin can be brought back to the Lord and find forgiveness (Jas 5:19–20), while the person who actively and willfully rejects Christ cannot be brought back (Heb 6:4–6). Unintentional sins could be forgiven via the sacrificial system, but intentional sins could not and meant rejection and removal of the covenant status as an Israelite

The results (10:26b–27) parallel 6:6 in their terrible nature. First, "no sacrifice for sins is left" (v. 26). As we just saw, sins with a high hand could not be forgiven, and no sacrifice would suffice. So this is a metaphor for an unforgivable sin against God (Mark 3:28–30). Moreover, Christ has become high priest of heaven, and his blood sacrifice on the cross has ended the sacrificial system. So when he and his sacrifice are rejected, there is no other way to find forgiveness.

The only thing remaining for such people is "a fearful expectation of judgment" (v. 27). Several have noted that in this context, *phobera* might better be translated "terrifying," for nothing could be more terrible than the end that is awaiting these people. For these people, judgment is not merely a possibility but a certain prospect. Nothing can keep them from this end, for they have gone over the cliff in their rebellion against God and become his implacable "enemies." The "judgment" is the final judgment of Revelation 20:11–15, the Great White Throne that will end with the "raging fire that will consume the enemies of God" (Heb 10:27)—namely, the lake of fire.

The language here is of *pyros zēlos*, a "fiery zeal" that consumes those who oppose God. Here it is seen as the inevitable destiny of these apostates. This fiery end is more than a mere metaphor. Jesus spoke of it as Gehenna (Matt 5:22, 29–30; 10:28), speaking of them being "thrown into the fires of hell" (Matt 18:9). This is an allusion to Isaiah 26:11, which spoke of "the fire reserved for your enemies [that will] consume them." We will not know until the end arrives how literal this is, but it seems to speak of an actual judgment event at the close of history.[4] The universality of this image makes me think it is more than a mere metaphor.

THE SEVERITY OF THE JUDGMENT (10:28–29)

The writer uses another of his *a fortiori* arguments (lesser to greater; see 2:1–4; 9:13–14) to underline the necessity of strict judgment. Under the Mosaic law an apostate "died without mercy on the testimony of two or three witnesses." The person who had turned to idols and repudiated the God of Israel for foreign gods was to be executed without mercy (Deut 13:8; 17:1–6). But this involved only physical death. Under the new covenant it was "much more severe," involving spiritual death, eternal in scope (Heb 10:29).

Three reasons are provided for so severe a penalty (paralleling 6:6):

1. "Trampled the Son of God underfoot"—The open contempt of 6:6 ("subjecting [the Son of God] to open disgrace") continues here (see also Zech 12:3; Matt 5:13; 7:6), likely including a denial of his deity (seen in "Son of God" here). God has made Christ his Son and part of the Triune Godhead, but these arrogant rebels have

---

4. See the emphasis on "fiery" punishment in Num 26:10; Ps 21:9; 78:5; Zeph 1:18; Matt 3:10–12; 25:41; 1 Cor 3;13; 2 Thess 1:8; 1 Pet 1:7 among others.

mocked that and, in effect, "trampled" him underfoot into the dust. No wonder God will make them "a footstool for his feet" (Ps 110:1 in Heb 1:13)!

2. "Treated as an unholy thing the blood of the covenant that sanctified them"—The entire central section of the letter has stressed the sacred character of the "blood of the covenant"—that is, Jesus' blood sacrifice that has instigated the new age of salvation. Those who apostatize will have mocked that sacrifice and "treated it as an unholy thing." The Greek is *koinon hēgēsamenos*, "considered it common or profane." While the first reason involved contempt, this one looks at indifference. These people consider Christ's sacrificial death irrelevant and of no worth. His was just another tragic death of an innocent person. Both Christ's person and his work are of no consequence and simply don't matter.

3. "Insulted the Spirit of grace"—The movement has been from contempt to indifference to insult. It is clear that those who have committed these despicable acts are no longer Christians. The Spirit of grace is, of course, the Holy Spirit. The title sums up the grace of God evident throughout this letter. The Spirit is the means by which God's grace is given to his people and experienced by them, and these rebels have "insulted" all that he is and has done on their behalf. They have been given the gifts of the Spirit (2:4) and become partakers of the Spirit (6:4) and then have thrown it all away. The verb (*enybrizō*) means not only to "insult" but to "outrage." It is possible there is a double meaning here—and that this connotes the wrath of God behind his reaction to such hubris on the part of these apostates.

THE TERRIFYING JUDGMENT (10:30–31)

Two quotes from Moses' farewell in Deuteronomy 32 close this section. This was the Song of Moses, which celebrated God delivering his people and punishing their enemies. These apostates have now joined the enemies of God and must suffer the consequences. The two quotes are from the latter part of the hymn and come from the same context: divine justice, which both vindicates his people and destroys their enemies. The first, from 32:35a, is "It is mine to avenge; I will repay," where God promises he will repay all the hurts inflicted on his people. It is also used in Romans 12:19 and shows God will extract his vengeance against all enemies, including those of Israel and the church who turn against him. No one is exempt, and his justice will prevail.

The second quote stems from the very next verse, 32:36a: "The Lord will judge his people." This makes explicit what was implicit in the preceding quote, that God's own people are included in the extremely serious warning. The readers of this letter cannot consider themselves free of responsibility just because they are members of the church. The warning of 1 Peter 4:17 is a apropos: "For it is time for judgment to begin with God's household." We are all mandated to remain faithful to the Lord at all times and in all things. God will vindicate his people, but they must remain deserving of his mercy and grace. That vindication will mean the judgment of the unfaithful.

The whole argument of this section (10:26–31) has led to this conclusion: "It is a dreadful thing to fall into the hands of the living God." Being the covenant people is a joyful, wondrous privilege but also an incredible, terrifying responsibility. The awesome persona of the Holy God is in view. He is not like dead idols but is a living, terrifying God. To fall into his hands is to experience his wrath and judgment. This could be an allusion to Deuteronomy 32:39–42, where God declares, "I put to death, and I bring to life ... and no one can deliver out of my hand ... I will take vengeance on my adversaries and repay those who hate me." God is a God of love and grace to those who remain true but a terrible, fiery God of judgment to those who flaunt his mercy. Those who allow themselves to be drawn back to the world should quake in fear.

THE CALL TO PERSEVERANCE (10:32-39)

REMEMBER PAST FAITHFULNESS (10:32-35)

After the severe warning against apostasy in 6:4-8, the writer turned to encouragement to persevere in 6:9-12, and he follows the same pattern here with 10:32-39 after the warning of 26-31. They are a second-generation church, and he is asking them to bring to mind the previous group of believers, many of them undoubtedly the parents of current members. They had passed through every bit as difficult a time of persecution as these people had and triumphed over the hard times.

These weak Christians are told to "remember those earlier days" when things were different and no warning was needed. This was when they were young believers who were thrilled at having "received the light"—namely, the light of God in Christ that had launched their faith journey. After their "enlightenment" they had undergone "a great conflict full of suffering." The NIV's "conflict" is actually "contest" (*athlēsin*, transliterated "athletic"), an athletic metaphor for the arena sports like the Olympics that were very popular in the first century (see 12:1-3). "Suffering" was an important concept in these events, depicting the disciplined training that gave them victory in these sporting contests. So enduring suffering was seen as the path to victory. Such imagery is frequent in the New Testament for the disciplined Christian life as the path to victory over sin and evil (1 Cor 9:24-27; Phil 3:12-14; 2 Tim 2:5; 4:6-8; Heb 12:1-2, 12-13).

The writer then reminds them (10:33-34) of particular times when their predecessors had passed through difficult times to say, in effect, "You can do this too." Both in times of personal trials and public mockery, they had been called upon to endure greatly for Christ. "Exposed to insult" parallels 11:26 and 13:13, where we are called to bear the same "disgrace" (*oneidismos*) that Christ suffered. Property was confiscated, and both homes and businesses were frequently plundered. They not only were persecuted privately; they often had to "stand side by side with those who were so treated," a good illustration of Galatians 6:2, "carry each other's burdens." The persecution was not only verbal but physical, as *thlipsesin* often indicates physical afflictions. Like Stephen and Paul in Acts, they were beaten and at times slain for being Christians.

As said in the introduction, these house churches were probably in Rome, where, in the early years of the church, fellow Jews were the main oppressors. The riots against Christians became so severe that in AD 49, the emperor Claudius expelled the Jews and Christians from Rome. From that time on, Roman persecution predominated, which included loss of property and jobs, imprisonment, and, in extreme cases, loss of life.

There is an A-B-B-A **chiastic** pattern between verses 33 and 34, with A = their suffering and B = helping others who have suffered. In verse 34 several of these are mentioned. Imprisonment would occur when they were designated enemies of the state, often because, as Christians, they refused to worship the Roman gods, while participation in the Roman religious cultus was legally required. The Jews had received a Roman exception to worship Yahweh, and for a time Rome extended this exception to Christians, whom they thought were a Jewish sect. However, the Jews argued strongly this was not the case, and that often led to trouble.

The reason they could "joyfully accept" the loss of their property was the knowledge that "you yourselves have better and lasting possessions" in heaven. It was superior both in quality (better) and quantity (lasting), for it would never fade away or disappear. This is knowledge gained through trials—that worldly possessions are fleeting and don't count, while heavenly reward is eternal in scope. We are "citizens of heaven" (Phil 3:20) and aliens to the things of earth (1 Pet 1:1, 17; 2:11). It takes trials of the faith to learn that critical lesson.

This lesson is made explicit in Hebrews 10:35 and is a challenge but also an indictment of these second-generation Christians who have failed to apply this to their lives. They are to cling to their "confidence" and refuse to "throw [it] away." In mind are these weak, lethargic Christians who are discouraged and on the verge of giving up on their faith walk with Christ. "Confidence" is *parrēsia*, "boldness," an important term in Hebrews with a twofold thrust: bold access to God (4:16; 10:19) and courageous confession of Christ in the face of opposition and persecution (3:6 and here).

There are two antidotes to apostasy in Hebrews, the vertical side (centering on the Triune Godhead in our lives) and the horizontal side (confessing Christ and admonishing one another). The previous generation had done so (vv. 32–34) and triumphed over their adversity. The readers had better get their act together while there is still time, lest they go down to ignominious spiritual defeat.

They need to center on the promise: if they do so, they "will be richly rewarded." This is another major concept in Hebrews, negatively picturing the "just punishment" for sin in 2:2 but primarily describing God repaying those who have sacrificed for him (here and 11:7, 26). While the "reward" to an extent is earthly and spiritual, referring to God's blessings poured out in the lives of the faithful, the primary thrust is final heavenly reward, linked to God's promises in verses 36–37. In 11:13 the patriarchs "did not receive" the promises but "welcomed them from a distance." In 11:39 this "great reward" is not given in the present but is heavenly, since God has "planned something better for us." So we are called upon to await the fulfillment of his promises in the great heavenly reward that will be ours for faithful service.

THE NECESSITY OF PERSEVERANCE (10:36–39)

This is the positive counterpart to the previous prohibition not to "throw away your confidence." In light of the terrible consequences of failure, the greatest "need" in their life is to "persevere" in Christ. Inspiring "endurance" (*hypomonēs*) is the goal of this entire last portion of the letter (10:19–13:20) and one of the primary themes of this work as a whole. The danger noted in every section is "drifting away" (2:1) from the faith, which characterized the wilderness people of 3:1–4:13, whose failure was caused by a hardened heart and a failure to persevere in their faith/belief. Overcoming faith is the reason the first-generation Christians of Rome triumphed (10:32), and here it is the greatest need the current generation has. In chapter 12, running the race with perseverance is to be the hallmark of the mature Christian community (12:1, 3, 7).

Perseverance is defined in what follows, where we see it is "continuing to do the will of God." This is the true heart of the issue. Christ has set the model for the life of obedience to the will of God (10:7, 9–10), and it can be said that following his will is the true sign of the victorious Christian life. As Paul says in Romans 12:2, the goal of such a life is to "test and approve" that God's will is best for us, leads to a lifestyle that is pleasing both to ourselves and God and is absolutely perfect for a successful and satisfying life.

In Hebrews, promise and reward are closely intertwined, and that is now made absolutely clear, where the reward is defined as "receiving what he has promised." Promise is a critical component earlier (4:1, 8; 6:12, 17; 8:6) and will become the primary concept in chapter 11, where the faith heroes of the past are seen to strive for God's future promises rather than for present glory or riches (11:9, 13, 17, 33, 39). The promised reward is the inheritance in heaven awaiting those who persevere (1:14; 6:12, 17; 9:15), and we have the same choice as the saints of the past: to live for earthly, temporary riches or heavenly, eternal reward. Will we believe and heed the secular voices of this world or the promises of God?

This paragraph follows the same pattern as the previous, with challenge (26–29 = 35–36) followed by two Old Testament citations (30 = 37–38) and then a conclusion (31 = 39). These are used to show that both testaments center on the need to persevere in the light of the imminent coming of the day of the Lord / return of Christ. The passage chosen here is Habakkuk 2:3–4, a judgment oracle against the sins of Israel and of the Babylonians. God used the Chaldeans to punish the evils of Judah, but Habakkuk wonders when he will punish the even more evil Babylonians. The message is that he would not tarry, and her condemnation is every bit as certain. Building on 10:25, "the Day approaching," the writer applies this theme to these weak Christians, warning them that God remains just, and they had better get right with him.

Three changes are made to the original Hebrew text and form the basis of its message, in which the Masoretic Text (MT = Hebrew) is impersonal, the **Septuagint** (LXX = Greek) is messianic, and the author applies it to believers in the present:

1. The writer begins with a short addition from Isaiah 26:20, "In just a little while" (Heb 10:37), where in a similar judgment context Isaiah speaks of patience in light of God's imminent action. He is quite alarmed with the spiritual condition of these people and so wants to highlight the "today" side of decision (see 3:7, 13, 15) and the imminence of judgment for those who fail to respond.

2. The text is largely drawn from the Septuagint version of Habakkuk 2. The LXX changed the impersonal coming of judgment to the personal coming of the Messiah to bring the judgment day by adding the definite article to "will certainly come," producing a messianic title, "he who is coming." Also, the MT speaks of the pride of the invader, and the LXX changes it to the need for faithfulness on the part of the Messiah ("the righteous one"). The author makes it faithfulness on the part of the messianic community ("my righteous one").

3. The final form is not actually too different from the MT or LXX in its basic message, which is: the Lord is

coming soon. Be faithful and do not shrink back. The
writer is, in effect, saying that if they do shrink back,
they will be like unfaithful Israel, and the judgment
will fall on them.

The first half of the quote centers on the imminent return of
the Messiah and the judgment he will bring. The Coming One in
Habakkuk 2:3 is God himself, but for the Septuagint and the text
here, it is the coming Messiah. Justice will finally be served, and
the evil that has characterized these people will receive its just
reward. Even though God seems to delay his justice, it is still certain and coming soon. Since his coming judgment is framed with
"a little while ... will not delay," that message is strongly emphasized. God and Christ are not weak and uncertain Lords of the universe; messianic judgment is coming in their own time, and that
time is very near.

The second part (Heb 10:38) shows the expected response to
this incredible news, completely thrilling for the faithful and
totally devastating for the unfaithful. Both in Habakkuk and
Hebrews, "the righteous one" is the persevering believer whose
behavior matches their commitment and who "will live by faith."
"Faith" comes to the fore in the next two chapters (twenty-four
times in chapter 11) and depicts not the believing mindset of the
faithful but their active lifestyle. To "live by faith" means to make
the Christian faith the barometer for all decisions. Habakkuk 2:3–4
was a major text for the early church, becoming a critical text in
both Romans 1:17 and Galatians 3:11.

The author is saying that a new crisis has arisen similar to
that faced by God's people in Habakkuk. Back then, their failure to respond in faith led to the exile, and that is the danger in
the present time as well. In fact, it led to a similar result for the
Jewish people just a few years from the penning of this letter, as
the destruction of Jerusalem and the temple occurred in AD 68–70.

For the church, many decades—even centuries—of serious persecution awaited.

God warns the church as he did Israel in Habakkuk, "I take no pleasure in the one who shrinks back" (Heb 10:38)—namely, the failed apostate. This is deliberate on the part of the writer, for in the LXX of Habakkuk 2:3-4, the clauses ("live by my faith" and "draws back") are reversed, and the latter applies to the Messiah who delays coming ("If he is late, wait for him"). By changing the order, it is God's people who are in danger of living by faith and then shrinking back. So this is an emphatic warning against weak Christian commitment that can fall away from the faith and, at the same time, a positive encouragement to boldly march forward in faith, trusting the Lord to enable us to triumph over the opposing forces of evil.

As in 6:9 ("we are convinced of better things in your case"), the author tries to encourage them that this dim picture does not apply to them (10:39). He includes himself with them ("*we* do not belong to those") as not to be included among the apostates ("who shrink back and are destroyed"). There is a strong sense of assurance in the midst of the frightening danger, for he is convinced that they like himself belong "to those who have faith and are saved." This is tied closely to verse 38 and reverses the order to provide a counter to the danger of "shrinking back" from 'the faith." Still, the danger is very real and demands immediate attention.

As a result, they belong to those followers of Christ who persevere in their faith and "are saved." The Greek is actually "of faith for the preserving of the soul" and pictures the spiritual security that persevering in faith produces. The apostate will be destroyed, but the faithful will be preserved by God and attain eternal rewards. This leads quite naturally into the faith chapter (11:1-40), where the heroic faithful of the past provide a plethora of examples as to how this faith-life can be lived out and triumph in the end. Those who persist in trusting God and Jesus in the midst of pressure and opposition from the world will join these great names of the past on the podium of heaven as they receive their gold medals from Christ.

———

This is the second turning point of the letter (with 4:14-16) and leads into the closing admonitions to persevere in Christ. It is an incredible passage, with the opening paragraph (10:19-25) summing up what it means to be a Christian as well as anywhere in Scripture. The first part of the paragraph is the why (vv. 19-21) — we must turn to Christ and grow in him because he has opened up the most holy place to us and made access to God permanent and complete with his one-time sacrifice. At the same time, he has become the heavenly high priest who has brought final salvation and forgiveness of sin into this world.

This leads to the three commands that describe the Christian life for those who put their faith in Christ (vv. 22-25). The first is the unbridled and bold worship that is now ours to enjoy, as we come to God single-mindedly—fully assured that God will hear and respond—and completely clean, cleansed, and devoid of guilt thanks to our faith in Christ. Second, we have the joy of boldly confessing our hope that has been guaranteed by Christ: our future is absolutely secure. And third, we have the privilege of stimulating our brothers and sisters in Christ so that they can enjoy serving one another and forging together a dynamic community in him. The Lord is returning soon, and we must be ready to meet him.

The next section gets us back into the problem of apostasy (vv. 26-31). The severity of the sin (vv. 26-27) brings a corresponding severity of judgment. This apostasy is not just a passive sliding into sin but an active provocation of God, called "sin with a high hand" in Numbers 15:22-31 because it is deliberate and committed continually as an act of contempt for the Lord. Therefore, the judgment itself is both severe and eternal. These people have moved from contempt to indifference to insult, and the result has been God's "outrage" at their hubris and studied rejection. They have rejected him; he is now rejecting them, and there is now no hope for them for eternity. God will avenge such wrongs (vv. 30–31), and no one should think they can act with impunity and get away with it. Nothing is more terrifying than final judgment, and it is time for all of us to get very serious about our walk with Christ. God is judging his people, and these warnings are part of that. We had better act and do so quickly and deeply, for nothing in our entire lives is as serious and important as this.

So this chapter concludes (vv. 32–39) with another exhortation to persevere in Christ. He begins by reminding them of the past experiences of their house churches (vv. 32–35) when they endured a great deal of pressure and persecution for their faith. Yet at that time, their difficulties drew them closer to the Lord and each other, and they successfully endured and triumphed over it, even when Claudius evicted them from Rome in AD 49. They actually grew in Christ during that time, and God has for them a present and future reward for their triumph.

Out of this comes a renewed emphasis on the necessity of persevering for Christ (vv. 36–39). He cites Habakkuk 2:3–4 and applies it to the fact that Christ is returning soon and will bring judgment with him—of the Babylonians in Habakkuk and of failed Christians here. God and Christ are not wavering by holding back but are giving these people time to wake up, repent, and get right with him while they can. Persevering believers who "live by faith" will inherit a huge reward. However, those who shrink back and apostatize will have the reverse, absolute judgment. However, at the close, the writer follows the lead of 6:9 and pulls back, saying he is convinced of better things for them and encouraging them to work even harder at enduring hardship for Christ and triumphing over the current situation.

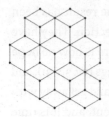

HEROES OF THE FAITH, PART 1

(11:1–22)

The last statement of chapter 10 declares that the readers are those "who have faith and are saved" (10:39). Now the author tells them extensively what the lives of the faith-people of the past look like. This is the third time he has stressed models from the past to show the readers what a life of faithfulness to the Lord should resemble. The first was 3:1–4:13 and the anti-example from the wilderness people whose hardened hearts led them into apostasy, and this chapter is intended to reverse that and guide the readers into the proper life for the people of God. The second was 10:32–34, when he used the previous generation of this church as examples. Now he goes further back to their ancient ancestors. In both, he is asking these Christians to follow their model and learn to live a life of faith. Both groups exemplify what the life of enduring hard times and serious opposition will look like.

The first part of this section (10:19–39) challenged these people to persevere in the life of faithfulness and become a contributing part of the history of the saints. Now he shows them what that life would look like. He takes them through that entire history, from creation (11:3) to the **eschaton**/end (11:39–40), hoping that they will turn themselves around and become one of the valuable parts of that story. He wants them to be the counter to the wilderness generation who never learned that lesson and perished without reaching the promised land.

This type of a historical list of examples was fairly common in Jewish writings, and this type of narrative resembles Stephen's compendium of the history of the Jewish people in Acts 7. However, there he was tracing the history of failure, while here the writer is tracing a history of faith and victorious living.

INTRODUCTION: THE NATURE OF FAITH (11:1-2)

This is one of the deservedly famous passages of the Bible, and it is one of the few places I still tend to prefer the King James Version. The two key terms are *hypostasis* and *elenchos*, and the question is whether they are translated objectively ("substance" and "evidence," as in the KJV), or subjectively ("assurance" and "conviction," as in the ESV, NASB). The NLT and NIV are alternative versions of the objective—"the reality of what we hope for ... the evidence of things we cannot see," and "confidence in what we hope for ... assurance about what we do not see." The objective emphasizes the actual content of faith, the subjective the impact it makes on us as we exercise faith.

Both the terms themselves and the context make the objective understanding preferable. Christian hope is not uncertain and ephemeral. It is not insubstantial but concrete and certain because it is based on the promises of God (see 10:36). I really like the translation "reality" here, for our future is far more secure via Christian hope than via the so-called real world we live in. That world is doomed and will be short-lived in every way. In the Greek papyri, *hypostasis* is used for a "title-deed" that guarantees ownership of a property; in this sense, faith "guarantees" the future, highlighting the "reality" behind this world that God controls on our behalf.

It is certainly true that we cannot see the future, but faith provides actual "evidence" that proves the future is guaranteed by the omnipotent God. This is where the subjective interpretation may possess some viability, though many doubt this is part of its meaning at all. Still, based on this "evidence," we are assured, and our convictions are strengthened. The message is that faith is the only way to operate successfully in the unseen world. What we cannot see or know is both visible and known to God, and even more, he is in control of it. So when we turn and rely on him, he guides us through its intricacies. What God has promised now remains future, but at the same time, becomes real and evidence that proves his sovereign control. We need not worry whatsoever regarding what awaits us at the end of the road for this world.

In verse 2 the "ancients" (*presbyteroi*; literally, "the elders") again become a model for us, this time exemplifying the kind of faith that they "were commended for." This is not fame in the world or community but literally "were witnessed to" or "approved" by God himself. So it is referring to the divine testimony that these lives were well lived. There is a public aspect to this, but it is God telling all around that he was pleased with them. In the **Hellenistic** world, this verb ("attests") often was used of people gaining civic honors. So the entire chapter begins with a note attesting God's approval of the "faith people of old." They bore witness to the Lord, and he bore witness of his pleasure in them.

FAITH AMONG THE ANTEDILUVIANS (11:3–7)

FAITH AND CREATION (11:3)

The pattern for the chapter as a whole is now set, as this is the first of the "by faith" openings that will guide us through the ancient witnesses. The primary unseen reality concerning this world, of course, is the creation of it in the first place. No human being played any part at all, and "the universe was formed at God's command." So this is the only section without a biblical figure behind it; God is that figure. Obviously, the writer is taking us back to the creation story in Genesis 1–2. Each "day" of creation was controlled by the divine proclamation, "Let there be light / a vault between the waters / water under the sky," and so on. The "let there be" command initiated each day's creative activity, and so it took place "by the word (*rhēmati*) of God."

Interestingly, "universe" is *tous aiōnas*, which means both "the worlds" and "the ages." It likely connotes both here, referring to the worlds that make up the universe and the ages that will determine how God controls world events and the process of salvation. In other words, God orders both the historical and temporal dimensions of life.

The result (*eis to*) is that we readers are called upon by faith to accept the fact that "what we now see did not come from anything that can be seen." There has been considerable debate over the meaning of this. A popular understanding has this as connoting *creation ex nihilo* or "creation out of nothing," seeing this as restating the "in the beginning God created" of Genesis 1:1. However, that is reading a lot into the wording here. Some think it stems from Plato's idea of the real and ideal worlds, with this real world a copy of the unseen world of God. However, there is little evidence that such thinking was behind the writer and his thoughts in Hebrews.

The most likely is probably to link "the unseen things" in verse 3b with "the word of God" in 3a, and in this sense, the second half of the verse restates the first half and means the faith-people live by God's commands rather than the mandates of the world. They have identified themselves with the reality of the unseen realm of God (v. 1) and follow its dictates, refusing to be "people of the world." The future belongs to the Lord and his followers, not to the secularists. This creation principle—that the God of the unseen world is in sovereign control of what can be seen—is the guiding principle of their lives. His word, not the false musings of the people of this world, is upmost in all things.

FAITH AND ABEL AND ENOCH (11:4–5)

Several interpreters see these two as a pair who establish the principle that will be followed in the list of heroes—namely, the

criterion finalized in Christ (12:1-3): that suffering is the path to
glory and victory. The story of Cain and Abel is one of the archetypal stories that reverberate throughout Scripture. The principle is stated well in Proverbs 15:8: "The LORD detests the sacrifice
of the wicked, but the prayer of the upright pleases him." It is the
internal reality of the heart that matters more than the surface
acts of religious observance.

Cain was a farmer and so brought offerings from the ground,
while Abel as a shepherd brought firstborn sheep. God honored
only Abel's offering, not because crops were unacceptable but
because of Cain's heart condition. He had serious heart trouble.
While many Jews interpreted this as God's ritual demand for a
blood sacrifice, the sacrificial system actually allowed both types of
sacrifice (Lev 2:1-16; 6:14-23). Abel's offering was "by faith," while
Cain's was not. God witnessed to this here by taking his as a "more
acceptable offering" because it "gave evidence that he was a righteous man." Both Christ (Matt 23:35) and John (1 John 3:12) stressed
the righteousness of Abel.

The final statement, "And by faith Abel still speaks, even though
he is dead," stresses that Abel has joined God in attesting as a heavenly witness to the validity of a life of faith. This, of course, is a
reference to his murder at the hands of his brother, with his blood
"crying out" to the Lord "from the ground" (Gen 4:10). His blood
is seen still "speaking out" and witnessing to this very day, imagery also found in Revelation 6:9-11, where the blood of slain mar-
tyrs cries out for justice. Suffering is seen here as a mechanism by
which faith still speaks of righteousness to a lost world.

Enoch adds to this in 11:5. He was a popular figure in Jewish
speculations, receiving special revelations about the world to come,
and was even considered in some circles a mediator between God
and his creation because of his pure life—for instance, as the
"righteous man" in the Wisdom of Solomon. The compendium of
material in 1 Enoch is 108 chapters of mostly **apocalyptic** material.
He was the ideal righteous man, proven by his disappearance when

God "took him away" to heaven. This continues the theme from Abel regarding the connection between faith and righteousness. This indeed was the basis of his fame, for "he was commended as one who pleased God." This, not his "translation" to heaven, is the primary emphasis here. He lived such an exemplary life that God deemed him too worthy to remain on earth and took him home to heaven. So Abel and Enoch are archetypal models of righteous people who pleased God. As a result, he becomes the first in Scripture to be taken up into heaven, the first proof that there is a heaven awaiting the righteous. He and Elijah are critical figures in discussions regarding a view of the afterlife in the Old Testament.

THESIS: FAITH AND PLEASING GOD (11:6)

Clearly, the reader's choice is between self-sufficiency and trust in the world versus a God-centered "faith." It is stated quite directly: "Without faith it is impossible to please God." No one—not Enoch nor anyone else—would be able to do so. This means believing and accepting his mandates and placing our trust in his promises. Abel was "commended as righteous" (v. 4), and Enoch "was commended (by every generation) as one who pleased God" (v. 5). Now we are asked to join these two, but we can only do so "by faith" (the organizing principle of this entire list). Several have pointed out that this verse actually sums up not just this section but the entire letter, for persevering in faith and pleasing God are concepts stressed in every chapter. The old sacrificial system was unable to sustain access to God and a life that was pleasing to God, and so it came to completion and was fulfilled in the new system instituted by Christ. In Christ we draw near to God (10:22) and discover a life pleasing to him. There are two areas in which *pistis* functions:

1. Believe that God exists—This is not so much a pure denial in the reality of divine beings; there were not many true atheists in the ancient world. When the psalmist declares, "The fool says in his heart, 'There

is no God'" (Ps 14:1; 53:1), this was not a denial of the
actual existence of God but rather that the God of
Israel was present and sovereign. They are living
their lives "as if" he isn't there and denying that this
God has any control over them. So this means that
God's people must center on the fact of God in their
lives and surrender control over to him. So "faith in
God" in 6:1 and "belief that he exists" here both mean
the acceptance that the God of the Bible is who he says
he is and directing one's life accordingly.

2. Believe that he rewards those who sincerely seek
    him—"Seek" is the present tense *ekzētousin* and
    emphasizes the ongoing nature—that is, persistence
    in seeking a closer relationship with him. Once more
    the perseverance of the saints is strongly stressed.
    "Rewards" is actually a noun (*misthapodotēs*) and
    becomes a virtual title, God as "the Rewarder." Those
    who please him will be rewarded for their trust. The
    doctrine of rewards is essential for Hebrews, refer-
    ring to the "rest" God gives in 3:1-4:13 and to the new
    salvation and access to God that we possess in the
    middle section (5:1-10:18). We don't seek God out of
    greed, to get a reward, but he wants us to know that
    when we do seek him, he will pay us back for all we
    sacrifice for him (2:2; 10:35; 11:26). Moreover, our
    reward will not be earthly and temporary but heav-
    enly and permanent.

Faith and Noah (11:7)

Like Abel and Enoch, Noah was a righteous man who reverenced
God and was rewarded for his persistent faith. The point here is
Noah's incredible act of obedience in building "an ark to save his
family." The instructions for building the boat (Gen 6:14-16) are

themselves remarkable, and the fact that no such flood had ever occurred before and that he worked so hard to build and ready the ark far inland, away from any water, shows the extent of his faith and the obedience that resulted from it.

All this resulted from his heeding God's warning "about things not yet seen" (Heb 11:7), wording taken from verse 1 and part of the meaning of faith. This unseen reality was the judgment about to fall on the unbelieving world, and this spurred Noah to enormous effort readying the vessel that would save his family. He took God at his word and obeyed to the letter in an impossible situation, with everyone around undoubtedly mocking his actions all the way (stressed in the Jewish *Sybylline Oracles*). As we now know, this became a harbinger of the final judgment at the end of history that would usher in the eternal reward for the faithful (see 11:13–16, 26; 12:28).

It is with "holy fear" (*eulabētheis*) that he did so, translated "reverent submission" when describing Christ in 5:7. All of these ideas are part of the meaning of the term—reverence, submission, and obedience to God. This becomes a term that should depict all of us as we grow in Christ and learn both reverence and submission, the hallmarks of the victorious Christian life. True faith produces godly fear, and this results in radical surrender and obedience.

Two final realities, one negative and one positive, emerge from this. Negatively, by Noah's actions resulting from faith, he "condemned the world," as this final judgment upon the evil world of his day reverberated down through the centuries to be finalized in the great white throne judgment of Revelation 20:11–15. The evil world of unrepentant humanity stands condemned and is simply marking time until its true end comes to pass. Positively, he "became heir of the righteousness that is in keeping with faith." Noah was the first man in the Bible called "righteous" (Gen 6:9; 7:1), but here he is "heir of the righteous," stressing his reward from God—partly his deliverance through the flood in which he and his family received divine "justice," the righteous result of their faith. At the same time, he inherited that righteousness in God's sight that would typify those who came after—namely, the other heroes of the faith mentioned in this chapter.

FAITH AMONG THE PATRIARCHS (11:8-22)

ABRAHAM AND SARAH (11:8-19)

Call to a promised land (11:8-10)

Abraham, of course, is the archetype of "righteousness by faith" person (Gen 15:6; see Rom 4). His deep faith is demonstrated first in his willingness to leave the home of his ancestors (Ur in the Chaldees) based on God's promises. He had no idea what the result would be, only that he would later "receive [that land] as his inheritance" (note the link with Noah as "heir" in v. 7). The amazing thing is that God never told him where that land was but just asked Abraham and his family to trust him and follow the path God set out for him. By faith alone he "obeyed and went" (v. 8). This was God's way of working with people throughout the Old Testament. He made it impossible to trust in their own resources, for those were all removed from the scene. Rather, they were forced to follow step by step without knowing the next one.

All Abraham had was the divine promise that this place would be his "inheritance," wherever it was and whatever it was. Very soon this earthly inheritance of a "promised land" would become the basis of a far greater promise that would demand trust in an eternal inheritance in a "city with foundations, whose architect and builder is God" (11:10; see also 11:13-14, 16, 19, 39-40).

When he reached this "promised land," the demand for absolute faith in God continued (11:9), for when he "made his home" there, he became not a settled resident but a semi-nomad who "lived in tents" and migrated from place to place depending on the seasons (Gen 12:8; 13:3, 12, 18). His true final home still lay in the future, and he was, in reality, "a stranger in a foreign country" (Heb 11:9). He was the first pilgrim among God's people and established the pattern so endemic to this letter of the Christian life as a pilgrimage. It is God who empowers and guides each step at a time. The pilgrim trusts and follows the Lord's directions. Abraham as a stranger and alien in this world is picked up by 1 Peter 1:1, 17, and 2:11 as the model for us. The classical spiritual says it so well: "This world is not my home, I'm just a-passin' through."

The writer notes that Isaac and Jacob were "heirs with him of the same promise" (Heb 11:9) to show that this became the principle for the patriarchs as a whole and therefore a paradigm for God's true people as a whole. We are all called on this pilgrimage through life to live as strangers in this world who look forward to God's inheritance and live by God's promises rather than those false principles set out for us by the world.

Abraham was able to live this way because he refused to live in the present for what he could get out of life in this world. Rather, he "was looking forward to the city with foundations" (11:10). "Looking forward" is *exedecheto*, to "look with great expectations," and refers to an eagerness to see God's promises come to light. A "city with foundations" is the opposite of a nomadic life in tents that have none. His would be a settled existence, and he would cease to be a stranger but become a citizen (Phil 3:20) of God's "city." This settled existence will not be when the people of Israel cross into Canaan but the eternal city this entire section is looking forward to (11:13-14, 16, 19, 39-40; 12:22-24, 28). In actuality, these are eternal foundations, and the heavenly city is a picture taken from Jewish apocalyptic (2 Bar 4:1-7).

Since this is a heavenly city, its "architect and builder is God." It is both designed and erected by the Triune Godhead (some think the architect and builder are meant to be the Father and the Son). Psalm 87:1, 5 states that the Jerusalem temple was "founded" and "established" by God, and Revelation 21:12-21 provides an extensive blueprint for the design of the new Jerusalem (building on Isa 54:11; 65:17-25). It is no wonder that it is "a kingdom that cannot be shaken" (12:28).

Sarah and the Abrahamic progeny (11:11-12)

Sarah had a great deal more trouble believing God's promise to Abraham that he would have a child in his old age. We would have had the same difficulty, for he was a hundred years old and Sarah ninety (Gen 17:17). When Sarah overheard him and his visitors, she "laughed to herself" (Gen 18:12), and the Lord took this as a lack of faith (18:13-14). Sarah denied this, and we are told she lied when she did so (18:15). Then at the actual birth, she laughed once more, this time in amazement (21:16).

The writer here wants to highlight not their struggle to find faith but the end result of the whole process and so says, "by faith ... she was enabled to bear children because she considered him faithful who had made the promise." There is a great deal of discussion as to whether Abraham, not Sarah, should be the subject of this verse because he is the subject in verses 10 and 12, and the phrase "enabled to bear children" elsewhere normally stresses the father's side in bearing children. However, Sarah is the subject of this scene in Genesis, and it was more she who had the problem with faith and triumphed over it in the Genesis story. This follows Genesis in making Sarah the subject here, and so she joins the other patriarchs in winning the victory "by faith."

Verse 12 does return to Abraham's faith, showing the ultimate result: "from this one man, and he as good as dead, came descendants as numerous as the stars in the sky and as countless as the sand on the seashore." Abraham and Sarah had been completely unable to have children all those years, and now they were far too old. Only divine intervention could have made it possible, the fact stressed with every hero of the faith in this chapter. God takes an impossible situation and turns it completely on its head for the sake of his glory and his peoples' faith.

Not only was Abraham allowed children, but his progeny were too numerous to be counted. The imagery of the stars in the sky and the sand on the seashore is taken from Genesis 22:17 (and Exod 32:13) and was completely appropriate from the fact that whole nations stemmed from Isaac (the Jews) and Ishmael (the Arab peoples). We have a God who delivers on his promises in ways that go far beyond our feeble attempts to understand and apply them. His generosity and faithfulness to us are more than we can comprehend.

Wanderers in search of a home (11:13–16)

This is a critical section establishing a message meant for us as well as the patriarchs. So long as we are pilgrims in this world, we will never truly find the home we long to have. We may live on a thousand-acre ranch that has belonged to our family for generations, but it will not turn out to be the "home" intended by God for us, and it will not truly satisfy in the long run. We will find our home when we, like the patriarchs, reach "a better country— a heavenly one" (11:16).

The patriarchs like us "were still living by faith when they died" (v. 13). This means their hopes had not been realized and they still had to place their trust entirely in the Lord throughout their lives. That is a need that never stops. The point that they "did not receive the things promised" (v. 13) points forward to the end of this chapter which repeats the message: "none of (the heroes) received what had been promised" because God had "something better planned for us" that could only be realized when they like us reached heaven (11:39-40).

Faith points beyond the years we live on earth to the greater reality of the heavenly world that will be ours. This does not mean God never answers prayer, but earthly requests are temporary in nature, and the true promises center on eternal reward. Our prayer life has an earthly component, and God is heavily involved in our earthly needs, but there is an ultimate dimension to prayer that goes beyond the earthly, and that is the subject here. Earth-centered issues can only go so far in satisfying the deeper needs of the soul. In his nomadic wanderings, Abraham "saw them and welcomed them from a distance" (v. 13), but they still "saw" them with the eyes of faith, as we do as well. The true reality is still unseen (11:1); nevertheless, we—like them—participate in it.

Their faith allowed them to welcome these promises "from a distance" (v. 13) and experience them through the hope that belongs only to the faithful. In Genesis 23:4 Abraham described himself to the Hittites as "a foreigner and stranger among you," and the writer here generalizes this to depict the stance of all God's people on this earth. Like them, we don't belong, for we are citizens of heaven (Phil 3:20) and foreigners and exiles in this world (1 Pet 1:1, 17; 2:11). In the ancient world, this meant that they were doomed always to be outsiders who didn't belong and had few rights and no legal protection.

In Hebrews 11:14-16 the author comments on Abraham's confession in verse 13. The basic premise occurs first: such a confession as he made in Genesis 23:4 means, "they are looking for a country of their own." They realize they do not belong to the place they are now inhabiting and that their true home is elsewhere. For most people, this was their birthplace to which they long to return (for **diasporic** Jews that would have been Jerusalem), but for Abraham and his family, this was the "homeland" God had promised for the—not the promised land in Canaan but the "city with foundations" (11:10) in heaven.

So verse 15 now clarifies this further. Abraham was not thinking of Ur, his original homeland he had "left" to follow God's promises. If that were the case, he explains, "they would have had opportunity to return." To do so, of course, would have meant turning their back on God's promises and denying their faith. Thus it had never entered their mind to do so. So when Abraham called himself "a foreigner and stranger," this did not entail a desire to go back to their birthplace. In fact, they did not even think of Ur any longer as home. Later, Jacob considered Canaan to be "the land of [his] fathers" (Gen 31:3).

Their true homeland is now made clear in verse 16. The reason neither the original home (Ur) nor the current home (Canaan) sufficed is that God's true promises were leading to "a better country—a heavenly one." This returns to the theme of "superior" or "better" (*kreittonos*) things given to us in the new covenant by the Godhead.[1] This is the ultimate reason for being a believer in Christ: with him comes a superior end—eternal life in a heavenly home.

The final homeland will be explored further in 11:40; 12:22–24, 28; 13:14. The author finishes by saying, "Therefore God is not ashamed to be called their God, for he has prepared a city for them" (v. 16). Since they were focused on their heavenly Father and the heavenly dwelling awaiting them, he was focused on them and not ashamed but proud to be the Father of such faithful children. In the narrow sense, "their" referred especially to the patriarchs, and throughout Scripture, God was quite often called "the God of Abraham, Isaac, and Jacob." However, we are definitely included in this, as we are equally his children. Every child is excited when their parents are proud of them and watch out for them.

The idea of God preparing a city for them is quite important. This is the "city with foundations" in verse 10 and corresponds to the new Jerusalem in Revelation 21, which is 1500 miles in every direction, exactly the length of the Roman Empire from Spain to the Euphrates River in Babylon. This wondrous city is in process of being prepared for Jesus' followers, and he will, at his second coming, "come back and take you to be with" him for eternity (John 14:2-3). Here we have the final and true "promised land."

Faith and the sacrifice of Isaac (11:17-19)

The Jewish people called this "the binding of Isaac," and it always signified the ultimate exemplar of faith in the Old Testament. The

---

1. See Heb 1:4; 6:9; 7:7, 19, 22; 8:6; 9:23; 10:34.

writer calls this the time when "God tested" Abraham (Gen 22:1), a test exactly like the "testing of your faith" in James 1:2-4, when a trial or difficulty would force a person to exercise their faith and trust in God.

The shocking nature of the test is explained in Hebrews 11:17b, which states that Abraham had already "embraced the promises" God had given him, undoubtedly meaning the promises of an heir, with Isaac as the promised seed through whom God's promises to Abraham of a great nation descending from his loins would come to pass. Ishmael was not the son of promise and so didn't count, and Abraham had to exile him and his mother in Genesis 21:1-11. Isaac was the "only begotten" or "one and only son" (v. 17; used of Christ in John 1:14; 3:16) who was to fulfill Abraham's destiny. Yet God had asked Abraham to surrender that very son to God and offer him as a sacrifice, against everything in which he believed.

No greater "test" could be imagined. In verse 18 the writer quotes Genesis 21:12 on this, "It is through Isaac that your offspring will be reckoned." It provided the ultimate contradiction. Isaac was to be the means Abraham and his "offspring" would live down through the generations of God's people, yet he was commanded to take that son's life on behalf of the very God who had made the promises! God's own promises were to be obviated. Yet it at the same time proved the extent of Abraham's faith and its intended result: his willingness to obey God to the ultimate extent. There was no hesitation, and he carried out the instructions immediately and to the letter. The knife was about to descend into Isaac's heart when God called it off. The level of obedience had been reached.

Abraham's reasoning is now explored (11:19). God had commanded, and he had to obey, but he reasoned there was still one way God's promises regarding Isaac and his offspring could be kept: God "could even raise the dead," and in that way, Abraham could "receive Isaac back from death." This is an important verse for the debate over whether the early people of the Old Testament believed in the afterlife. This would certainly show that the author of Hebrews thought so, and I would concur with his assessment. Life after death is essential for the thrust of this entire chapter. As Paul said about Jesus, "if Christ has not been raised, our preaching is useless and so is your faith" (1 Cor 15:14).

The author's point here is that Abraham's faith encompassed life after death and that God had the power to raise Isaac from the dead and still fulfill his covenant promise even if Abraham were to sacrifice him. As several have pointed out, this could be implicit in Genesis 22:5 when he told his servants, "We will worship and then *we will come back*" (emphasis added)—meaning, come back alive after Isaac had been sacrificed and then raised from the dead. This has implications for his current readers and us as well. Death is no detriment for God's faithful followers, for he is in control.

He concludes that "in a manner of speaking he did receive Isaac back from death" (v. 19). The actual phrase is *en parabolē*, "as a symbol or type," and it most likely means that the near-death of Isaac pointed forward figuratively to the sacrificial death of Christ and the future resurrection of believers as a result of his sacrificial death. So the binding of Isaac is a "type" both of Christ and of our future resurrection.

FAITH AND ISAAC (11:20)

The patriarchal blessing of Jacob and Esau took place in Genesis 27:27-40 and 28:1-5. The full story is not recounted, and the way Jacob received his blessing through deceit is ignored. All attention is on the basic thrust of this chapter: the forward look of faith and its relation to the future. First in the sentence for emphasis is "in regard to their future" ("concerning things to come" NKJV, KJV, CSB). The stress is not so much on the individuals than what God planned to do with them and through them. Even Esau, as earth-centered as he is, is under God's purview, and he had a plan for his destiny as well. The point is that God is sovereign over every person and every detail in their lives, and his people must learn to acknowledge his sovereignty over their lives. Jacob in his faithfulness and Esau in his unfaithfulness are both under God's control, and faith allows us to relinquish this control to the Lord.

FAITH AND JACOB (11:21)

Faith is still seen in its connection with death and future resurrection, so the author mentioned that Jacob's patriarchal blessing was bestowed "when he was dying." Since he was the father of the rest of the patriarchs, he blessed the rest of them in Genesis 48:1–22 (Joseph's two sons) and 49:1–28 (his own twelve sons). The point is that faith moves beyond death to the fulfillment of God's will. The stress is on the blessing of "Joseph's sons" rather than of his own sons. There are several reasons. As with Jacob and Esau, the younger (Ephraim) is preferred over the older (Manasseh). When Joseph brought them before Jacob, he deliberately crossed his hands and gave the blessing to the younger (48:14). The result is that Joseph received a double portion of the blessing, and both his sons (not him) founded two of Israel's tribes. The future belonged to him, and his faith was doubly rewarded.

The writer concludes this by having Jacob worship "as he leaned on the top of his staff."[2] This stems from Genesis 47:31, a different episode in the story—namely when Jacob had Joseph promise to bury him back in Canaan. This is used here to teach that the act of faith is God-directed, not just directed to the patriarchs who are blessed. Joseph is at the close of life, and at that time, bows his head over his staff, indicating that all of his life has been lived in submission to God. So the patriarchal blessings are ending on a note of worship.

FAITH AND JOSEPH (11:22)

Joseph both ends the patriarchal period and leads into the Egyptian period of Moses. Joseph's entire life could be called a faith narrative,

---

2. This is the Septuagint (Greek) reading, preferred by many versions. The Masoretic Text (Hebrew) has "the head of his bed," but there are indications that reading came later and that the Greek reading in this instance is superior.

but the author follows precedent by choosing an episode "when his end is near" and the future was to be in "the city with foundations" (11:10). That time when he speaks of the "exodus" and gives "instructions concerning the burial of his bones" takes place at the very end of Genesis in 50:24–25 where he said, "I am about to die. But God will surely come to your aid and take you up out of this land to the land he promised" and then adds, "you must carry my bones up from this place."

Joseph demonstrates a twofold sign of faith—first, believing God's promise that Israel would return to Canaan, that that the promise regarding the promised land still held secure. He would not live to see this, so in this the promises transcended death. Second, requesting that his bones be buried there showed faith that the promise concerned him as well, even though he was soon to die. In fact, this was virtually a prophecy fulfilled first by Moses (Exod 13:19) and then by Joshua (Josh 24:32). The Israelites carried his bones throughout the exodus (Exod 13:19), and they were buried in Shechem (Josh 24:32).

———

Hebrews 11 presents an "example list" meant to challenge the readers to be people who live by faith. Such a list worked by driving home example after example of something, providing overwhelming evidence. As we have seen in our first movement of the chapter, "Heroes of the Faith, Part 1" (vv. 1–22), the author wishes to challenge his readers to be people who, like the examples from biblical history, take a bold stance as marginalized people in a difficult world, trusting the unseen God. This first part of the chapter has three movements: an introduction on "The Nature of Faith" (vv. 1–2), "Faith Among the Antediluvians" (vv. 3–7), and "Faith among the Patriarchs" (vv. 8–22).

In the introduction, the author first defines faith as something objective (v. 1). Unlike the understanding of many modern people

who see faith as a "blind leap" against all the facts, biblical faith
has to do with trusting God concerning certain realities that God
has made known. Although we can't see the future, it is "guaranteed" because it rests in the hands of the one, true God. Christian
faith produces "evidence" as people of faith trust God and see him
accomplish things in the world, a reality to which the whole of
Hebrews 11 bears witness. "The ancients," that is, "the elders," are
wonderful examples for us in this pattern of living (v. 2), and God
applauded the way they approached following God in the world.
Their lives bore witness to God, and he, in the Scriptures, bore
witness to their faithfulness!

So with verse 3 the author of Hebrews begins making the case
that this life of faith is the only way to live for God in the world.
In verses 3-7 he focuses on that period of history prior to the rise
of the patriarchs, what we have in our Bibles as Genesis 1-11. By
beginning with the creation account itself (Heb 11:3), the author
demonstrates that the life of faith is grounded in reality itself.
God, the main actor of the biblical story, is the author of both history and time, and his pattern is to bring "seen things" out of the
unseen. Faith-people live by what God has revealed as being true,
especially by living out the Scriptures rather than living by the
principles and dictates of the world. Abel and Enoch are the first
examples tapped from human history (vv. 4-5). Abel's story demonstrates that the condition of the heart is critical for a proper
stance of faith. Faith was a manifestation of a heart rightly related
to God. So Abel is considered "a righteous man" whose story "still
speaks," bearing witness ultimately to God's reality. Enoch's story
is different from Abel's since he did not see death (v. 5), but they
have God's approval in common. God approved of Abel's gifts as the
manifestation of his righteous heart, and God approved of Enoch,
with whom he was pleased. Following on the heels of these two
righteous exemplars, verse 6 challenges us to live by faith, which
is the only way to please God. Living this out boils down active
faith to two salient points. First, we must believe that God exists;

and we must believe that God rewards those who trust him. So the section on the Antediluvians wraps up with the example of Noah (v. 7), who acted on God's revelation, building the ark and trusting God in things that had never been seen in the world, and he was rewarded by God as an heir of righteousness.

It is fitting that the author next turns to the "Faith among the Patriarchs" (vv. 8–22), since in Judaism, Abraham was seen as the preeminent example of faith in God (Gen 15:6). In obedience to God's word, he left his homeland on the basis of God's promise concerning a land Abraham had never seen. Once he arrived, he lived as an alien in that land but trusted God's promise that it would be his inheritance (Heb 11:9). Ultimately his hope was set on a heavenly city, "whose architect and builder is God" (v. 10). One of the great challenges to Abraham's faith came with the promise of children, for both he and Sarah were elderly. Sarah was able to triumph over her own lack of faith by trusting in God's faithfulness, and she was enabled to have a child of the promise (v. 11). Therefore, despite Abraham and Sarah being well past the age of childbearing, God fulfilled the promise in ways much beyond what anyone could have expected, making Abraham's offspring more numerous than stars and sand (v. 12).

At 11:13–16 we come to a critical reflection in the chapter, the author pointing out that the life of faith recognizes that our ultimate destination is an eternal, heavenly reality. Thus a looking forward in trust of God must be the believer's posture all the way to death. This life will never fully satisfy our longings. It was never intended to do so.

The remainder of Part 1 of Hebrew's account of "The Heroes of the Faith" focuses on Abraham's descendants (vv. 17–22), treating the fulfilment of God's promise that the patriarch would have children. The test of Abraham concerning the sacrifice of Isaac is one of the foundational stories of faith in all of Scripture, for Abraham believed that God could raise his promised son from the dead if necessary (vv. 17–19). At the heart of the story, Abraham was willing to obey the word of God, trusting God, even though he did not understand God's command and it seemed to contradict God's promise. Isaac expressed faith by blessing Jacob and Esau concerning things in the future (vv. 20–21), and the examples quickly turn to Joseph, who also anticipated the future from a posture of faith, speaking of the exodus (v. 22), trusting God's sovereignty over history and his promise concerning the land.

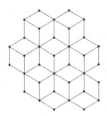

HEROES OF THE FAITH, PART 2
(11:23–40)

This great chapter continues with its reworked history of Israel considered from the standpoint of the faith required for those who serve God. The message is that following the Lord demands not only an ongoing trust in him but a forward-looking vision for the Lord's future promises. Life for the godly will never be culminated in this life but only in the kingdom reality of heaven. With the patriarchs, the crisis for faith was the promises of God and inheriting the promised land. Now with Moses and the historical books the crisis is opposition and persecution faced by God's people. In both sections the message is that God controls our future and we must surrender to his sovereign will.

FAITH AND MOSES (11:23–28)

There are four "by faith" sections, and that will form the outline for this portion. The message here is that faith gives boldness and courage that enable us, like Moses, to act decisively when faced with adversity. At the same time, it demands that we refuse to give in to the blandishments of this world and proceed through life God's way.

FAITH AND MOSES' BIRTH (11:23)

The birth of Moses (Exod 2:1–10) centered on the faith of his family and their decision to refuse the demands of the authorities and to hide him for three months (Heb 11:23). Pharaoh had commanded his soldiers to drown every Hebrew baby boy (Exod 1:22), so it was a life-and-death decision. We aren't told where Moses was hidden, but surprisingly, we are told why: "she saw that he was a fine [beautiful] child" (2:2). Here in Hebrews 11:23 it states, "they saw he was no ordinary child." This almost certainly means that they recognized God had chosen this child for extraordinary things. This is where their faith was at work—they knew God would protect the child from the monsters who had so turned against their people. The present was filled with difficult times, but the future was secure in the sovereign power of the Lord.

So the result is that "they were not afraid of the king's edict." If caught, their lives would be forfeit as well as the child's, but they trusted God far more than they did Pharaoh. They would much rather obey God than any human authority. As Jesus said in Matthew 10:28a, "Do not be afraid of those who [can merely] kill the body." The saints down through history have looked with disdain at despots and their threats that could never go beyond this life. The reality of eternal life changes everything. Moses' parents knew the Egyptian powers could do nothing to turn aside from God's will and so acted boldly in faith to protect the baby Moses.

FAITH AND REFUSING THE WORLD'S RICHES (11:24-26)

Like Exodus, Hebrews skips Moses' childhood in Pharaoh's courts and goes straight to his adulthood. He was faced with a major decision: to embrace his royal upbringing or to identify with his beleaguered Hebrew people. The first thing we learn is that he "refused to be known as the son of Pharaoh's daughter." He had been raised as such (Exod 2:10), but immediately upon adulthood, he had defended a Hebrew worker who was being beaten by an Egyptian, killing the Egyptian and incurring Pharaoh's wrath as a result (2:11-15).

We should note that the Israelites are called "the people of God" (11:25) here to identify their true allegiance and make clear their major difference with the Egyptians. In so doing, he is connected not only with his fellow Israelites but also with God's people down through the ages in their suffering. Faith allowed Moses to see the big picture and join the true victors rather than the seemingly powerful Egyptians.

Moreover, he also triumphed over "the fleeting pleasures of sin" (v. 25). As a member of Pharaoh's royal court, these pleasures were more than most of us could even imagine. The movies try to show it, and the reality was probably far greater. But his faith in God gave him the wisdom to realize these were indeed "fleeting" or transitory. This is something every one of us struggles with. In our day, there are more of these "fleeting pleasures" than at any other time in history, with the computer games, smartphones, and social media outlets. None of them ever suffice, and they become just another demeaning addiction.

Yet the choice was as stark as it could get, and it truly dealt with polar opposites—the pleasures that only royalty can enjoy versus "disgrace" with his despised people (11:26). The writer shows the extent to which Moses identifies with the whole people of God down through the ages by having him endure not just the sufferings of the Hebrew people but "disgrace for the sake of Christ." Moses is aligned with all God's saints throughout history in the choices he had to make in Egypt. We all go through the same process "for the sake of Christ."

When he relates "the treasures of Egypt," we must remember that Egypt was renowned throughout the ancient world for its gold and vast wealth. However, Moses realized that God controlled all the riches of the world accumulated through all history, and so Egypt could offer nothing compared to the eternal treasures of heaven. When he writes, "he was looking ahead to his reward" (v. 26), this eternal reward in heaven was in the author's mind. It is impossible to imagine what awaits us in heaven—for we are mere human beings—but Moses recognized that it made his sacrifices worth it.

This is the theme of this "roll call of heroes of the faith"—namely, that they were waiting with Enoch to be translated to heaven (11:5), with Noah for "things not yet seen" (11:7), with Abraham for "the city with foundations" (11:10), and with Moses for "the reward ahead." The eternal heavenly glory awaiting us far outstrips anything this world can offer. Yes, the suffering and struggle our pilgrimage entails is extremely difficult to endure, but that very perseverance is its own reward.

FAITH AND LEAVING EGYPT (11:27)

Interestingly, the writer presents this almost as Moses leaving on his own volition, while Exodus 2:14-15 has Moses fleeing to Midian in fear after killing the Egyptian overseer because Pharaoh thought he was rebelling against him as well. But there is a second flight from Egypt, one that takes place forty years later and involves the nation, namely the exodus itself. The main argument for understanding this of the flight to Midian is the order of the events, as the Passover (v. 28) follows the first flight but not the second. Those who take it this way believe the answer is that his surface and immediate response was fear, but his long-term reaction at the deeper level was trust in God.

This is how I understood this passage in the past, but after further reflection, I think it best to understand this from a broader perspective. Chronology is not the determining factor; rather, theology controls the story. When it says he was "not fearing the king's anger," the account in the book of Exodus favors it reflecting the ensuing battle between Moses as God's champion versus Pharaoh, the personification of the forces of darkness. In all ten plagues and in the exodus itself, Moses was fearless and stood up to the king magnificently. This is a far better understanding, so his "leaving Egypt" was at the head of the nation at the exodus itself, one of the great stories of the entire Old Testament. This makes a great deal more sense.

Continuing the mega-theme of chapter 11, the author adds, "he persevered because he saw him who is invisible" (v. 27). Some take this as a quasi-title for God, "the Unseen One," going back to the definition of faith in 11:1, "assurance about what we do not see." This is not a reference to an actual vision of God as at the burning bush (Exod 3:4) or on Mount Sinai (Exod 24:9-10) but a realization of what kind of God we serve and a testimony to the faith that is required. Moses was able to endure and persist in that extremely tension-filled time because he felt God's presence and knew he was at work behind the scenes. This is how we all must operate. Moses' boldness before the most powerful ruler in the world is beyond belief, but the reason is he knew the unseen God of the universe was behind him. Both the readers in the first century and we today must identify with Moses here and refuse to be cowed by the pressures of the world but place our complete trust in the God who is at work in our lives.

Faith and the Passover (11:28)

This was the last of the twelve plagues (Exodus 11-12), with the angel of death passing over every Egyptian home and taking the firstborn of each household. We are told this "destroyer of the firstborn" did not "touch the firstborn of Israel." The first three "by faith" passages on Moses centered on his perseverance through trials. Now the author turns to the victories that God gave him and the faithful over the purveyors of evil.

At the Passover, the Hebrew homes placed the blood of a slain lamb on the doorposts and lintels of their homes (Exod 12:22), bringing life rather than death to their families. This became the most sacred of the seven Jewish feasts and was the harbinger of the sacrificial system but also provided background to the Christian celebration of the Lord's Supper.

FAITH AND THE EXODUS EVENTS (11:29-31)

The second scene of victory over evil (with the Passover) was at the crossing of the Red Sea (Exod 13:17-14:22). The story is deservedly well-known and demonstrates the power of God on behalf of his people when they trust him. Not only did the waters recede, but the seabed dried up immediately when the Israelites began to pass through. Moreover, this was not a company of a hundred or so people. Exodus 12:37–38 tells us there were 600,000 men on foot along with innumerable women and children and a huge amount of livestock. It would have taken a great deal of time to get across to safety, and the amount of water held back would have been prodigious.

The Egyptian cavalry and chariots followed them, but when they were in the middle of the seabed, God released the millions of gallons of water and drowned the entire army (Exod 14:33–41). This became the archetype for future deliverances of God's people and the punishment of the wicked. As such, this provides a further warning regarding apostasy.

The final two instances of faith in Hebrews 11:30–31 take place after the people have entered the promised land. In this case, all the armies of Israel, not just one single person, were the exemplars of faith. The command to march around it for seven days must have seemed ridiculous. Armies often did strut around a fortification to show their superior power (as in *The Iliad*), but for seven days? And seven priests with seven trumpets? God was clearly testing their faith, and the triumph was spectacular, as at the end of the seventh day, at the shout of the people, "the wall collapsed; so everyone charged straight in, and they took the city" (Josh 6:20). Jericho was one of the strongest city-states in that part of the world, and God caused it to fall with hardly any effort on Israel's part.

Rahab is the only gentile and the only woman to appear in the list in verse 31, but she became quite well-known in Jewish circles for her faithful and brave act and appears in James 2:25 as an example of justification by works since she acted on her faith. In Joshua 2:1–3 she hid the two spies (Caleb and Joshua) who were scouting out Jericho and saved their lives. Her life was spared as a result. Then in 2:11 she confesses that "the LORD your God is God in heaven above and on the earth below." Jewish writers later took this as a sign of her conversion, and she was highly regarded (*b. Megillah* 14b–15a; *Exodus Rabbah* 27:4). By naming her as a "prostitute," the author shows how forgiveness can be achieved and how the failures of the past can be turned around by faith. In Matthew 1:5 she is one of the ancestors of David and thus of Christ himself.

FURTHER EXAMPLES OF FAITH (11:32–38)

The writer now shifts into overdrive and finishes at breakneck speed. He wants his readers to realize how essential faith was to the history of Israel and encourage them to join the list of heroes, so he keeps his message succinct but still powerful, addressing first the kind of life these heroes lived and second the kind of difficulties they endured, emerging victorious from it all. He wants the readers to realize they are a part of this history and that future generations will recall them as well, hopefully with an appreciation for the lives of faith they too exemplified.

He begins, "And what more shall I say?" While he obviously has not finished the Old Testament period, he has made his point about what a life of faith should look like and what that life can accomplish. Here he uses a rhetorical move, giving a rapid-fire series of examples meant to evoke the rest of Israel's history. Two themes dominate, restating what has already been said. First, with God in control, the faith-person will perform miraculous deeds and have a life that makes a huge difference (32–35a). Second, they will still face huge obstacles and endure tremendous difficulties in following the Lord, for the world will have turned against them (35b–38). But the end product will be victory and glory both now and in eternity (39–40).

THE WONDROUS DEEDS OF THE PERSON OF FAITH (11:32–35A)

The writer recognizes that the material of this chapter could have become the message of the entire book, stating there isn't time or space to recount the lives of the great men and women of faith.

The first four names (Gideon, Barak, Samson, and Jephthah) sum up the period of the judges, David and Samuel the monarchy, and finally the prophets. This covers the entire time to the end of the Old Testament period. David and Samuel are reversed because Samuel was the first of the order of the prophets and initiated that movement.

The mind-boggling ten things they did in the name of faith are covered in verses 33–34. Their exploits done "through faith" would impress anybody who read them. They have been organized into three groups of three each, with a concluding event centering on resurrection. The NIV has designated this by the way it words the three sections slightly differently (following the Greek):

1. Military and political victories—There is an A-B-A pattern here, as the first and third are fairly synonymous, since "what was promised" is wording taken from the conquest of the promised land. Gideon, Barak, Samson, and Jephthah were judges and kings, the subjects of this first set of accomplishments. Both the Mosaic and Davidic covenants were part of this set, and the judges centered on the middle one, administering justice.

2. Overcoming life-threatening situations—The first two are derived from the book of Daniel, with Daniel shutting the mouths of lions (v. 33; see Dan 6:22) and Shadrach, Meshach, and Abednego quenching the flames in the fiery furnace (v. 33; see Dan 3). This is a mega-theme, as nearly all of the faith heroes in this chapter were the recipients of miraculous events that took place when they placed their dependence wholly on God (think of Gideon here). Every military hero "escaped the edge of the sword" (v. 34) on numerous occasions. David's escapes from Saul may be especially in mind.

3. Power over Israel's enemies—These three return to the military successes of the first set and tell how they were accomplished. Israel's weakness turned to strength when God took over (think again of Gideon). There are so many examples of this. In fact, the conquest of Canaan followed this theme throughout, as the "grasshoppers" overcame the giants (see Num 13:33). Their power in battle that allowed them to rout foreign armies (v. 34) was always due entirely to God and not anything they had done themselves.

4. The concluding wonder is the greatest of them all: "Women received back their dead, raised to life again" (35a). The two prominent examples would be Elijah and Elisha raising the sons of the widow of Zarephath (1 Kgs 17:17-24) and the Shunammite woman (2 Kgs 4:18-37). Needless to say, the writer wants us to see this as a type of the raising of Jesus and of ourselves. It is the greatest miracle of all and will be experienced only by the faithful.

THE TERRIBLE SUFFERING OF THE PEOPLE OF FAITH (11:35B-38)

Triumph through adversity is the name of the game. The world of darkness hates light (John 3:19-20) and will always turn against those who belong to God. What follows (Heb 11:36-38) comes in another series of threes:

1. Persecution and opposition: This first instance in verse 35 is worded strangely, telling of those who were tortured for their faith, "refusing to be released so they might gain an even better resurrection." The term "tortured" refers to being tied to the rack and beaten to death, possibly referring to Eleazar, an

elderly scribe in 2 Maccabees 6:18-31 who refused to reject God to be "released" and chose death over apostasy. The writer says he did so to "gain an even better resurrection" than just being allowed to live an earthly existence. The other two are mockery and imprisonment: all of the prophets faced the jeers of those opposed to them, and several were imprisoned—Jeremiah was put in the stocks (Jer 20:2) and later thrown in prison (Jer 37:15).

2. Martyrdom: Jeremiah was also said to have been stoned to death (Jerome, *Against Jovinian* 2.37), though Zechariah may have been more in mind (2 Chr 24:21). Isaiah was said to have been sawn in two (*Martyrdom of Isaiah* 5:1-11). In 1 Kings 19:10 several prophets are reported put to death with the sword, as was Uriah in Jeremiah 26:23.

3. Persecuted prophets: These form a trio with an A-B-A literary pattern, with A = two terms and B = a single term. The "sheepskins and goatskins" (Heb 11:37) depict the garments of Elijah and Elisha (1 Kings 19:13, 19; 2 Kgs 1:8). The other two descriptions are of the persecuted prophets in general and depict all they went through in speaking out for God: they lost everything in a monetary sense and were severely mistreated at pretty much all times. The author's conclusion is apt: "The world was not worthy of them" (v. 38). In an evil world, the power and resources belonged to the purveyors of wickedness, and they used it against those who were worthy of having everything but instead were forced to give it up and have nothing. This reverses reality, for in truth, this world is not worthy of them. This comment prepares for verses 39-40.

4. Wandering pilgrims: The final trio shows that many of them were forced into hiding and lived nomadic lives but in a far worse state than Abraham. Wandering in deserts, of course, describes the forty-year sojourn of the wilderness generation (see 3:1–4:13) but also describes Elijah and Elisha, as well as other prophets who were forced into hiding (1 Kings 18:4; 19:3–9). In a sense, this whole chapter calls us to be wandering pilgrims, living fearlessly for God in an evil world.

THE PROMISED CULMINATION (11:39–40)

These verses conclude the entire chapter, but they are especially related to this final section, so I have chosen to situate them in that way. It is a very difficult message, but it is essential that we learn it. We sacrifice and go through extremely hard times because we believe God's promises and trust that he will turn everything around in his own time. But that is the key. It is in his time, not ours, and the writer is challenging us to realize that these great warriors for God, these true heroes of the faith-camp, never saw the realization of those promises until after they died. God fulfills every promise, but many of them must await the time of heavenly reward.

While every person mentioned in chapter 11 was "commended for their faith," "none of them received [in this life] what had been promised" (v. 39). This goes back to the declared "evidence" that made their faith real (v. 1)—namely, God's promises as stressed in verses 9 and 17 (Abraham), 11 (Sarah), and 13 and 33 (all the faithful). This is the conundrum—the life of faith is not just a this-worldly phenomenon. It stretches beyond our earthly existence into the next. We are called upon to trust God and his promises that will not culminate until we reach heaven. Verse 13 tells us this same thing and then adds that they "welcomed them from a distance, admitting that they were foreigners and strangers on earth." It then continues that the promises actually related to a "country of their own ... a heavenly one" (vv. 14-16)—namely, "a city with foundations" (v. 10). They all looked ahead to the reward (v. 26).

The truth behind all this is made clear in verse 40: the reason is that "God had planned something better for us," vastly superior to Egypt's treasures (v. 26) or the plaudits of the world. For the Old Testament saints, however, the attainment of "something better" (v. 40) had to await the coming of Christ, his atoning sacrifice, and the new covenant age he would establish. What is "better" is that "together with us they would be made perfect" (v. 40), probably meaning both the completion of Christ's redemptive work at his second coming and the sinless perfection we and they would at that time enjoy in eternity. We come to perfection when our sins are forgiven and we become children of our heavenly Father, and then when we enter eternity. We will share our heavenly home together, the people of the two covenants who are united under Christ.

———

The latter half of Hebrews 11 ("Heroes of the Faith, Part 2"; 11:23-40) consists of four movements: the first reflections on Moses (vv. 23-28), the second recounting events of the exodus (vv. 29-31), the third a section on further expressions of faith (vv. 32-38), and the fourth a conclusion concerning the culmination of faith (vv. 39-40). In the first half of the chapter, we saw the foundations of biblical faith laid with God's creation of the world, by which what is seen was created out of what is unseen, and the faith stories associated with the patriarch Abraham. Now the author pushes further into biblical history, probing especially the ways that true faith responds to opposition and persecution.

The first movement of Part 2 focuses on Moses (vv. 23-28) with four "by faith" sections illustrating courage in the face of seemingly overwhelming odds. This would have been very encouraging to the first readers of Hebrews, who were struggling in their own experience of persecution. In 11:23 Moses' parents, seeing that God had given them an extraordinary child, hid him; they trusted God more than they feared the king, acting in bold faith. The second section, illustrating Moses' life of faith, concerns his adulthood in Pharaoh's courts (vv. 24-26). Moses chose to identify with God's people rather than the Egyptian elite, which had two implications. It was a path of suffering and a path away from prosperity, and Moses took the path by faith because he saw something better in his future. The third "by faith" section tells us, therefore, that Moses left Egypt in the face of the king's anger because his life was oriented to God and God's reward, a key theme in this chapter (v. 27). Finally, Moses' faith story concludes with a final "by faith" section focused on the Passover (v. 28). Trusting God's instructions concerning the Passover lamb, Moses acted in obedience, making a distinction between the Israelites and their Egyptian oppressors. With the sprinkling of blood, the destroyer passed over the houses of God's people.

The second major movement in Part 2 concerns "Faith and the Exodus Events" (vv. 29-31), the example list naturally transitioning from Passover to exodus. One of the great events of Israelite history, the crossing of the Red Sea, illustrates the active nature of faith. The people of Israel crossed the Sea as if they were walking on dry land, while the Egyptian army was drowned. The final two instances of faith in this unit are in verses 30-31, jumping ahead to entrance of the promised land. Although the command to march around Jericho seven times seemed ridiculous, the people obeyed, and the walls came down. Amazingly, the author concludes this second movement with the faith of a Canaanite prostitute! Rahab courageously welcomed the spies in peace, bearing witness to the power of God!

The third major movement in Part 2 provides a rhetorical flourish of examples meant to evoke the rest of Israel's history. Two key themes stand out. First, the author focuses on the wondrous deeds people of faith have performed (vv. 32-35a), and second, the terrible suffering they have endured (vv. 35b-38). Among the wondrous deeds performed, we find victory in battle and politics, overcoming life-threatening situations, and even the dead being brought back to life! On the other hand, faith is also expressed through suffering in the form of persecution, martyrdom, and wandering the world as homeless. In all of these situations, faith is expressed—and God commends it.

Finally, the chapter concludes with a fourth movement, a fitting conclusion to the chapter as a whole (vv. 39-40). The promised culmination of this small but powerful unit has to do with the eternal posture of true faith. All of these great examples of faith in Hebrews 11 demonstrate that the ultimate aim of faith was to be commended by God and the reception of a reward that is beyond the present time. The heavenly reward, the "something better," is a consistent focus of this chapter. The "something better," which was promised but not yet realized in the old covenant era, would eventually be realized by "someone," Christ himself, who would inaugurate the coming of an eternal kingdom and bring his people decisive forgiveness for their sins.

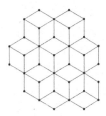

A CALL TO DISCIPLINED ACTION
(12:1–29)

The pattern for the life of God's people under the new covenant has been introduced in chapter 11—a life of active faith not only dependent on God and lived for the future reality he has promised and guaranteed but actively persevering in that lifestyle for the whole of our lives. Using a great deal of sports imagery, he pictures us as spiritual athletes growing in strength in the short term and persevering in that faith for the long term. We are both 100-meter dash specialists and marathon runners, ready for whatever life sends our way. Moreover, the Christian life is a team sport, and we face its trials and obstacles together as a family who is there for each other at every turn.

PERSEVERING IN THE RACE (12:1–3)

The Christian life is pictured here as a great summer Olympics event in a huge amphitheater, with the heroes of chapter 11 sitting in the stadium as "a great cloud of witnesses" (v. 1). They "witness" not in the sense of spectators watching us race but as witnessing to us regarding the value of persevering in the life of faith (11:2, 4–5, 39). A "cloud" is a metaphor for a vast number of people congregated together, and they testify by their example as presented in chapter 11. They "surround" us, filling the front rows of the stadium, with the first tiers containing row upon row of the great saints of the past sitting there wearing their gold medals and giving us the thumbs up, telling us how we can be victorious as well by following their example. Imagine what it would mean for a runner in the great race looking up and seeing Jesse Owens, Carl Lewis, Michael Johnson, and Usain Bolt all giving encouragement and advice. Here it is Enoch, Abraham, Moses, David, and the great prophets shouting that we can win as well.

In light of this great scene, the exhortation flows: "let us run with perseverance the race marked out for us" (12:1). He begins with the marathon, depicting our pilgrimage through life as a great long-distance run. Yet it could also be designated a steeplechase, for there are difficult obstacles throughout the race. There are four rules presented in verses 1–2a for winning the race:

1. Throw off entangling sin—Before an athlete can compete, they have to get in shape by working out assiduously and building their speed and strength. The author describes this two ways—"everything that hinders" and "the sin that so easily entangles" (v. 1). This might well be the clothes that could hinder running and lifting (Greek runners would run nude) as well as (and primarily) the excess weight that makes a person weak and unable to perform. For the believer, this means all distractions, anything that will encumber one's walk with God. These impediments both hinder and entangle us and so must be eliminated as quickly as possible.

2. Run with endurance—Life is definitely a marathon race, and we can only persevere through its ups and downs. For the Christian who is opposed by the world and its anti-Christian sinners, that often means opposition and persecution. That is the thrust here, and

this "endurance" (*hypomonē*) is a feature of this final section. In 10:32 the readers were reminded of the earlier generation who "endured in a great conflict full of suffering," and then in 10:36, they were exhorted that they, too, "need to persevere so that ... you will receive what he has promised." In this section, this occurs four times (12:1-3, 7), with Jesus the great example as he "endured the cross" (v. 2) and "opposition from sinners" (12:3). In that light, they must "endure hardship" (12:7) like Jesus did. The term for "race" is *agōn* (English: "agony") and designates a brutal contest that demands strenuous effort.

3. God has "marked out" (v. 1) the race for us—"Marked out" is a divine passive and means God has established the path we are to run and the rules for the race, and we must run it his way, not whatever way we please. The annals of sport is replete with stories of people who have tried to cheat or have made a mistake, like the famous Super Bowl mistake where the runner dropped the ball just before crossing the goal line. We must follow the rules of the particular race God has "appointed" (another meaning of the verb) us to run.

4. Fixing our eyes on Jesus—The verb *aphoraō* means to "fasten your gaze" or "focus your attention" on what would be the finish line in a race. At the end of our race, that is Jesus, and he is presented here as the final and greatest of the "heroes of the faith" for us to emulate. At his incarnation he was "made like" us (2:17) and was tempted "in every way, just as we are" (4:15), and his complete triumph over every obstacle we face makes him the perfect model for our life of faith.

Hebrews 12:1 describes the race we must run, and verse 2 tells us why Jesus is the perfect model we fashion our lives after in running the race of life. In the movie *Chariots of Fire*, the British runner, Abrahams, studies the running style of all his rivals to learn from them. We are challenged to study the life of Jesus and pattern ourselves after him, and this tells us why. He is "the pioneer and perfecter of faith" (v. 2). "Pioneer" (*archēgon*) was used first in 2:10 of Jesus as the "pioneer of their salvation" whose office was completed ("made perfect") at the cross. There I pointed out that it depicts Jesus both as the pioneer who leads his people through their pilgrimage in this life and the champion who triumphed over suffering and guides us to that same victory. This is also the thrust here. He is the gold medal winner who has returned to teach us how to forge that self-same victory over adversity. To use the American West as an example, he is the Daniel Boone who has pioneered the way across the wilderness and now has come back to lead us along the same path.

At the same time, he is the "perfecter" (*teleiōtēn*) or "finisher" of the faith pilgrimage. The two (pioneer and perfecter) are linked by the same direct article and thus form, in a sense, a single description—several have suggested it could be paraphrased "the beginning and end" of the faith journey, the one who initiated the path and now brings it to completion. Our faith walk is complete in him, and every step is orchestrated by him. The way we persevere is to surrender and follow him at all times and in everything.

His model is especially exemplified in the fact that "for the joy set before him he endured the cross" (v. 2). "Set before" is the same verb as in the first verse and means this was God's appointed path for Jesus. The language is an extremely important development, describing the process and suffering of the cross as "for joy." "For the joy" is *anti tēs ... charas*, and the *anti* can mean either "instead of" or "for, in order that." If the former, Jesus is turning his back on the joy or earthly glory and status and "instead" chooses the path of suffering. If the latter, he suffers "in order that" he might experience the joy of the cross, bringing salvation to humanity. With the athletic metaphor, the positive thrust makes a lot more sense, with the "joy set before him" as the prize for the victor in the race. Christ triumphed and brought redemption, resulting in eternal joy.

When the author says he "endured the cross," this must be tied to the "shame" that was associated with crucifixion. For the Jew to be crucified was to be cut off from the covenant, and for the Roman it was the most disgraceful form of death imaginable, so much so that no Roman citizen could be crucified except by direct edict of Caesar. There are two possible translations here: he endured, "scorning/despising the shame," or he endured "disregarding the shame." If he disregarded it, it could be a reflection of Gethsemane, as Jesus turned his back on the horror and shame and willingly accepted his God-given destiny. If he "scorned" it, it refers to the utter sinfulness of humankind that was associated with it. He refused to yield to the shame of the cross and took the sins of humankind on himself as he sacrificed his blood on the cross. Both options fit the context well, but I slightly prefer "disregard" and the Gethsemane imagery behind the comment.

The result is Psalm 110:1 once more (see 1:3, 13; 8:1; 10:12–13). Jesus gave himself as the one-time atoning sacrifice on the cross and then "sat down at the right hand of the throne of God" (v. 2). Enthroned and exalted, he became the high priest of heaven. He went from shame to glory, from suffering to absolute triumph, and in all this he has taken us with him. We are called to a life of sacrifice and suffering in order to win our way to victory and share in his glory forever. Both the original readers and we current readers are being asked to write our names on the roll call of heroes of the faith.

Verse 3 is often seen as the opening verse of the next section, but I prefer to see it as the third passage in the opening section, forming the conclusion and exhorting us to "consider him who endured such opposition from sinners." Of course, as a transition passage, it both concludes 1–3 and introduces 3–11 with the mega-theme of endurance/perseverance in the midst of great difficulties, continuing verse 2 with its emphasis on running the race with endurance. The author is saying that the persecution they are experiencing is uniting them with Jesus, who endured as the model for them. We must remember that when we are called upon to sacrifice for God that Jesus went through it first and did so on our behalf. "Consider" (*analogisasthe*) means not only to be aware but to study with concentration and carefully reflect on the implications. Jesus and all he went through must consume our thoughts as we go through the difficulties of life.

The danger is that if we try to get through it on our own strength, we will "grow weary and lose heart" like the wilderness generation in 3:1–4:13. They lost heart and began grumbling against God because they were living for themselves rather than for him. With the athletic metaphor that predominates, this pictures us out of shape and running out of gas in the middle of the race, then giving up and stepping off the track. It is probably meant to lead to the next discussion of the danger of apostasy in 12:15–17, 25–29. "*Such* opposition" uses the Greek *toiautēn* and might be better translated "such great" or "intense opposition." That is clear in the passion narrative, especially in the crucifixion scene (Matt 27:20–31, 38–44) when every group there taunts Jesus and calls for his death.

DISCIPLINE AND SONSHIP (12:4–17)

THEIR LIMITED EXPERIENCE (12:4)

They have gone through very little compared to Jesus or their forefathers (see 10:32–34 and the whole of chapter 11), for while they have indeed struggled against sin, they have not yet "resisted to the point of shedding your blood" (v. 4). The persecution is probably verbal thus far, and no one has been beaten or martyred to this point in complete contrast with the heroes of the past (see 11:32–38). Thus far, their race has been fairly easy and uncomplicated, making their discouragement and thinking about giving up all the worse. With the imagery of "struggling" and "resisting," the athletic metaphor has moved from the footrace to boxing or wrestling, and in the ancient world, they were much more violent than today, often ending in the death of one of the fighters and with blood everywhere. With this, the writer is hinting that more difficult days may well be on the way, and they must be ready.

CHALLENGE: REFLECT ON YOUR SONSHIP (12:5-6)

The author is clearly aghast at their shallow reactions to the situation thus far and wants them to wake up and grow up by reflecting on their true status with God and Christ. They have gone through so little yet have acted like cataclysm has taken place. They have "completely forgotten this word of encouragement" regarding their place in God's family. He rebukes them, reminding them that they are sons and daughters of God (returning to 2:10-14 for this emphasis) but are not acting like it in the least. Sonship contains both privilege and responsibility, and they need to change their behavior accordingly.

He turns to Proverbs 3:11-12 to make his point. The message is that sonship by necessity involves discipline, and so all they are going through is the result of God's loving discipline intended to help them grow as his children. The citation contains two parts: the proper reaction to this discipline (Heb 12:5) and the reason why God as a loving Father must take them through such experiences (v. 6). The passage is looked at as the admonition of a father addressing his beloved son. Both passages contain two clauses linked by synonymous parallelism and making the same point twice for emphasis.

The first (v. 5) warns of a dangerous reaction to divine discipline that leads the people to "make light" of the situation and thereby to get discouraged and "lose heart" when difficult times arrive. To "make light" means to "belittle" or "treat something as unimportant." God has been the perfect Father, encouraging or reproving when needed, but his children have ignored his loving actions and treated them as irrelevant. Instead of gaining courage from his presence in their lives, they have focused only on the surface events and "lost heart" or become discouraged by them (like Israel in the wilderness). Not only the general suffering but even the opposition and persecution by pagans is seen here positively as "discipline" from the Lord. This is a critical point. God uses everything, even suffering and persecution, to help his children grow spiritually in dependence on him. However, they have forgotten and ignored this essential truth.

The next two clauses (v. 6) tells us why we should take it all positively as from God.[1] Putting them together, the Lord "disciples/chastises" his sons and daughters because he loves them enough to know this is for the best for them (Rom 8:28). There is no reason to give up because things are going wrong in our lives. Our loving Father is in complete charge of them all and will turn them around for our benefit. The trials are temporary, but the spiritual blessings that arise out of them will be eternal. The next section (12:7–11) will develop this further and tell us how and why he does so. Since every believer is part of his family and is his child, he loves them enough to send discipline to help them grow up in him. "Chastise" is *mastigoi*, the word for "scourging and stresses the severity of the discipline when needed. God, like any loving parent, will punish a child when he or she needs it.

THE UNIVERSAL NEED FOR DISCIPLINE (12:7–8)

Because every true child of God is the object of his loving care, it transpires that every true child will have to undergo "hardship." The important part here is that negative hardship becomes

---

1. There is a chiastic pattern in the Greek order, A-B-B-A, with A = the Father's love and B = him disciplining his children. The literal translation is: "Whom the Lord loves, he disciplines, and he chastises everyone whom he accepts as a son." This stresses the synonymous use of "disciplines / chastises."

positive discipline when the Lord is given control. Our task is not to let ourselves fall into despair but to "cast all [our] anxiety on him bcause he cares for [us]" (1 Pet 5:7). When God allows trials into our lives, he is "treating [us] as his children" (Heb 12:7). So life's difficulties, in this sense, are loving gifts from a Father who cares enough to bring into our lives what we need to grow. The readers' problem is that, in their spiritual lethargy (5:11; 6:12), they have forgotten this fact and must be reminded of it as the negligent children they are.

Discipline and sonship are interconnected and a perfect sign that God has accepted us into his family as his children. After all, the author remarks in verse 7, "what children are not disciplined by their father?" There has to be discipline in any parent-child relationship (Prov 13:24; 22:15; 23:13–14). In Scripture it is the parents who are responsible for raising a child and making them a contributing and mature adult. The point is that if this is true on an earthly plane, it is even more the case on the heavenly plane. God must discipline his children, and only he has the wisdom to do it properly and well.

Verse 8 continues this thought and states the same point negatively: "If you are not disciplined ... then you are not legitimate, not true sons and daughters at all." Criminal records are replete with stories of kids who were neglected by parents completely or given too much, where they never had to pay for their mistakes. Both are tragic errors and signs of the lack of both love and basic wisdom. That is not how God operates. Every child needs discipline for their own good. We need a different mindset to realize that God will use our troubles in a myriad of positive ways in our lives.

In the Roman world, an illegitimate child was not considered part of the family and was given no attention or help. However, the readers are legitimate children and as such should expect a great deal of loving discipline in their lives. This is further proof that God deeply loves them and is involved in their lives, so they should consider this a divine gift meant for their good.

HUMAN FATHERS AND THE HEAVENLY FATHER (12:9–11)

Using another *a fortiori* (lesser to greater; see 9:23; 11:28–29) argument, the writer contrasts the limited, finite decisions parents can make with the perfect decisions of our heavenly Father. As a father and a grandparent, my discipline decisions are loving but rarely perfect. Still, my kids recognize the care I have for them and respect me and my discipline. Like all fathers, I am severely limited, as I am earth-bound and do not know the future. I can only do my best and pray for wisdom. The word for "disciplined" here is *paideutas* and was used for the Greek "pedagogue" or "disciplinarian, tutor, teacher" who helped raise the child to adulthood. They were essential components in the ancient family (Alexander the Great's pedagogue was Aristotle himself) and highly respected.

If we do love and respect our human parents for disciplining us, the argument goes, "how much more should we submit to the Father of spirits" (see Num 16:22; 2 Macc 3:24–25; it is extensively in the Similitudes of Enoch, 1 Enoch 37–71). We are fathers of flesh and bone and have the human perspective in every decision we make. God is Father of "spirits," referring both to the eternal spirit behind each of us and the heavenly eternal beings. The rhetorical question expects a resounding "yes" response: "Why, of course we should submit!" Our God is Lord of the universe and Creator of all that is in it, so of course, we should surrender all to him.

The value of such submission is that in doing so we shall "live," referring to the "indestructible life" (7:16) that is ours in Christ now and especially awaits us in heaven. Currently, the Triune Godhead will both empower us and fill us with the wisdom to make the right decisions in living our life on this earth. Even more, with our sins forgiven and Christ as our Savior, death becomes merely a step up to the eternal life that will be ours in heaven.

He explains this further in verse 10, relating two areas of inferiority in the guidance of earthly parents. As much as they wish to do what is best for the child, their discipline is temporary, and the perspective is that of "a little while"—that is, with temporary

benefits that may turn out well and may not. We can only see a bit
into the future, and even that is partial. Moreover, parental discipline only works until they go off to college, and then they are on
their own in effect. Second, our decisions are as we think best, that
is, finite from start to finish. I am hoping I made the correct decision, but I cannot know for sure. No matter how good my intentions, the discipline is finite in both quality and quantity.

In contrast, God's discipline is "for our good" (*sympheron*; "beneficial") in an absolute sense. He never makes a poor decision, and
every single one will benefit us in the end. Like the human counterpart, they will not always be pleasant or welcome, but they
are always for the best (Rom 8:28). This is where Christian ethics
differs from Greek ways, which prized mastery of self. For them,
maturity was being sufficient in self, while Christians sought to
be sufficient in God and selfless in relation to others.

The purpose of divine discipline is now spelled out—"in order
that we may share in his holiness" (v. 10). They are already "holy
brothers and sisters" (3:1) who have been "made holy" via his "one
sacrifice" (10:14). They are set apart from the world for God and
are called upon to progressively grow in that holiness. The term
used here (*hagiotētos*) only appears here in the New Testament
and refers to holiness as a divine quality that we humans need to
inculcate. So discipline is intended to help us to be more like him
and less like the world. Second Peter 1:4 calls this participating in
the divine nature. Our trials mold us and help us to realize that we
can only surmount our struggles in him and in dependence on him.

Verse 11 concludes this entire section (12:1–11) and puts the
teaching together for us, beginning with a huge truism: "No discipline seems pleasant at the time, but painful." Every one of us can
agree with that. I have never yet gone through a trial and enjoyed
it, nor will I ever. However, the end result of that tough situation
is always positive when looked at from God's perspective, and that
is the subject of the second half of the verse: "Later on, however, it

produces a harvest of righteousness and peace for those who have been trained by it." This, too, is further athletic imagery, with God the coach who devises discipline or training exercises to get us in shape for the race of life. None are pleasant, but all are essential in order to be ready for the surprises coming in every game once the season starts.

The second image used here is an agricultural metaphor, "producing a harvest." Before a crop can be finalized, the soil must be plowed, the seeds planted, and the manure packed around it. All this is pictured here as the necessary spade work for a successful harvest. Few are more hardworking than farmers (see 2 Tim 2:6), and we must go through the hard times to have the final product. By its very nature, divine discipline must entail hardship and difficulty, for its purpose is to combat sin and produce holy living (note Elihu's classic statement, Job 22:19-28).

The Greek has "the peaceful fruit of righteousness." Two crops are specifically named in the harvest. First, peace flowers in our lives. One of the fruits of the Spirit in Galatians 5:22, peace here refers to the tranquility of the soul and inner contentment flowing out of the tumult of the situation. The difficult earthly trial forces us to rely on God more deeply, and that produces the peace of God in our hearts and lives. Philippians 4:6-7 says it so well: "Do not be anxious about anything, but in every situation ... present your requests to God. And the peace of God ... will guard your hearts and your minds in Christ Jesus." Then 4:9 adds, "The God of peace will be with you." After extensive training in the gym of hard knocks, the spiritual athlete is more and more confident in her ability to react properly to all future problems and feel the empowering presence of God and the Holy Spirit, resulting in contentment of soul.

"Of righteousness" is placed at the end of the sentence and serves as the conclusion of the whole. When the conflict is finished and the harvest is in, the main crop produced is a righteous life in which God has taken over and refashioned the person in his own image, as well as brought a new-found peace into her life. God's righteousness and justice have been inculcated in us. This is seen in athletes at the end of a successful race, with their arms high in triumph and the entire face suffused with joy. That is us now and especially in eternity. Some even see this mainly as pointing to the heavenly reward, but I believe it equally describes us in this life as we grow in Christ.

THE CORPORATE DIMENSION IN THE RACE (12:12–13)

This is a crucial addition, forming a second conclusion with the promise of the harvest. Both in the Roman world and our society today, rugged individualism ruled the culture, and people tried to be self-sufficient and handle all their problems by themselves. The result was failure, for no one can deal with life's complexities in their own strength. We need the wisdom of others, lest we fool ourselves into making bad decisions (which all finite individuals often do). The key is that the commands here are in the plural and mean that we are not to do this in our own strength but to bring other believers into our lives to help us accomplish this strengthening process in the corporate community.

The athletic imagery continues here as well, with two points, the first in line with the maxim, "when the going gets tough, the tough get going" (v. 12). There is always a point in a race when strength begins to falter, and the prepared athlete needs to find a second wind in order to finish well (I think of what is called "heartbreak hill" in the Boston Marathon, where so many fail). Then there is the need to overcome the obstacles life throws your way (v. 13).

The "feeble arms and weak knees" (v. 12) combines the boxing and running metaphors of verses 1–3 and is taken from Isaiah 35:3–4: "Strengthen the feeble hands; steady the knees that give way." The writer may well intend us to recall two things from the Isaiah passage: the need for the weaker brothers to receive help and the promise of God's soon coming (35:4: "your God will come"). There it is God who will give you that strength, while here they also are to draw strength from each other.

In the midst of the pressure-laden struggle, the runner/boxer is at the end of their rope and about to give up. They desperately need to get help, as they are about to be knocked out by their opponent. Worst of all, their struggle is still in the beginning stages, for they have "not yet resisted to the point of shedding your blood" (12:4). In their weakened spiritual condition (5:11–6:12), apostasy is a very real danger.

The race of verse 13 is the marathon we saw in 12:1-2, with an extremely long straightway that demands endurance and strength. They dare not deviate from the path God has set before them (v. 2), lest they collapse and fall into the ditch. The spiritually strong are to "smooth the way" or point out the true path for the weak among them. The members of God's family are responsible for one another. Here the allusion may be to Proverbs 4:26-27: "Give careful thought to the paths for your feet.... Do not turn to the right or the left; keep your foot from evil." This recalls verse 1, "throw off everything that hinders and the sin that so easily entangles."

For the race, it is obligatory to keep to the straight and narrow way of God and not to get sidetracked by life's (and the world's) distractions. This is clearly a call for faithful living and perseverance in the Christian life. As Matthew 7:13-14 makes clear, we must "enter through the narrow gate, for ... small is the gate and narrow the road that leads to life, and only a few find it." What the narrow road leads to is told us in 12:22-24 below, and it is unbelievably significant. So we are challenged to "make a straight path" at all times to the heavenly city of verse 22 and to make sure we are not distracted by life's temptations.

The "lame" are those on the verge of failure and apostasy, and they are in danger of being "disabled" or unable to finish the race. Here is where the community becomes so critical, as we often need the help and support of others to find the strength to continue.

One of my favorite sports scenes of all time came in the Special Olympics a few years ago. Three runners were straining to the finish line when one of them suddenly lost footing and fell to the track. The other two didn't hesitate but stopped, helped the fallen competitor stand, and all three crossed the finish line together. That is the perfect model for the church to follow. Every one of us need that support often in our lives.

"Disabled" is *ektrepomai*, "to be turned aside," and may well combine medical along with athletic imagery, as it can mean "put out of joint" and refer to a knee giving way in the midst of the fight or race, causing the participant to fall and fail to finish. We need "healing" and constant strengthening so we can finish the race and attain the heavenly prize. As in Philippians 3:14, we must "press on toward the goal to win the prize for which God has called me heavenward in Christ Jesus."

Warnings Concerning Failure (12:14–17)

"Make every effort" is *diōkete*, "pursue" or "strive for," the same term as "press on" in the Philippians 3:14 passage above. The athletic imagery continues here, as we are commanded to energetically pursue this in our church and our life. This combines the horizontal (peace with everyone) and vertical (holiness) sides of the Christian life. Both aspects must be constant goals we strive to attain. As our troubles have produced a harvest of God's peace in our lives (v. 11), we need to extend that to our relations with everyone around us, both believers and non-believers alike. This is similar to Galatians 6:10, so we will paraphrase (replacing "do good" with "seek peace"): "Seek peace with all people, especially with those who belong to the family of believers." Peace is the result of our salvation, increases as we grow in Christ, and must govern our external relationships even as it develops as we grow in him. So we seek a harmonious relationship with all, even with our persecutors (Ps 34:14, cited in Matt 4:9; Rom 12:18; 1 Pet 3:11).

This sense of peace with God and with those around us is part of our holiness (see on 12:10). We seek the two together. So the author adds, "without holiness no one will see the Lord" (v. 14). This does not so much mean experience God's presence but is more emphatic and means see the Lord in eternity. Without basic holiness, a person cannot be truly saved or know Christ. So seeing God is literal and not just metaphorical. On this earthly plane, no one can literally "see" him (Exod 33:20; John 1:18); we will actually "see" him when we get to heaven. Holiness is an absolutely essential part of being a Christian. The writer is well aware that the spiritual lethargy of many of these church members means a corresponding lapse of holiness and wants to warn them most severely. So this statement leads into the next two verses and the next warning about apostasy.

When he says in verse 15, "See to it that no one falls short of the grace of God," he is returning to 2:1 and 4:1 and the danger of "falling short" or apostasy. This is one of the dominant issues of the book, discussed in depth in 2:1–4; 3:7–4:13; 5:11–6:12; 10:19–31; and 12:14–29, so this begins the final warning passage. The "grace of God" would encompass all he has done in sending his Son to die on the cross for our sins and the new era of salvation that has resulted. In 4:16, divine grace is intended "so that we may receive mercy and find grace to help us in our time of need." The wilderness people fell short and lost their place in God's promised land, perishing in the wilderness. Esau here has joined them and becomes another negative example of what *not* to do if one wants to inherit eternal life.

Two other comments clarify this. First, there is the "bitter root (that) grows up to cause trouble and defile many" (v. 15). The resulting bitter fruit is the opposite of the "harvest of peace and righteousness" that brings life in 12:11. This alludes to Deuteronomy 29:18 in a context of idolatry, which is seen as a "bitter poison" that destroys, a spiritual contamination that defiles the entire community as a result of sin, producing people who have become calloused with a false sense of security due to their hardened hearts.

The second comment (12:16) provides the terrible example of the "sexually immoral" and "godless" Esau, who married Hittite women in Genesis 26:34 (see Jubilees 25:4-10) and was spiritually unfaithful (*pornos*, used for both types) to God. He was completely centered on his needs and was so shallow that he "sold his inheritance rights" to Jacob for the price of a "single meal" (Heb 12:16), bringing terrible shame on his birthright and his gift from God (Gen 25:29-34). His contempt for the things of God rendered him an apostate.

So when he later "wanted to inherit this blessing," he was "rejected" by God (12:17) in the same way that all apostates will be rejected (Gen 27:1-40), echoing the point of Hebrews 6:4-6 and 10:26-27 that such an apostate has committed the unpardonable sin and will never be accepted back. Some think that when he repented and "sought the blessing with tears" (12:17) he should have been forgiven as in the New Testament. However, we must realize that these were not tears of repentance but merely a secular "change of heart" that reflected a desire only to get his inheritance back, not get right with God. He never really turned back to God and merely desired the greater wealth and prestige of his birthright. His was worldly sorrow, not godly grief. He never could "change what he had done" because, like in 6:6, he had in reality "subjected (God's offer of blessing) to public disgrace" and never truly sought an actual new relationship with God. In addition, his apostasy removed him from ever deserving God's forgiveness. Deuteronomy 29:20 says, "The LORD will never be willing to forgive them. ... All the curses written in this book will fall on them, and the LORD will blot out their names from under heaven."

THE TERROR OF THE EARTHLY SINAI AND
THE JOY OF THE HEAVENLY ZION (12:18-24)

The contrast between the old and new covenants is now expressed
in a new way, returning to 2:2-3 on Sinai and adding the scene of
awesomeness that permeated it. This is not a warning but centers on the contrast between the fear of the old covenant and the
festive joy that attends the new covenant. The antithesis is introduced with the catch-phrases "you have not come" (v. 18, like Israel
at Mount Sinai) and "you have come" (v. 22, like believers at Mount
Zion). Each of the two subsections (vv. 18-21, 22-24) contains a
balanced set of descriptive phenomena connected by *kai* ("and")
and thus clearly in contrast to one another. Therefore, the antithesis is between the fear permeating the old ways of Judaism and
the blessings that infused the new ways of Christ. So once more it
asks, "Why would you want to return to the lesser when you have
the supremely greater in Christ?"

EARTHLY SINAI (12:18-21)

At Sinai, God—more than at any other time in human history—
showed physically the shock and awe that portends his **Shekinah**
presence in this world. Sinai "cannot be touched" (see Exod 19:12),
seen particularly in the palpably visual elements of fire, darkness,
gloom, and storm (Exod 19:16-19) and the auditory image of the
trumpet blast (Exod 19:16, 19; 20:18). The result is always terror at
the actions of Almighty God. The "blazing fire" took place when
the top half of the mountain was wrapped in smoke and fire at the
arrival of the Lord (19:18), meaning he was present in his awesome
power. The darkness, gloom, and storm describes what Moses himself entered when he ascended Sinai "where God was" (20:21). The
trumpet and voice caused the people to quake in fear (19:16; 20:18).

It says in Hebrews 12:19 that they "begged that no further word
be spoken to them," pleading that Moses alone speak, lest they die
(see Deut 5:24-27). The writer is not saying that they wanted no
further messages but no messages *directly from God*, for the divine

power was too great for them to bear. It is this awestruck fear the writer wants his readers to catch, for their indifference and lethargy are getting them into serious trouble.

The absolute terror is clear throughout Sinai as presented here. With the sovereign God infusing the mountain with his presence, if either man or animal so much as touches the ground of Sinai it will die. In Exodus 19:12, 13 (reflected in verse 20 here), God's holiness will be so palpable that no crested being dare live. The people would have to stone them or kill them with arrows from a distance, lest they touch one of the doomed beings and have to die themselves. All of us must learn from this. We, like Israel of old, too easily take the holiness of God for granted. The absolute might and glory of his sacred Person is more than we will understand in our finite existence.

Even Moses himself (12:21), who had met and spoken with God numerous times, had to admit, "I am trembling with fear." This statement does not occur at Sinai but reflects the golden calf incident when Moses said, "I feared the anger and wrath of the LORD, for he was angry enough with you to destroy you" (Deut 9:19). The true holiness of God is more than we can bear. As 10:31 has already made clear, "It is a dreadful thing to all into the hands of the living God." This sums up so well the true divine-human encounter. There is both privilege and responsibility in or relationship with the living God. The privilege leads to joy and peace as we reflect on the loving Father who watches over us. The responsibility leads to awe and fear as we realize how seriously we must take the necessity of our faithfulness and obedience to him. We do not want to stand before him in shame and have to confess the extent of our failure (2 Tim 2:15).

HEAVENLY ZION (12:22–24)

This is another of the truly beautiful passages in Scripture, especially because it contains a thrilling double meaning in which our current experience of worship is completely linked with our future heavenly enjoyment of the Godhead. As our spirits sore in current contact with our heavenly Father, we right now have a touch of heaven in our lives. In our "Zion" encounter, we enjoy not the unapproachable God of Sinai but the indwelling God of Zion, entailing a festive atmosphere of worship and joy. The reason is that we are entering "the city of the living God, the heavenly Jerusalem" (12:22). In Revelation 21:1–8 this is an **apocalyptic** metaphor for heaven itself. We will take each in turn to show how they accumulate to describe the incredible privilege of being worshiping Christians.

1. "Mount Zion ... the city of the living God" (Heb 12:22): Mount Zion in Jerusalem was not only the place of David's residence (2 Sam 5:6–9) but also and more importantly, the resting place of the ark of the covenant (2 Sam 6:2). So it stood for the earthly home of God and his Shekinah glory (1 Kgs 14:21; Ps 78:68–69). When Solomon later built the temple on Mount Moriah, the name Zion was extended to the whole area and became synonymous with Jerusalem (Ps 87:1–7). As the "city of the living God," we have entered his true home and joined him in residence there. This is "the city with foundations, whose architect and builder is God" (11:10), portrayed in its present as well as future reality.

2. "The heavenly Jerusalem" (v. 22): To the earthly image of Zion is added the apocalyptic image of the heavenly reality, but it is a current and not just a future one. It borrows the language of "the new Jerusalem" of Revelation 3:12; 21:2, 10 and extends the image to the present experience of God. The pilgrimage portrayed so well in Hebrews is not just a journey to a future entering of the heavenly Jerusalem but the present enjoyment of this reality in our current walk with

God (Gal 4:26). The theme of this is God currently dwelling with his people and his self-manifestation to them

3. "Thousands upon thousands of angels in joyful assembly" (v. 22): I love this picture, for it tells me that right now, I am surrounded by the angels of heaven as I serve the Lord. At Sinai these angels had the solemn task of mediating the law (2:2), but now they are engaged in joyous celebration of the Lord with us. This is a festal gathering like the Feast of Tabernacles, with everyone dancing and singing with joy at the harvest celebration. Exaltation is the emotional response. The absolute joy of heaven becomes a present anticipation as we reflect with the myriads of angels on all God has done and is doing in our lives.

4. "The church of the firstborn, whose names are written in heaven" (v. 23): Some say these are angels, who are described this way in the early Christian writing *Shepherd of Hermas* (*Vision* 3.4.1), but angels are never depicted as "enrolled in heaven," and God in Exodus 4:22–23 calls Israel his "firstborn," in contrast to Esau who gave up his birthright. So these are believers whose names have been written in the book of Life (Luke 10:20; Rev 20:15; 21:27). Others think it may have been the Old Testament saints, but the context is centering upon all believers of every age. These are the people of God as citizens of heaven (see 11:8–10), and the idea of the "firstborn" is not temporal but privileged status, looking at our dignity as "firstfruits" who are members of the "city of God."

5. "God, the Judge of all" (v. 23): The Greek order is "to a Judge, who is God of all," and this is likely intended both ways. God is universal Judge, and every person

will answer to him and him alone. This is a positive blessing for the faithful (= reward) but a critical warning for the weak. They will indeed stand before him, and they had better remember the awesome, terrifying God of Sinai from verses 18–21. This becomes the basis of our trust and confidence in our leaders in 13:17, who are described as those who will make good decisions because they know that they will "give account" to this God, the Judge of all (also 4:13). God is actually the central figure of this whole section, and it is so important for us to realize this and make certain he is central in our lives.

6. "The spirits of the righteous made perfect" (v. 23): There is some difference of opinion as to whether these are the Old Testament saints in heaven or New Testament saints who have died, but there is little reason not to realize both are included in this. These are the saints of all the ages who are now with the Lord. Behind the idea of "the righteous made perfect" is primarily Christ, whose "one sacrifice" has "made perfect forever those who are being made holy" (10:14) but also the saints, depicted in 11:40 as part of the process ("together with us would they be made perfect")—meaning that the final destiny of the saints of the old covenant is intertwined with us new covenant people. The point here is that even now the saints in heaven celebrate with us. We together are the "righteous" who belong to God (10:38). We and they have both experienced God's complete work in their lives and belong to him fully.

7. "Jesus the mediator of the new covenant" (12:24): This is an essential core emphasis in this letter, as seen in 8:6 and 9:15. This entire Zion scene is a new covenant

blessing, made possible by the high priestly work of Christ on the cross. Christ has stepped between us and the God we ignored before our conversion and created a new reality and era of salvation that has eternal ramifications.

8. "The sprinkled blood that speaks a better word than the blood of Abel" (v. 24): The Greek simply has "speaks better than Abel," and some think this means simply that the new covenant message was superior to the speaking even of the first "righteous" person, Abel (11:4). While possible, it was Abel's blood that "cried out" from the ground (Gen 4:10), and this more likely means that Jesus' blood sacrifice for sins was superior than that of Abel, for Abel's cry was for vengeance and judgment while Jesus' message brought redemption and forgiveness to sinful humanity. The "sprinkled blood" stems from the sacrifice for sin in the old covenant, and Jesus achieved that once-for-all with his one-time high priestly blood sacrifice that launched the new covenant.

CONCLUDING WARNING AGAINST APOSTASY (12:25-29)

This warning paragraph both concludes the chapter on perseverance (12:1-29) and acts as a summary of many of the themes in the book related to our walk with God (our pilgrimage) and the danger of falling by the wayside and losing our salvation birthright. The second half of the chapter (vv. 14-29) is framed by warning (vv. 14-17, 25-29) and extends the obstacles of the race of life that demand endurance (vv. 1-3) to the danger of stumbling over those obstacles and losing it all. Repeating the basic message of 2:1-4, the vast superiority of Zion over Sinai and the incredible benefits of being under the new covenant make it all the more critical to grow and maintain our walk with God at all times.

THESIS: DO NOT REFUSE HIM (12:25A)

This begins with the same verb as 3:12 (*blepete*; "be very careful, watch out"), where it also introduces a warning against apostasy (a sinful, unbelieving heart). With the emphasis on Sinai in verses 18–21, this also likens them to the wilderness generation that failed and perished without reaching the "promised" land. A hardened heart is once again leading them to disregard the admonitions of Yahweh. Here the danger is refusing to listen to "him who speaks," which denotes an active rejection of both God and his revealed truths. God speaking began this letter (1:1–2, the contrast between the old [prophetic] and the new [Jesus] revelation), and the stress is on his eternal truths. Here he has spoken at both Sinai (12:19) and Zion (v. 24), and so it is even more critical to hear and respond to that voice.

TWO EARTH-HEAVEN DICHOTOMIES (12:25B–27)

The *a fortiori* argument (lesser to greater) of "how much less" in 12:25b parallels 2:3 with its earth-heaven contrast. If Israel "did not escape" God's "earthly" voice of warning,[2] how much less will we (note the emphatic *hēmeis*, "we") not escape if we repudiate his "heavenly" warning? This is defined in strong terms as "turning away," not simply a gradual withdrawal from awareness of God but a studied and deliberate rejection (compare 2 Tim 4:4; Titus 1:14). They at first "begged" Yahweh not to speak further (12:19), then they refused to listen or heed his commands (v. 25). God is now speaking through his Son, and the admonition is all the more binding and severe.

---

2. Some think the earthly voice is that of Moses, but it is better to see this as the divine voice commanding on earth, then in heaven. The contrast is not between the two speakers but between the two covenants, the one earthly in origin, the other heavenly.

At Sinai we are told God's voice "shook the earth," and in verse 18, that was described as "burning with fire … darkness, gloom, and storm." The divine earthquake shook the mountain to its very foundations (Exod 19:18; Ps 68:7), and this signified the establishing of the law and the old covenant. The contrast is seen in verse 26 via a citation from Haggai 2:6: "Once more I will shake not only the earth but also the heavens" (also 2:21). In Haggai it portends God judging the nations and establishing the glory of Israel, and here it is that and more, as this entails also a new heavens and new earth (Rev 21:1). The wicked nations will be no more, and all who have turned against God and his people will suffer eternal torment.

The point here is that this will include apostates, and nothing can be more fearsome than this realization. In fact, the only group for which this terrifying scenario is guaranteed are the apostates, for there is no more hope for them (6:4–6; 10:26–27),[3] while the unsaved still have the opportunity to repent and escape this judgment.

The writer goes on to explain that "once more" refers to a future shaking and "indicates the removing of what can be shaken—that is, created things" (12:27). The "once more" means not just a repetition of the earlier shaking at a later time but the completeness and finality of the act. The temporal and finite is now giving way to the eternal and perfect final reality. All creation partakes of the temporal and the incomplete, and there are, in a sense, three "shakings"—at creation (implicit), at the giving of the law (removed and replaced with the coming of Christ), and at the **eschaton** (the end of this world order). Thus the "removal of what can be shaken" refers to the end of the created order, that which since the fall of humanity into sin became incomplete and imperfect, needing to be replaced by the infinite.

---

3. Remember the earlier discussion at chapter 6 and 10. Active, final apostasy of the Hebrews type cannot be forgiven, but the more passive type of James 5:19–20, in which sin crowds Christ out of your life, is redeemable.

The shaking of the heavens will take place at the final judgment when the new heavens and new earth replace not only this
world but heaven as currently constituted. This world will be
destroyed by fire (2 Pet 3:7, 10). This, of course, will not take place
with heaven. Rather, it will be amalgamated with the new creation and form one final united dwelling place for God, his angels,
and the redeemed, called "the new heavens and new earth" (Isa
65:17; Rev 21:1). There will no longer be two separate places but one.

The final result is "that what cannot be shaken can remain."
This will be called "an unshakeable kingdom" (NET, LEB) in the next
verse, and this will include not just the place but the people, those
who will inhabit the eternal heavenly kingdom. This is what will
"remain" for eternity (menō; "remain, dwell"), as we make our home
with God forever. This is a terrifying prospect for the unsaved and
the apostate but a wondrous prospect for the righteous and will
constitute a final, complete, and eternal moment of glory.

CONCLUDING EXHORTATION (12:28-29)

Out of the dire warning emerges another reason for confidence
("since") for true believers—namely, the certainty of what God is
giving us. "We are receiving" (v. 28) is present tense rather than
future, meaning that the process by which this world will end
has already begun. This is a marvelous example of what we call
"inaugurated **eschatology**"—namely, that God has already started
to act, and he has initiated our final future. As we just said, the
"unshakeable kingdom" is the final resting place for God's people,
no longer finite but perfect and complete. This is the "city with
foundations" of 11:10. It exists now in the believer's heart and is
experienced spiritually, but it will become a physical reality after
the "Day" arrives (10:25).

The command in light of this spectacular future is to "be thankful" (v. 28) or "have grace" (echōmen charin)—namely, to acknowledge God's mercy and glory by way of praise and gratitude. This
thankful heart of gratitude is then interpreted in terms of worship,

and we are to do so "acceptably with reverence and awe"(v. 28). In one sense, this goes beyond the act of worship, for *latreuō* describes a life of Christian service in which everything we do for God is part of our worship.

Two characteristics define this worship and service. It is "acceptable" (*euarestōs*), meaning the desire to please him in all things. This will guide every decision. Second, the attitude is "reverence and awe" or "reverential awe" in which we serve him "with fear and trembling" (Phil 2:12), wanting desperately to obey and glorify him in everything we do. This is a proper reaction to his holiness, as we bow before it and throw ourselves on our knees in submissive awe.

The reason for this worship and awe (*gar*; "for") is that "our God is a consuming fire" (12:29), a citation from Deuteronomy 4:24 (also Isa 33:14). The fire of Sinai is reinterpreted as both the holy awesomeness of God (= reverence) and the fiery divine judgment against all who are unworthy and stand against him. As 10:31 concludes, "It is a dreadful thing to fall into the hands of the living God." All of us have two choices with the divine "consuming fire": to be enveloped with his holiness or his judgment. It is a choice with eternal ramifications. We dare not ignore the God who speaks, for these are eternal truths that will determine everything. Nothing compares to this set of decisions in importance. We must remain right with him.

With Hebrews 12, the author moves to the climax of the book, using various word pictures to describe a life of discipleship that endures in following Christ. The first describes the Christian life as a race (vv. 1–3) and the faithful of Hebrews 11 as a great cloud of witnesses. Rather than spectators, they bear witness to us concerning God's faithfulness and the fruitfulness of the life of faith, encouraging us as we run. So, like a runner, believers are called to throw off those things that would hinder them, run with endurance, follow God's established path for the race, and keep our eyes on Jesus as our ultimate example, for Jesus shamed shame itself and took his seat at the right hand of God (Ps 110:1). In following his example of endurance in the face of opposition, we do not lose heart. The situation of the original hearers is that they have not yet faced a level of persecution that involved the shedding of their blood (unlike the great heroes of the faith in Hebrews 11!), but that could be coming in the future, and they need to be ready (Heb 12:4).

The author next takes up an encouraging image from Proverbs 3:11-12, the discipline afforded a child by a loving father. The Lord's discipline, in the form of the persecution the readers are facing, is a gift and, therefore, should not be taken lightly (Heb 12:5). God uses such experiences to strengthen his children and, as such, they are an expression of his love (v. 6). They also are expressions of legitimacy, God treating us as his children (vv. 7-8). The point is underscored in verses 9-11 by drawing an analogy to the discipline offered by earthly fathers, the author again using an argument from "lesser to greater." If we respect human fathers who have disciplined us, we certainly should respect God as our heavenly Father, embracing his discipline, which leads to "indestructible" life and holiness. The truism that discipline is painful is put in perspective when we grasp that it is wonderfully fruitful in our lives (v. 11), bringing a bumper crop of righteousness in life.

With Hebrews 12:12-13 the author comes back around to the athletic imagery used at the beginning of the chapter, but now the emphasis is on the importance of running the race with others. With words taken from Isaiah 35:3-4, the readers are encouraged to "Strengthen the feeble hands; steady the knees that give way." In context, the emphasis is both on helping weaker runners in the race and depending on God for strength. In community and with God's help, we can keep on the straight path, rather than being disabled in taking wrong steps. We need the Lord and each other to finish the race well.

The series of warnings at 12:14-17 are varied but focused on the real spiritual danger of falling short of God's grace. In relationships with both believers and unbelievers, we should seek peace and holiness (v. 14). The "bitter root" of verse 15 alludes to Deuteronomy 29:18, which in context speaks of idolatry and a hardened heart, dynamics involved in turning away from God's covenant of grace. When people do fall away, it affects others around them in a devastating way. Selling out one's inheritance, like Esau, shows a shallow and self-centered contempt for the things of God, and such will be judged by God.

The section entitled "The Terror of the Earthly Sinai and the Joy of the Heavenly Zion" (12:18-24) forms the climactic moment of the whole book as the author paints a striking comparison between the old and new covenants. The imagery of wandering in the wilderness evoked at various points in the book to this point (for example, 3:7-19) now is brought to bear on the idea of "having arrived" somewhere, particularly one of two mountains. Mount Sinai stands for the old covenant, a place of terror and separation (12:18-21). This mountain sums up what it is to meet the all-powerful, holy God outside of the grace and hope offered in the new covenant. By contrast, Mount Zion represents that new covenant, and the imagery here is of celebration and welcome, joy and blessing (vv. 22-24): the heavenly city Jerusalem as the dwelling place of God; thousands upon thousands of angels in joyful assembly (v. 22); the church of the firstborn with their names written in heaven; God as vindicator of those who obey him and the spirits of righteous people—those still living and those who have died— made perfect (v. 23); and Jesus as mediator of the new covenant, his sprinkled blood speaking better than Abel's blood (v. 24).

Chapter 12 concludes with a warning and exhortation (vv. 25-29). The author reinforces the warning "do not refuse him" (12:25a) with language from earlier in the book and an argument from lesser to greater, much like the warning found in 2:1-4. If

those who trembled at Mount Sinai did not escape when they
rejected the word of God, those who reject God's word today certainly won't escape! God shook the earth at Sinai, but according to
Haggai 2:6, there is another shaking coming, which will involve
both the heavens and the earth (Heb 12:26–27). In other words,
when the final judgment takes place, only the "unshakable kingdom" will remain in God's a new heavens and earth. This reality
forms the foundation for a final, encouraging exhortation in the
chapter (vv. 28–29). Since believers are receiving an unshakable
kingdom, they should thank God and worship him with reverential awe, prompted in part by the realization that "our God is a
consuming fire" (v. 29).

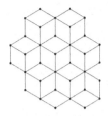

PRACTICAL INSTRUCTIONS
AND PRAYER
(13:1–25)

The purpose of this material is to sum up the themes of the letter and provide practical exhortation telling us how we can serve God with reverence and please him (12:28). The practical content and style have led some to speculate it is inferior to the grand rhetorical quality of the rest of the letter and even to conclude it was added by a later hand. But it does fit well with the rest of the letter as an exhortation. The first part especially would form a fine mini-series of messages on living the Christian life, moving from the corporate (vv. 1–3) to the individual (vv. 4–6), with a meditation on the relationship between leaders and those they serve (vv. 7–9).

ETHICAL INJUNCTIONS (13:1-6)

THE SOCIAL LIFE OF THE CORPORATE CHURCH (13:1-3)

There are two sets of instructions providing a balanced look at how the church and its members are to live out a life that pleases God, first in the social aspects of life together (vv. 1–3), then in the private lives of each member (vv. 4–6). We begin with "brotherly love" (*philadelphia*) between those who are "brothers and sisters" in our Father's family. This has special relevance for the persecuted people who desperately need each other and apparently have lost this sense of unity in the community. Some had neglected this and endangered the rest, which relied on togetherness and mutual support.

As we have seen throughout (for instance, 12:12–13), God holds us responsible for the spiritual well-being of one another. If Christ loved us enough to pay the price for our sins on the cross, we must continue his love as we become part of God's people. So the command is for perseverance in love, and this should become a lifestyle that controls all we do together in the church. Moreover, this is not merely emotional caring or even spiritual concern but concrete, tangible acts of love and help on a continual basis. In churches today, this is often not done well, but not just because people don't care. Those who are hurting have too much pride to share their needs with others. This is where the sense of family is so critical. In the nuclear family, such sharing is much more common, for the ties together are much more apparent. We need this family togetherness in the lives of our churches.

This is endemic not just inside the corporate life of the church but should also be visible in our relationships with outsiders. So the author adds, "Do not forget to show hospitality to strangers" (13:2). This was a major stress in pagan as well as Jewish and Christian circles. As a present-tense prohibition, this could be translated, "Do not ever forget" or even "stop forgetting," implying this was being neglected in these house churches.

Both central terms in these two verses are wordplays—brotherly love is *philos* + *adelphos*, "love of brothers"; and hospitality is *philos* + *xenos*, "love of strangers." Today as well, caring for those passing through one's territory is an obligation upon everyone. If we were to pass through enemy territory, the people there would have to welcome us as guests. For Christians there is also the added element of witness, as we care for them and share our faith with them. Zeus and the gods often visited homes and punished those who were unkind to strangers (see Acts 14:11–13). Moreover, inns in that day were centers of pagan practices and often housed the criminal element, so housing was especially needed (see 1 Pet 4:8–9; 3 John 5).

We must remember that Christians did not begin erecting separate buildings for Christian worship until the fourth century (after Constantine), and so they met in private homes (labeled "house churches"). So the idea of the church as a family was, from the beginning, at the heart of the self-consciousness of every church group. This also made showing hospitality to strangers much more natural, for the private family and the church family acted in concert in doing so. It was both a social obligation and part of the mission of the church.

The writer inserts an interesting comment to add emphasis to the practice: "for by so doing some people have shown hospitality to angels without knowing it." I especially like the well-known KJV translation, "entertained angels unawares." This, of course, built on Abraham's experience, as well as Lot (Gen 18–19), who were blessed by caring for God's angel-messengers. It was the three mysterious visitors at Mamre in Genesis 18 who gave Abraham and Sarah the promise that God would give them a son in their old age. This is the positive example of unexpected heaven-bound visitors that provided a counter to the negative example of Zeus and Hermes visiting in Acts 14.

Finally, the writer turns to a particular problem due to the extensive persecution the church was undergoing in Rome: believers that had been arrested and thrown in prison (13:3). This was an ongoing problem, for it had taken place in the previous generation of their church (10:32–34) and now was occurring again. Sadly, this was a common first-century difficulty, as Paul himself testified (1 Cor 12:26; 2 Cor 11:23; 2 Tim 1:16). The command here is for empathy and spiritual sharing.

"As if you yourselves were suffering" is literally "as you yourselves also are in the body." Some versions have "since" (NASB, ESV), but I prefer "as if" with NIV, NLT, NRSV, LEB, and NET. I believe it is important to retain "in the body" (counter the NIV), and the question is whether it refers to the church body or the physical body. If the former, the stress is on identifying with one another's suffering in Christ. If the latter, it is on sharing together the bodily suffering that persecution entails. The other instances of *sōma* in Hebrews feature the physical body (10:5, 10, 22; 13:11), and this is the more likely here. Christ became incarnate and suffered physically on our behalf, and it is our privilege to share both with him and with one another.

OUR PRIVATE LIFE AS CHRISTIANS (13:4-6)

The first item is Christian marriage, and this does not act as a summary here, for the topic has not arisen as yet—perhaps Esau in 12:17-19 who married pagan wives. Some think the Essenes are in mind; they did not countenance sexual relations, believing it defiled the participants, so marriage for them was out. However, it is more likely that the "purity" leads to the next clause—namely, defiling a marriage by immorality. The gentiles could also be in mind, as in the gentile churches of Corinth and the profligacy there.

There are two issues in this admonition: honoring marriage and avoiding sexual sin. Several point out the close relation of this to the exhortation regarding brotherly love. Love in the community and house church begins with marital relationships, so this continues the theme of verse 1. It is organized as a chiasm:

A Honored
   B Should be marriage
   B' The marriage bed should be
A' Kept pure

This format highlights the close connection between the institution of marriage and the sexual love that keeps the parties close to one another. The message is quite clear. God has established husband-wife marriage as the heart of marriage and of society, and all should "honor" (*timios*), more than respect—hold sacred—that God-given enterprise. This is the same adjective used of the "precious" blood of Christ (1 Pet 1:19) and speaks of that which is greatly valued by God and by his people. By shifting to "the marriage bed," the emphasis is also on the sexual side of the marriage relationship and means that, too, is precious as a divine gift. However, it is a gift within only marriage, and it must be kept "pure"—that is, free of unfaithful liaisons outside marriage. Sexual immorality is more than breaking the marriage bond. It is contrary to God's new covenant order and so "defiles" everyone it touches.

As a result, those who commit such heinous acts against God as well as the institution of marriage will be judged by God as adulterers (= what they are) and sexually immoral (= what they do) (v. 4). This is a likely reference to the final judgment, and it means there are eternal ramifications for those who place sexual pleasure above their commitments to God and their marriage partner. Such self-centered acts will be severely punished. He is the dreadful "living God" (10:31) who is "a consuming fire" (12:29), and we do not want to fall under his wrath.

This is followed by the danger of greed and "the love of money" (13:5). Instead of a life of avarice and consumerism, the writer calls for contentment apart from material needs. Money is just as addictive as sex, and so we are commanded to "keep our lives free" from such coveting. Coveting covers both sexual and material desires, so these two are intertwined. In the Ten Commandments, they are together (the seventh and eighth, combined in the tenth, Exod 20:14–15, 17; Deut 5:18–19, 21). Several other passages connect them (1 Cor 5:11, 6:9–10; Eph 5:3; Col 3:5).

The problem of riches is a frequent emphasis in Scripture (Matt 6:24: "You cannot serve both God and money"). It is entirely an earthly phenomenon concerned with the procurement of worldly goods. Of course, much of it deals with necessities to maintain life, but it also leads to luxury and the pleasure principle.

The writer employs a third compound noun for "love of money," *a-phil-argyros*, literally, "not-loving-money." A meaningful term has recently been devised to portray the danger: "affluenza," the disease of affluence. We need to develop an antidote, for it has now become a pandemic of greed.

The polar opposite of covetousness is contentment—namely, "be content with what you have." Our society is moving in precisely the opposite direction, for as wealth spreads further and further over the Western (and much of the Eastern) world, people cannot get enough of it. Entitlement has replaced contentment, as everyone says, "I deserve that." Paul states this well in 1 Timothy 6:8-10: "But if we have food and clothing, we will be content with that. Those who want to get rich fall into temptation and a trap and into many foolish and harmful desires that plunge people into ruin and destruction. For the love of money is a root of all kinds of evil." The answer to poverty is quite simple—trust and dependence on God. It is not easy to do when the hard times hit, but it is the secret of contentment, which means sufficiency in Christ rather than sufficiency in self—the opposite of **Hellenistic**, especially Stoic, thinking.

As often in this letter (10:8-9 16-17, 30, 37-38; 12:20-21), the author anchors this in two Old Testament citations (13:5b-6). The first is a key theme from the patriarchal period and the conquest of Canaan, "Never will I leave you, never will I forsake you," repeated in Genesis 28:15, Deuteronomy 31:6, 8, and Joshua 1:5. When God's people face insurmountable odds, they need to know that there is no such thing as impossible when God is involved. Joshua and his small army had to conquer a land containing one of the most powerful opponents on earth, and he was scared. But God was with them in the ensuing years to accomplish this task. This would be all the more true in terms of earthly needs in general. We can trust our compassionate Father and "cast all [our] anxiety on him" (1 Pet 5:7).

The second citation stems from Psalm 118:6, "The Lord is my helper; I will not be afraid. What can mere mortals do to me?" In the Triune Godhead there need be neither fear nor discontent, for they are watching over us and "helping" in our every trial. Psalm 118 is the last of the Hallel (Thanksgiving) Psalms (113–18) and is especially concerned with God's covenant care in times of suffering and trouble. The recurrent theme is, "His love endures forever."

In light of his help, this is no place or need for fear at life's obstacles. In fact, Hebrews 13:5b–6 hints that divine love is best evident in the crucible of earthly struggles, for it adds here, "What can mere mortals do to me?" This is answered forcefully in Matthew 10:28, "Do not be afraid of those who kill the body but cannot kill the soul." They can only take away the earthly side of life, but when that takes place, God's people enter the heavenly and eternal phase of life, and all suffering is gone forever. All of chapter 11 on the heroes of the faith point to this quotation, for all of heaven is involved in us and our true needs.

RELIGIOUS LIFE IN THE COMMUNITY (13:7–19)

IMITATING THE LEADERS (13:7–9)

Several models have been adduced for these believers to follow throughout the letter—the triumphant community of the past in Rome (10:32–34), the heroes of the faith from the past (chapter 11), Jesus himself, the champion of their faith (12:3), and now the current leaders God has placed over them. Here in verse 7 it is the past leaders once more, and in verses 17 and 24, it is the present leaders who are addressed. The leaders have never been mentioned specifically before now, though they were implicit in 2:3, speaking of the era of salvation that was "confirmed to us by those who heard [him]" (the apostles and subsequent leaders). While many of the members themselves have grown weak and undernourished spiritually, their leaders are still holding strong, but they need to listen more closely to them (v. 17) and remember the successful examples from the past (here).

These are concretely identified as those who "spoke the word of God to you" (v. 7). This is more than meaning they were teachers in the community, for the "word of God" is highly prized in Hebrews as God's revealed word (2:3; 4:12–13; 6:1), and they are identified as Christian oracles directly inspired by God so they speak his truths to these people. They must listen, heed, and emulate what they have spoken, for it has come directly from God.

They are enjoined to "remember your leaders" (v. 7), and "consider the outcome of their way of life." Most of them have passed away, and they need to bring to mind their previous triumphs in living for the Lord in hard times and change their ways accordingly. Note the three stages—remember, consider, imitate. The process of discipleship and Christian growth begins with bringing the lessons to mind, then thinking and meditating on their significance and how to emulate them, then "imitating" or putting the lessons into practice in day-to-day life. This is called *imitatio Christi*, and in the early church, it meant to model Christ to others in the church. The leaders become walking examples of the Christlike life, and the goal is "attaining to the whole measure of the fullness of Christ" (Eph 4:13).

Though times and leaders change, Jesus Christ does not (13:8; see also 1:12; 7:24). This is likely a creedal affirmation asserted here to anchor the injunction of verse 7 but at the same time provide an absolute contrast to the ever-shifting views of the false teachers in verse 9. The doctrine is called "the immutability of God," the belief that he is entirely stable and the only anchor for eternal truth. Here we recognize it is the Godhead, all three members of the Trinity, who are never-changing. Whether eternity past (yesterday, 5:7; 10:32–34), the present-day (today, 3:7, 13; 4:13), or eternity future (forever, 6:20; 7:17), he is the same.

Christ has been the past anchor for God's leaders; he is today the same mighty Lord of the universe and of the church, and he will ever be so throughout eternity. The leaders they had relied on are now gone, but the Christ who undergirded and guided them is still present, and he both grounds them in himself and is the never-changing reality they can at all times count on.

Most likely, many readers are not overly impressed. We live in a day that prizes innovation, creating new things to impress and amaze us. As a scholar, I have been trained since my master's and doctoral days to produce studies that are "new contributions" to my field. Scholarship that fails to rework its material in brand-new directions will not be passed. Yet when God revealed his word, he did not say something in the time of Christ and Paul that was meant to be replaced by new understandings. Yet people are constantly enamored with just those so-called insights, many of them undoubtedly false. When we study God's word, we seek to discover what he inspired his ancient author to say, not some recent so-called insight that has never been thought before. There are new discoveries, but they relate to background and theological insights we had not known before. As such, they aid us in uncovering more deeply what was originally intended, not in reading things into the passage never before meant.

The problem of false teachers was frequent in the early church (Eph 4:14; 1 Tim 4:1–3; 2 Tim 3:1–9; 1 John 4:1–3). The resulting pernicious doctrines wreaked havoc in many congregations, and the early church developed creeds and catechetical teachings to protect believers from being deceived by such people.

This is applied in 13:9 to the situation and teaching in these house churches. In place of the immutable truths of Christ's revealed word, many in these churches were reading new meanings into the new covenant truths that would allow them to return to their previous Judaism and escape the persecution they were currently experiencing. This likely involved following the food laws and the festival calendar. These are "strange teachings" because they go against the new covenant freedom from such laws that Christ instituted.

The way the author devised to protect his readers from being "carried away" into heresy and apostasy by such evil teaching is for them to recognize that "it is good for our hearts to be strengthened by grace" (v. 9)—namely, the grace that ensued with the teaching about Christ as Son of God and high priest and the new era of salvation and liberation he brought to the new Christian reality. This is a "heart" religion, not a bondage of required "ceremonial foods" (v. 9) that replace God's grace in Christ. Such an external religion is "of no benefit" (v. 9) to participants. They have been cleansed by the blood rather than forced to eat certain foods to establish a relationship with God.

Some think this refers to a Jewish-gnostic type of syncretism similar to Colossians and the Pastorals, but I see no need for this. The contrast is simply between the spiritual food that comes from the grace of God in Christ and the old covenant practice of eating undefiled food and participating in the sacrificial system. It is law-based rather than faith-based Christianity and both "strange" and "of no benefit" in the new covenant age of Christ and salvation.

TRUE PARTICIPATION IN CHRIST (13:10-14)

The "strange teachings" were clearly Levitical in origin and had no place in a Christian context. So the writer sets the record straight beginning here. "Those who minister at the tabernacle" are the Jewish priesthood, and they "have no right to eat" at the new "altar" of Christ (v. 10). This is another analogy from the Day of Atonement (chapters 9-10) in which the flesh of animals slaughtered was not eaten but instead was taken outside the walls of Jerusalem and the temple and was burned (Lev 16:27). The reason is that this sin offering for the nation became unclean unless blood had been taken into the holy of holies. When this didn't take place (the other days of the year), the priests ate the flesh. The present tenses indicate that the ritual was still practiced in Judaism; the destruction of the temple had not taken place yet, so this was pre-AD 70.

There are several "having" or "we have" statements that define what it means to know Christ: a great high priest (4:14; 8:1), things to do with salvation (6:9), hope as an anchor (6:19), entrance to the most holy place by the blood (10:19), a better and lasting possessions (10:34), a kingdom that cannot be shaken (12:28), a city that is to come (13:14), and a clear conscience (v. 18). The altar we currently have with Christ is heavenly, not the altar of the Day of Atonement ritual. Some think it a reference to the cross or even the Eucharistic table, but the latter is unlikely, as it was not called an altar in the early church.

Most likely, it is a broad metaphor depicting not only the cross but all aspects of the death of Christ as an atoning sacrifice. It refers to the means of the sacrifice and so not only to Jesus' sacrifice on the cross but to Christian involvement in it via worship (present tense "we have"). The emphasis is on the continuous activity of worship and the salvation experience, though that is also certainly found in the imagery of the sin offering. Ours is superior because it is once-for-all and eternal in scope. The idea of our "eating from the altar" of Christ pictures our participation in the redemptive effects of the cross.

This is further clarified by contrasting the Levitical Day of Atonement ceremony (v. 11) with Jesus' sacrifice (v. 12), which further contrasts the "then" and the "now" of the worship of God's people. In the "then" ceremony of the Day of Atonement (Lev 16:27), the animals (a bull and a goat) were sacrificed on the altar of the tabernacle, with the blood carried "into the most holy place as a sin offering" (Heb 13:11). As we have seen, that proved inadequate because it had to be repeated every year and only provided temporary forgiveness. The bodies of the animals were carried "outside the camp" (v. 11) and burned. The emphasis here is on the bodies of the sacrificial animals (deliberately not named to stress that they were merely animals in contrast with Christ). To be taken outside the camp signified that the sins of the people had been removed.

The ground outside the camp was unsanctified and thus defiled,
so the antithesis is complete. Jesus sanctified the people and paid
for their sins also "outside the city gate" (13:12) on defiled ground,
and his once-for-all sacrifice was eternal in scope. The cross was
also outside the gates of Jerusalem, and Jesus suffered for our sins
as one removed from God's covenant because he embodied our
sins. He fulfilled the Day of Atonement imagery perfectly and bore
our penalty on our behalf so we could be forgiven of our sins (see
9:11–15 above).

The purpose is to "make the people holy through his own
blood" (v. 12). The new covenant inaugurated through the sacrifice of Christ brought not only salvation but sanctification, making
it possible for God's people to be set apart from the world to God
and to belong wholly to him.

Verses 10–12 have told us what Christ has done for us on the
cross, and now verses 13–14 tell us how we participate in his wondrous gift to us. When we suffer persecution, we should rejoice
at the privilege (see Acts 5:41), for it is in reality suffering with
him in "participation in his sufferings" (Phil 3:10). We unite with
him "outside the camp" and share his despised status. This is the
supreme paradox: that we enter his glory by enduring his shame.
His exalted status "at the right hand of God" (Heb 10:12) came via
the cross, and we, too, are lifted up through suffering for him. We
dare not allow ourselves to fall into despair because of hard times.
Such is part of our oneness with him, and it brings us in a special
way into contact with the Godhead. For these believers, to join the
Jews in old covenant worship would constitute remaining within
the camp, and going outside means leaving the Jewish way of life
and turning to Christ. For us today it means we leave worldly pur-
suits and turn entirely to serve Christ.

The reason (Heb 13:14) is that "here we do not have an enduring city"—that is, life is temporary, and we do not belong since
we are citizens of heaven. Abraham and the heroes of chapter 11
were awaiting this "city with foundations" (11:10), and our hope

is built on the certain promise of a home beyond this world. As aliens in this world (11:9), we seek the heavenly city Christ is preparing for us (John 14:2–4). For these readers, the transitory nature of Jerusalem and its temple would especially be in mind. They have been replaced by Christ, and worshiping him is where eternal values are found.

So the solution is to look for "the city that is to come" (Heb 13:14). This is a reference back to the faithful men and women of chapter 11 (see 11:10, 14, 16), whose lives were oriented to the future, and therefore, refused to be discouraged by present problems. The same Jesus who suffered "outside the camp" is now exalted and enthroned in the eternal city of heaven, and we are called to follow him on this God-given path for champions of the faith. At present this life of faith involves realizing that the divine promises on which our hope is based make it certain, enabling us to live lives of victory. This means embracing the disgrace as part of our unity with Christ and entrusting both present and future with Christ, our champion and high priest.

ADMONITIONS THAT PRODUCE VICTORY (13:15–17)

A series of three commands now define how this victorious life may be lived. The first two are described as "sacrifices" and present the vertical (God-directed) and horizontal (people-directed) sides of this new life. First, we are to "continually offer to God a sacrifice of praise—the fruit of lips that openly profess his name" (v. 15). We inhabit a new city and worship at a new altar (v. 10). As "new priests" of the new covenant, we can enter directly into God's presence (10:19–20); we come "through Jesus"—Christ being the mediator who has made it possible for us to enter the heavenly holiest place, our sins having been decisively forgiven once for all time (9:9–14; 10:19–20). Consequently, we no longer have need for sacrifices for the forgiveness of sin; but in this new priesthood, we should offer up continually the "sacrifice of praise" (v. 15), a phrase taken from passages like Leviticus 7:12–15, 2 Chronicles 29:31, and

2 Chronicles 33:16, which describe it as an offering of thanks to God for his gracious works on our behalf. In the psalms we are challenged over and over to give thanks to the Lord (for example, Pss 26:7; 30:4, 12; 33:2; 97:12), and a vibrant Christian life should be characterized by praise and thanksgiving to God.

Hebrews continues by describing the sacrifice of praise as "the fruit of lips that openly profess his name" (13:15). The little phrase "fruit of lips" is taken directly from Hosea 14:2, the second part of which reads, "Forgive all our sins and receive us graciously, that we may offer the fruit of our lips." The author of Hebrews probably thought of this verse in light of Jesus' sacrifice for sins. Since God in Christ *has* forgiven us decisively and, therefore, received us "graciously," we have a wonderful reason to offer this sacrifice of praise to him! Yet there also is a bold, public dimension to this sacrifice, for our fruitful lips are to "profess his name" (v. 15). The author uses the word rendered "profess" (*homologountōn*) earlier in the book at 11:13, where he describes the people of faith as "professing" that the earth is not their true home. Part of the life of faith involves taking a bold public stance for Christ and with Christ's church, professing his name before a watching world. There will come a time when every knee in all of creation will bow and every tongue "confess" (a related word, *exomologēsetai*) that Jesus is Lord (Phil 2:10–11), but until that day, we as God's people lead the way by making that public profession before the world now (Heb 3:1; 4:14; 10:23)—even at great cost—calling people to allegiance to Jesus.

The second command gives attention to another type of "sacrifice," one oriented to our "horizontal" relationships with other people: "And do not forget to do good and to share with others" (13:16). The author already has emphasized the importance of good works done in ministering to people (for example, 6:10; 10:24, 34; 13:1-3), and a specific expression of "well-doing" is to share what we have with others in our new covenant community. The word translated as "share with others" (*koinōnias*) is a noun used to describe, for instance, fellowship, a close relationship, or generosity with fellow believers. In other words, doing good and meeting the practical needs of fellow Christ-followers should be rhythmic acts of worship for people of the new covenant. Hebrews assures us that "with such sacrifices God is pleased" (v. 16), a thought that should encourage us greatly. Here is a concrete way that we can know we are pleasing God!

At verse 17 the author comes back around to the topic of church leadership (see 13:7–9), and here he clearly has current leadership in mind. The relationship between leaders of a congregation and those who follow them stands as one of the most vital dynamics for a healthy church. Those of us who are not in the primary roles of leadership need to carefully consider how we might support and encourage the leaders, who bear the weight of tremendous responsibility. The author begins with twin exhortations, followed by a basis for those exhortations and then a motivation.

The first exhortation is to "have confidence in your leaders" (v. 17). The interesting word translated here as "have confidence in" (peithō) has a broad range of possible meanings and could be rendered, "convince," "be convinced by," "persuade," "strive to please," "pacify," "trust in," "believe," "obey," or "have confidence in." Given the context, the last of these options seems a good one, for the author encourages the readers with a second exhortation, to "submit" (v. 17)—that is, to work with the authority of those leading the congregation. Submission cannot be forced but must be embraced, ultimately in submission, yielding, to God himself. The basis of these exhortations the author expresses as: "because they keep watch over you as those who must give an account." Ultimately the leaders are accountable to God for caring for the spiritual welfare of those under their charge. The verb translated as "keep watch" (agrypneō) has to do with being alert, being vigilant in guarding something. Imagine guards set to watch over the crown jewels of England. Part of their job would be to stay alert for any threat to such a treasure. Of much greater value, God's people—his treasure—should be guarded, which is not an easy job. Therefore, members of the church should work with the leadership of the church, yielding to their direction and care, for that care is for the good of people in the church. Furthermore, church members should be motivated to "do this so that their work will be a joy, not a burden" (v. 17). Everyone who knows the responsibility of leadership in the church knows that the role can be burdensome at times. The word translated as "burden" in our verse speaks of doing something with a groan or a deep sigh. When we work against rather than with our leaders, we add to their responsibility a soul-crushing, emotional weight, which causes them to groan. The author reminds us that such a posture toward leaders of the church is no benefit or "help" to us. By contrast, we should relate to leaders in a way that brings them joy. This is beneficial to everyone.

Request for Prayer (13:18–19)

One of the greatest things we can do for our leaders or fellow church members is to pray for them. Rather than an optional spiritual discipline, prayer is God's way of involving his people in moving the world. Of course, God knows our needs and the needs of those for whom we pray before we mention them to him, but prayer constitutes a natural, ongoing conversation with God, an expression of intimacy in which we join in being concerned with the things that concern him (for example, Matt 6:10). So as the author begins moving toward the end of the book, he makes a personal and practical request, "pray for us" (v. 18), employing a stylistic device called an "authorial plural," which was used earlier at 5:11 and 6:9, 25. To use the plural "us" or "we" was an elegant way of speaking of oneself. Two things follow on the heels of this request and seem clear from the remainder of verses 18 and 19. First, the author has been detained (v. 19), for the content of his prayer request is that he "may be restored" to this congregation soon. Although we are not told the exact nature of his detention, the mention of Timothy's release in verse 23 probably means that the author has been imprisoned in the cause of Christ. If this is the case, it offers a fresh perspective on the earlier mention of those of this congregation who had been imprisoned (10:32-34) and the exhortation at 13:3 to visit those in prison. Evidently, the author had firsthand experience of what it was like to be imprisoned because of gospel work. In any case, there is a note of urgency to this prayer request ("I particularly urge you," [v. 19]), for the author wants to be restored to them "soon" (v. 19).

Second, concerning being imprisoned, the author evidently has been accused of misconduct since he writes, "We are sure that we have a clear conscience and desire to live honorably in every way" (v. 18). The author's conscience has been perfected by Christ through the cleansing from sin (9:9, 14), but here he probably speaks of innocence in relation to the authorities by which he is held. The term translated as "honorably," *kalōs*, could communicate action that was splendid or appropriate, carried out with high standards, or something done correctly or with excellence. So the author proclaims in no uncertain terms that he has been held unjustly. Consequently, in honoring his request to pray for him, the readers pray for his vindication and release.

FINAL GREETINGS (13:20-25)

BENEDICTION (13:20-21)

Benedictions were an important aspect of worship in Judaism of the first century, and they could be used in letters or sermons, shaped to address the specific needs of a group addressed. The benediction we find in Hebrews 13:20-21 unfolds basically in two parts: a blessing that anchors the benediction with reference to God (v. 20) and the content of the blessing, described as God's good work in the people being addressed (v. 21). Many themes in this passage as a whole have shown up earlier in Hebrews, for instance, "the blood" (Heb 2:14; 9:7, 12-14, 18-22, 25; 10:4, 19, 29; 11:28; 12:4, 24;

13:11-12), the concept of "covenant" (Heb 7:22; 8:6, 8-10; 9:4, 15-17, 20; 10:16, 29; 12:24), and "doing" God's "will" (Heb 10:7, 9-10, 36), all very important concepts for the sermon. So this benediction has been shaped as a fitting conclusion to the sermon as a whole.

The author launches the benediction by referring to God: "Now may the God of peace ..." Addressing God as a God of "peace" evokes the Jewish concept of "shalom," or well-being, which, by the time Hebrews was written, had become a standard way to open or close Christian letters (for example, Rom 1:7; 16:20; 1 Cor 1:3; 2 Cor 1:2; Gal 1:3; 6:16). In fact, with the verses before us, we begin to see elements normally associated with the ending of a letter, so it seems that an epistolary ending was attached to Hebrews once the author was finished crafting the sermon.

The reference to God is filled out with a description, "who through the blood of the eternal covenant brought back from the dead our Lord Jesus, that great Shepherd of the sheep" (v. 20). Throughout Hebrews, we have seen that God the Father and God the Son have been the two primary subjects of this amazing book. For instance, the book starts with God (1:1) as the "speaker" of revelation but quickly focuses on the Son as both identified with God the Father and the ultimate expression of the Father's revelation (1:2-4). The whole of Hebrews weaves together the relationship of these two members of the Trinity. This is the first time in the book that the resurrection of Christ has been mentioned overtly; it is normally assumed and alluded to with reference to the exaltation to the right hand of God (1:3, 13; 8:1-2; 10:12; 12:2). The concept of the Son's resurrection is especially vital concerning his appointment as a superior high priest, since, unlike the earthly priests, Jesus was appointed by virtue of his indestructible life (7:16) and always lives to make intercession for us (7:26-28).

But what might the author mean in 13:20 when he says that the resurrection was accomplished "through the blood of the eternal covenant"? The little preposition used (en) can mark a circumstance or condition under which something takes place.

Furthermore, "blood" in Hebrews is most often used in relation to death and sacrifice, whether of the Levitical sacrifices or the sacrifice of Christ himself (for example, 9:14, 25; 10:19-20). Christ's blood is the "blood of the covenant" since his death, the shedding of his blood, established the new covenant between God and people (9:12-17). So Christ's resurrection from the dead took place in relation to his death. That was the circumstance that "gave rise" to the event.

Most of us are familiar with shepherd imagery in the Bible because of wonderful passages like Psalm 23, and the word picture offers us a beautiful picture of God's provision for and protection of his people. Yet in the Old Testament, the image could also be used negatively of leaders who did not take care of God's people (for example, Isa 56:11; Jer 23:1; 50:6; Ezek 34:2, 7). So in longing for faithful leaders for the nation, the concept came to be associated with the coming of Messiah in Second Temple Judaism, as well as the New Testament (for example, John 10:11-18; 1 Pet 2:25). Jesus is our ultimate Shepherd, who has provided for us as his sheep through the ministry of the new covenant.

This is the foundation for the second half of the benediction, what the writer hopes for the recipients. Basically, his prayer is that God would "equip" them "with everything good for doing his will" (Heb 13:21). The author already has used the word rendered as "equip" at a couple of significant points in the book. At 10:5 it refers to the Father's *preparation* of a body for the Son, the incarnation, and at 11:3 the word speaks of God *forming* the universe at creation. So here the blessing consists of God shaping the believers—that is, "equipping" them in relation to what is good so that they will be people who do God's will, what is "pleasing to him" (13:21). As we live as people in the world who have been shaped by God, equipped with good things by his grace, God is working in us to live out his will in the world and thus bring him pleasure. This all, of course, works to the glory of our Lord Jesus, for none of it is possible apart from him.

It is a great thing to bless people. Although the benediction in Hebrews 13:20-21 serves as a formal closing to the book, it is also theologically rich, relationally warm, and expresses great hope for fellow believers. What more could we wish for one another than that we would live lives that are good, pleasing to God, and that bring glory to Christ?

Personal Notes (13:22-23)

As Hebrews draws to a close, the author adds several personal notes (13:22-23) before the final salutation and blessing (13:24-25). As Christ-followers, we are a part of God's family—his children and Christ's brothers and sisters. The author capitalized on this aspect of Christian teaching earlier in the book, where he points out that Jesus is "not ashamed to call" God's holy people "brothers and sisters," reinforcing this truth with passages from Psalms and Isaiah (Heb 2:10-13). The term translated as "brothers and sisters" (*adelphoi*) was used in the ancient world to refer to both men and women in religious groups and had come to be a common way of addressing fellow believers in Christian circles. Having used the address sparingly earlier in the book (3:1, 12; 10:19), the author now closes by exhorting his "brothers and sisters" to "bear with [this] word of exhortation" (v. 22). In referring to Hebrews as a "word of exhortation," the author gave us one of our best clues on the nature of the book since the same phrase is used in Acts 13:15, where upon entering a synagogue, the Jewish leaders offer an invitation, saying to Paul and Barnabas, "Brothers, if you have *a word of exhortation* for the people, please speak" (Acts 13:15). In response, Paul stood and preached a powerful sermon, in part recounting aspects of Israel's history, quoting Scripture, and speaking of Jesus as bringing salvation through the forgiveness of sins (Acts 13:16-41), characteristics also seen in Hebrews. This is one reason many scholars understand Hebrews to be a sermon. Synagogue homilies or sermons often alternated back and forth between exposition and exhortation, as does Hebrews. However, it is clear that the exposition of the book, which wonderfully unpacks a majestic Christology on Jesus' person and work, serves the purpose at the heart of Hebrews, for the exposition lays the foundation for the exhortation, challenging the hearers to persevere in their commitment to Christ. In urging the hearers to "bear with" the message, which he describes as brief, the author uses common, rhetorical language, a polite way of challenging the listeners to take the message seriously. The claim of brevity, in effect, suggests, "There was so much more I could have said!"

The reference to Timothy in verse 23 has led some in the history of the church to understand Hebrews as written by Paul, since the apostle mentions his young companion often in his letters.[1] But as noted in the introduction, there are several reasons why most scholars do not think Paul wrote Hebrews. At the same time, as also mentioned in the introduction to this commentary, it seems that the author was a member of Paul's mission, so it would not be surprising that he had a relationship with Timothy. It may be that Timothy had been held somewhere other than where the author was being held, since he speaks of the young man arriving. Yet he encourages the believers, noting that if Timothy joins him, they will travel together to the congregation.

CLOSING SALUTATION AND BLESSING (13:24–25)

A formal word of greeting and a final blessing grace the end of the book (13:24–25). Twice in chapter 13 the author has spoken about the "leaders" of the church (13:7, 17), and he now sends greetings to them along with "the Lord's people," a designation more straightforward rendered as "all the holy ones," tapping a prominent theme in the book, since Christ's work has effected the holiness of his people (3:1; 10:14–18). Offering greetings and blessings formed common social conventions at the end of ancient letters.

---

1. For example, Rom 16:21; 1 Cor 4:17; 16:10; 2 Cor 1:1, 19; Phil 1:1; 2:19; Col 1:1; 1 Thess 1:1; 3:2, 6; 2 Thess 1:1; 1 Tim 1:1–2, 18; 6:20; 2 Tim 1:1–2; Phlm 1.

To greet someone was to express hospitality in recognizing the other person.² That "those from Italy send" (v. 24) greetings to the believers addressed may indicate that the church is in Italy, and those with the author are from there, but this is disputed by some. In any case, the greetings flow both ways, speaking of the distribution of believers in different parts of the world at that time. Letters from the broader Greco-Roman culture often ended by saying "farewell," or "be well," but Christian writings at times closed as the author does here, with a blessing of grace (for example, Rom 16:20; 1 Cor 16:23; 2 Cor 13:13; Gal 6:18).

Chapter 13 begins with a series of very practical instructions for living well as followers of Christ, the first half addressing guidelines for corporate life (vv. 1-3) and the second half instructions for individuals (vv. 4-6). Here we have a mix of ethical injunctions for the community as a whole that include loving each other as brothers and sisters (v. 1) and showing hospitality to strangers (v. 2), the latter grounded in the biblical example of Abraham, who entertained angels without knowing it. The church as a whole is also encouraged to keep in mind and identify with the brothers and sisters in prison, who suffered because of their public stand for the faith (v. 3). The ethical exhortations for individuals, on the other hand, concern living honorably in the marriage relationship by remaining sexually pure (v. 4) and having proper attitudes in relation to money and material possessions (vv. 5-6).

Hebrews 13:7-19 deals with a variety of topics concerning the religious life of the community. Throughout the book, the author has offered positive examples for these beleaguered Christ-followers to consider, whether believers from their community

---

2. For example, Matt 5:47; 10:12; Luke 1:40; Acts 18:22; 21:7, 19; 25:13; Heb 13:24; 1 Pet 5:13; 2 John 1:13.

who had offered a bold public witness in the face of persecution (10:32–34), the heroes of Hebrews 11, or Jesus himself (12:3). Now the leaders who at some time in the past had spoken God's word to the hearers are held up as examples to imitate (13:7). As living examples of how to walk with God and live for Christ in the world, these leaders were worthy of emulation. Of course, all earthly leadership is transient; we are here today and gone tomorrow due to the frailties of human existence. But the example of these leaders remains relevant since Christ himself does not change but "is the same yesterday and today and forever" (v. 8). The stability offered by the witness of the community's first leaders and the unchangeable nature of Christ gives a strong guard against "strange teachings" (v. 9).

It seems the author's concern is for those in the community not to be drawn away from sound Christian teaching back to practices involved in mainline Judaism. These strange teachings probably related to food laws and practices of the Jewish festival calendar, which constituted a move away from new covenant teachings of grace. "Ceremonial foods" are of no benefit, as is the case with the Levitical worship practices in general (v. 10). As he has done throughout the book, the author counters the false teaching by pointing to the superiority of Christ and his sacrificial work. That work was foreshadowed in the Old Testament Levitical system, the high priest taking the blood of animals into the most holy place on the Day of Atonement, burning the bodies outside the camp (v. 11). Analogously, Jesus—the supreme sacrifice for sin and the great high priest, whose Day of Atonement sacrifice only had to be offered once (for example, 10:25–28), also suffered outside "the camp" to cleanse his people through the shedding of his blood (13:12). Consequently, his followers should continue to identify with him publicly, knowing that their orientation, rather than to an earthly city, is an eternal one (vv. 13–14).

Although we do not follow the old covenant worship system, we are "priests" who offer sacrifices, one being "a sacrifice of praise," the "fruit of lips that openly profess his name" (v. 15). This "vertical" sacrifice is directed to God in thanks for God's work on our behalf, but it also is public as we profess his name, identifying with him publicly before a watching world. A second sacrifice is horizontal, related to our brothers and sisters in the community of faith, and involves doing good and sharing with others (v. 16). With 13:17 the author also deals with relationships in the church, but this time he returns to the topic of leadership, focusing on the congregation's relationship with their current leaders, whose role is to "keep watch" over the congregation. Basically, people of the church are to "have confidence in" their leaders and work with their authority, supporting their leadership in a way that gives the leaders joy rather than grief.

Several dynamics mark the final movement of the book. The author makes a personal plea for prayer in 13:18-19. Asserting that his conscience is clear and his way of life honorable, he asks the community to pray that he will be restored to them soon. Having made that request, he breathes a prayer of benediction for this community to whom he writes (vv. 20-21). Invoking the "God of peace" who raised Jesus, the great Shepherd, from the dead and established the new covenant through his shed blood, the author cries out for God to equip them with good things that will lead to them doing God's will, pleasing him, which will bring glory to Jesus Christ. In closing, the author urges his brothers and sisters to bear with this sermon, the "word of exhortation" (v. 22). He speaks of traveling to them with Timothy, who has been released recently (v. 23), and then he closes with a round of greetings (v. 24) and a blessing of grace (v. 25).

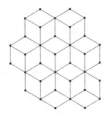

GLOSSARY

apocalyptic Refers to truths about God's plans for history that he has hidden in past generations but has revealed (the Greek *apokalypsis* means "unveiling") to his people. The name also describes a genre of ancient literature (including Revelation and parts of Daniel) that communicates these truths using vivid symbolism.

chiasm (n.), chiastic (adj.) A stylistic device in which a passage is organized into two sections, with the contents of the statements in the first half repeated in reverse order in the second half (ABC:C′B′A′).

christological (adj.), Christology (n.) Refers to the New Testament's presentation of the person and work of Christ, especially his identity as Messiah.

diaspora (n.), diasporic (adj.) Refers to the (often Greek-speaking) communities of Jews living outside Israel. The term comes from the Greek word for "scattering."

eschatological (adj.), eschatology (n.) Refers to the last things or the end times. Within this broad category, biblical scholars and theologians have identified more specific concepts. For instance, "realized eschatology" emphasizes the present work of Christ in the world as he prepares for the end of history. In "inaugurated eschatology," the last days have already begun but have not yet been consummated at the return of Christ.

eschaton Greek for "end" or "last," referring to the return of Christ and the end of history.

Hellenistic Relates to the spread of Greek culture in the Mediterranean world after the conquests of Alexander the Great (356–323 BC). "Hellenist" can refer to people, both Jewish and gentile, whose primary culture and language is Greek.

inclusio A framing device in which the same word or phrase occurs at both the beginning and the end of a section of text.

midrash (n.), midrashic (adj.) A Jewish exposition of a text using the techniques of ancient rabbis to give a detailed analysis of the meaning and theology of a text.

parousia The event of Christ's second coming. The Greek word *parousia* means "arrival" or "presence."

Qumran A site near the northwest corner of the Dead Sea where a collection of scrolls (called the Dead Sea Scrolls) was found beginning in the 1940s. The community that lived at this site and wrote these scrolls separated themselves from the rest of Jewish society. Many scholars believe they were a branch of the Essenes, one of the three major Jewish sects mentioned by Josephus (*Antiquities* 13.171–72). The Dead Sea Scrolls include manuscripts of Old Testament books as well as other writings that are not part of Scripture. They do not refer to Christianity but do shed light on aspects of Judaism around the time of Jesus.

Septuagint An ancient Greek translation of the Old Testament that was used extensively in the early church.

Shekinah A word derived from the Hebrew *shakan* ("to dwell"), used to describe God's personal presence taking the form of a cloud, often in the context of the tabernacle or temple (for example, Exod 40:38; Num 9:15; 1 Kgs 8:10–11).

soteriological (adj.), soteriology (n.) Relating to the doctrine of salvation (Greek: *sōtēria*), including such subjects as atonement, justification, and sanctification.

typological (adj.), typology (n.) A literary device in which Old Testament persons or events are the types that correspond to and are fulfilled in New Testament realities (antitypes).

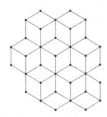

BIBLIOGRAPHY

Allen, David L. *Hebrews*. New American Commentary. Nashville: B&H, 2010.

Brown, Raymond. *The Message of Hebrews*. The Bible Speaks Today. Downers Grove, IL: InterVarsity Press, 1988.

Bruce, F. F. *The Epistle to the Hebrews*. New International Commentary on the New Testament. Grand Rapids: Eerdmans, 1990.

Cockerill, Gareth Lee. *The Epistle to the Hebrews*. New International Commentary on the New Testament. Grand Rapids: Eerdmans, 2012.

deSilva, David A. *Perseverance in Gratitude: A Socio-Rhetorical Commentary on the Epistle "to the Hebrews."* Grand Rapids: Eerdmans, 2000.

France, R. T. "Hebrews." In *The Expositor's Bible Commentary, Volume 13: Hebrews–Revelation (Revised Edition)*, ed. Tremper Longman III and David E. Garland. Grand Rapids: Zondervan, 2006.

Guthrie, George H. *Hebrews*. NIV Application Commentary. Grand Rapids: Zondervan, 1998.

Hagner, Donald A. *Hebrews*. Understanding the Bible Commentary. Grand Rapids: Baker Books, 2011.

Hughes, R. Kent. *Hebrews: An Anchor for the Soul.* Preaching the Word. Wheaton, IL: Crossway, 1993.

Koester, Craig R. *Hebrews: A New Translation with Introduction and Commentary.* Anchor Yale Bible. New Haven: Yale University Press, 2008.

Lane, William L. *Hebrews 1–8.* Word Biblical Commentary. Dallas: Word, 1991.

Lane, William L. *Hebrews 9–13.* Word Biblical Commentary. Dallas: Word, 1991.

Stedman, Ray C. *Hebrews.* IVP New Testament Commentary. Downers Grove, IL: IVP Academic, 1992.

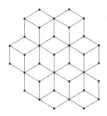

SUBJECT AND AUTHOR INDEX

and faith, 237–38
faithfulness of, 68, 242–43,
   251, 263–64
as forgiving sins, 167–68
grace of, 50, 99, 123, 221, 306
and his enemies, 219–20
and hope, 215
living, 8, 16, 72–73, 91, 115, 183,
   212, 222–23, 286, 293, 301
oath of, 71–72, 127–30, 147–48
and offerings, 199–200
of peace, 278, 314, 320
and perseverance, 124–25, 133–
   34
presence of, 28, 64, 132, 146, 155,
   166, 174–78, 210–11, 278
and the race, 269
as raising the dead, 246–47
rest of, 85–86
as rewarding the faithful, 225
and salvation, 50–52
scrutiny of, 92
of Sinai vs. of Zion, 284–85,
   290–92, 295–96
and the Son, 79
as the Unseen One, 256–57
and the unseen world, 233–35
wrath of, 71–72
See also Father
gold, and the tabernacle
   furnishings, 174
gospel, and rest, 84
grace
   of God, 50, 99, 123, 221, 306
   and the Spirit, 221
greed, 301–2
greetings, final, 313–18
guarantor, of a better covenant,
   147–49, 157
gymnazō, 112

H

hagiazō, 52, 204
hagios, 63
hagiotētos, 277
hands, laying on of, 115–16, 133
hapax, 119, 190–91
hardships, and unbelief, 78
harvest, of righteousness, 278–79
heart
   of Abel, 250
   of Cain, 236
   cleansing of, 179, 182, 213–14
   hardened, 20, 70–73, 205, 226,
      232, 283, 290, 295
   and the law, 166, 205–7
   losing, 272–74, 294
   new, 166, 169–70
   religion of, 306
   sincere, 212–13
   and the word of God, 91–92
heaven
   and Christ, 95–97, 153, 180–81
   vs. earth, 255–56
   purification of, 188–89
   sanctuary of, 159–63
heifer, ashes of, 182
heir, Christ as, 25–26, 39–40
heirs, of Abraham, 129
hell, and fire, 220
hendiadys, Hebrews' use of,
   216n2
heroes, of the faith, 126–28,
   232–66, 303, 308–9
heteros, 142–43
Hezekiah, 71
history, of faith, 233, 259, 264–66
holiness
   of Christ, 152, 201
   and discipline, 277, 294
   of God, 285
   of God's people, 204, 207, 317
   and peace, 281–82

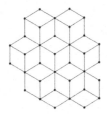

INDEX OF SCRIPTURE AND OTHER ANCIENT LITERATURE

Old Testament

New Testament

Deuterocanonical Works

Old Testament Pseudepigrapha

Dead Sea Scrolls

Josephus

Rabbinic Works

Babylonian Talmud

Apostolic Fathers

Other Ancient Writers

"Grant Osborne is ideally suited to write a series of concise commentaries on the New Testament. His exegetical and hermeneutical skills are well known, and anyone who has had the privilege of being in his classes also knows his pastoral heart and wisdom."

—**Ray Van Neste**, professor of biblical studies, director of the R.C. Ryan Center for Biblical Studies, Union University

"Grant Osborne is an eminent New Testament scholar and warm-hearted professor who loves the word of God. Through decades of effective teaching at Trinity Evangelical Divinity School and church ministry around the world, he has demonstrated an ability to guide his readers in a careful understanding of the Bible. The volumes in this accessible commentary series help readers understand the text clearly and accurately. But they also draw us to consider the implications of the text, providing key insights on faithful application and preaching that reflect a lifetime of ministry experience. This unique combination of scholarship and practical experience makes this series an invaluable resource for all students of God's word, and especially those who are called to preach and teach."

—**H. Wayne Johnson**, associate academic dean and associate professor of pastoral theology, Trinity Evangelical Divinity School